POSTPROCESS POSTMORTEM

T0289081

PERSPECTIVES ON WRITING

Series Editors: Rich Rice, Heather MacNeill Falconer, and J. Michael Rifenburg
Consulting Editor: Susan H. McLeod | Associate Series Editor: Jonathan P. Hunt

The Perspectives on Writing series addresses writing studies in a broad sense. Consistent with the wide ranging approaches characteristic of teaching and scholarship in writing across the curriculum, the series presents works that take divergent perspectives on working as a writer, teaching writing, administering writing programs, and studying writing in its various forms.

The WAC Clearinghouse, Colorado State University Open Press, and University Press of Colorado are collaborating so that these books will be widely available through free digital distribution and low-cost print editions. The publishers and the Series editors are committed to the principle that knowledge should freely circulate. We see the opportunities that new technologies have for further democratizing knowledge. And we see that to share the power of writing is to share the means for all to articulate their needs, interest, and learning into the great experiment of literacy.

Recent Books in the Series

Ryan J. Dippre and Talinn Phillips (Eds.), *Approaches to Lifespan Writing Research: Generating an Actionable Coherence* (2020)

Lesley Erin Bartlett, Sandra L. Tarabochia, Andrea R. Olinger, and Margaret J. Marshall (Eds.), *Diverse Approaches to Teaching, Learning, and Writing Across the Curriculum: IWAC at 25* (2020)

Hannah J. Rule, *Situating Writing Processes* (2019)

Asao B. Inoue, *Labor-Based Grading Contracts: Building Equity and Inclusion in the Compassionate Writing Classroom* (2019)

Mark Sutton and Sally Chandler (Eds.), *The Writing Studio Sampler: Stories About Change* (2018)

Kristine L. Blair and Lee Nickoson (Eds.), *Composing Feminist Interventions: Activism, Engagement, Praxis* (2018)

Mya Poe, Asao B. Inoue, and Norbert Elliot (Eds.), *Writing Assessment, Social Justice, and the Advancement of Opportunity* (2018)

Patricia Portanova, J. Michael Rifenburg, and Duane Roen (Eds.), *Contemporary Perspectives on Cognition and Writing* (2017)

Douglas M. Walls and Stephanie Vie (Eds.), *Social Writing/Social Media: Publics, Presentations, and Pedagogies* (2017)

Laura R. Micciche, *Acknowledging Writing Partners* (2017)

POSTPROCESS POSTMORTEM

Kristopher M. Lotier

The WAC Clearinghouse
wac.colostate.edu
Fort Collins, Colorado

University Press of Colorado
upcolorado.com
Louisville, Colorado

The WAC Clearinghouse, Fort Collins, Colorado 80523

University Press of Colorado, Louisville, Colorado 80027

ISBN 978-1-64215-126-8 (PDF) | 978-1-64215-127-5 (ePub) | 978-1-64642-223-4 (pbk.)

DOI: 10.37514/PER-B.2021.1268

Printed in the United States of America

Library of Congress Cataloging-in-Publication Data

Names: Lotier, Kristopher M., 1985– author.
Title: Postprocess postmortem / Kristopher M. Lotier.
Description: Fort Collins, Colorado : The WAC Clearinghouse ; Louisville, Colorado :
    University Press of Colorado, [2021] | Series: Perspectives on writing | Includes bibliographical
    references and index.
Identifiers: LCCN 2021012756 (print) | LCCN 2021012757 (ebook) | ISBN 9781646422234
    (paperback) | ISBN 9781642151268 (pdf) | ISBN 9781642151275 (epub)
Subjects: LCSH: English language—Rhetoric—Study and teaching (Higher) | Report writing—
    Study and teaching (Higher)
Classification: LCC PE1404 .L68 2021 (print) | LCC PE1404 (ebook) |
    DDC 808/.0420711—dc23
LC record available at https://lccn.loc.gov/2021012756
LC ebook record available at https://lccn.loc.gov/2021012757

Copyeditor: Don Donahue
Designer: Mike Palmquist
Series Editors: Rich Rice, Heather MacNeill Falconer, and J. Michael Rifenburg
Consulting Editor: Susan H. McLeod
Associate Editor: Jonathan P. Hunt

The WAC Clearinghouse supports teachers of writing across the disciplines. Hosted by Colorado
State University, and supported by the Colorado State University Open Press, it brings together
scholarly journals and book series as well as resources for teachers who use writing in their
courses. This book is available in digital formats for free download at wac.colostate.edu.

Founded in 1965, the University Press of Colorado is a nonprofit cooperative publishing
enterprise supported, in part, by Adams State University, Colorado State University, Fort Lewis
College, Metropolitan State University of Denver, Regis University, University of Colorado,
University of Northern Colorado, Utah State University, and Western Colorado University. For
more information, visit upcolorado.com. The Press partners with the Clearinghouse to make its
books available in print.

CONTENTS

ACKNOWLEDGMENTS

I could not have written this book without the necessary time and physical space, without the wise and knowledgeable guidance of others, without professional and institutional support, without the emotional encouragement and love of friends and family.

For the time, I thank the membership—and especially the leadership—of my labor union, the Hofstra University chapter of the American Association of University Professors. Were it not for the nine months of sustained research time provided by my Not-Yet-Tenured Faculty Research Leave, I could not have written this text so quickly, and I may never have completed it, at all. Special thanks, in solidarity, go to my department's union representative, Patricia Navarra.

For the physical space, I thank my fellow New York City taxpayers—citizen and non-citizen alike—for their willingness to fund the Brooklyn Public Library system, especially the Central Library at Grand Army Plaza, where I wrote and/or revised the vast majority of this book.

This book hardly resembles my doctoral dissertation from Penn State, except for one shared chapter, which was subsequently slashed and burned and re-written from the ground up. But, those pages launched all of this, in the end. I owe thanks to the Penn State Center for Democratic Deliberation, which offered me a research fellowship during the period in which I wrote that dissertation chapter, and to the writing group chaired by Cheryl Glenn that offered me my first feedback on it. I want to extend special gratitude to the director of my dissertation committee, Debbie Hawhee, for her steady support and encouragement over the course of several years. Thanks, as well, to my doctoral committee, John Christman, Jeffrey Nealon, and Mya Poe for helpful feedback on the dissertation itself.

In an entirely separate way, I will be ever grateful for the many supportive friends I met at Penn State. They helped me to thrive in a program where I would have settled for just surviving. I can't name everyone worth thanking, but I'll extend particular regards to Jake Hughes, Aaron Kimmel, Ethan Mannon, Jason Maxwell, Justin Mellette, Dan Radus, Sarah Salter, Daniel Story, Josh Tendler, Sarah Breckenridge Wright, and Paul Zajac. The next couple rounds are on me.

While I'm talking about institutional arrangements, let me say: I've been richly blessed to work in the department of writing studies and rhetoric at Hofstra University. I am grateful to many colleagues who have made my experience such a rich and positive one, but I extend special thanks to the three who have served as department chairs, Frank Gaughan, Jennifer Rich, and Ethna

Lay, and to my current associate chair, Daisy Miller. I acknowledge that the research in this book bears little resemblance to the business-writing role I was hired to fulfill within the institution's bureaucratic structure. So, I appreciate that I've always felt empowered to pursue my intellectual impulses, rather than compelled to conform to a mandate from on-high.

During course of writing this book, I reached out to three of the scholars about whom I was writing, Russell Hunt, Douglas Vipond, and Louise Wetherbee Phelps, for clarification on matters I felt unqualified to address on my own. Each of them was graciously hospitable to my questions and impressively forthcoming with insightful commentary and guidance. I extend them sincere thanks for their assistance.

I would also like to thank this book's editors and its anonymous reviewers for the critiques and suggestions they offered, which have improved the text tremendously.

An earlier version of Chapter Six was originally published as "Around 1986: The Externalization of Cognition and the Emergence of Postprocess Invention" in *College Composition and Communication* 67.3 (February 2016), pp. 360–384. Copyright 2016 by the National Council of Teachers of English. It is reprinted here with permission. Thanks to the journal's editors and to the Publications Director at the National Council of Teachers of English (NCTE) for those permissions to reprint.

Finally, I want to acknowledge and thank my family: my wife; my parents; my grandparents; my brothers and my sister; my step-parents and parents-in-law; my siblings-in-law and step-siblings; my nephews and my niece; my aunts and uncles and cousins. In so many ways, both large and small, they have encouraged and sustained me. I am ever grateful to them—inexpressibly so. I hope they all know that already. But, I also hope they never forget it.

POSTPROCESS POSTMORTEM

CHAPTER 1.

AN INTRODUCTION (AFTER THE DATE OF EXPIRATION)

In his 2008 article, "What Should We Do with Postprocess Theory," Matthew Heard credits postprocess with having offered a "fresh new look at the goals and strategies we use to teach students." Even so, he cannot help but note (quite correctly) the disappearance of postprocess "from recent critical discussion in composition." As an admirer of the underlying ideas, Heard considers this disappearance "surprising," the silence of scholars "puzzling." And so he asks, "Does the silence indicate that postprocess is dead, or have we simply been unable to figure out how to put the bold ideas of postprocess to use?" (285).

I appreciate Heard's implication that a (possibly) dead postprocess would not need to stay dead; it could be revitalized, even resurrected, through use.

I agree.

Still, in what follows, I want to pursue a different angle.

As the title of this book, *Postprocess Postmortem*, indicates, I *do* think that postprocess as a movement/theory/attitude with a name and a relatively stable core of premises has died. In my estimation, though, that death is not an altogether bad thing. As Heard himself implies, the movement or idea or attitude may have been better served by being called something else (285–86). Indeed, I would argue, it *has been*—and presently *is being*.

Before the name *postprocess* existed, Thomas Kent called the underlying approach a *paralogic rhetoric*, and the eponymous book in which he did so won the 1995 Conference on College Composition and Communication (CCCC) Outstanding Book Award. Marching under the banner of postprocess, the same concepts did not subsequently fair as well. Although the bombast of its name implied that postprocess had or would supersede Process, the movement/theory/attitude never acquired anything close to its predecessor's disciplinary standing.

Meanwhile, from the mid-1980s onward, many discernibly postprocess tenets have surfaced and resurfaced, with some even flourishing.

But, they haven't been *called postprocess*.

The name seems to be dead.

And yet, the ideas live.

I am therefore reminded of a passage from the twelfth chapter of the Gospel of John, the twenty-fourth verse: "I tell you the truth, unless a kernel of wheat falls to the ground and dies, it remains only a single seed. But if it dies, it produces many seeds" (*The Bible, New International Version*).

This book is not concerned with mourning over the plant.

Instead, in writing it, I wanted to study the seeds.

Before there was *postprocess*—a word, a name—there were some seeds: scattered ideas, tenets, and principles that hadn't yet been bound together in a conceptual package. I set out to determine where those seeds came from and who planted them. I wanted to know how they were treated when they were presumed to be independent entities versus when their inter-relations were accepted, taken for granted. I was also curious how and why and to what extent scholars resisted the hegemony of Process before their efforts were deemed *postprocess*.

For a time, postprocess blossomed. Though somewhat loosely, the conceptual package was bound together. A "three-part mantra" with "poster-ready brevity" was proclaimed: "(1) Writing is public; (2) writing is interpretive; (3) writing is situated" (Lynch 32). Scholars began to self-identify with the appellation. A cumulative, collective intellectual project emerged.

Still, inevitably, dust returns to dust. As postprocess was dying, more seeds fell. I set off to find out where they landed, and who picked them up, and whether they were scattered again. I wanted to know if they had taken root—and, if so, when and where and how and why—to find out if they were growing again, even now.

SOME NOTES ON HISTORIOGRAPHIC METHOD: CONTEMPLATING REVISION, OSCILLATION, RESOLUTION, CIRCULATION, RECEPTION

Over the last thirty years, if one desired to write a history of composition and/or writing studies, the advice would have been straightforward: go local. Select a marginalized group that's been overlooked in "standard" accounts of the field. Go to the physical archives: read syllabi, textbooks, teaching notes, student essays, peer review worksheets. Excavate ephemera—the more obscure, the less "authoritative," the better. Do not, under any circumstances, write a Grand Narrative or a teleological account of the "progress" of the discipline toward *reason* or *truth*. Instead, write a *petit recit* or a series of *petits recits* that complicate or expand large-scale histories. Tell some stories, not The Story.

Don't (just) write; *revise*.

This advice has been commonly and well heeded, so much so that revisionist historiography now holds the hegemonic high ground. Indeed, disciplinary historians have long taken for granted that "any claims to truth in rhetoric and composition are (yawn) partial, situated, and contingent" (Gallagher 843). And, even in 2001 Chris Gallagher could contend, "We already have too much revisionist history in rhetoric and composition" (842). In a 2012 text, Byron Hawk likewise suggests that "traditional historiography is no longer viable." However, he also concludes that "revisionary historiography has given way to bureaucratic mandates (retrieve the excluded)"—a tendency that Ryan Skinnell has called the "broadening imperative" (Hawk, "Stitching" 110; Skinnell 113). What was once a revolution is now the status quo.

These days, scholars offering innovative methods of history-writing position themselves in opposition to revisionist history—not against any sort of unified, teleological, Grand Narrative approach. The practice of disciplinary-history-writing has shifted so thoroughly that there's no historiography that isn't revisionist historiography, extended from it, or framed against it. Certainly, to the extent that revisionist methods produce better answers, this may all be for the best. At the same time, though, for someone to get to be a revisionist, someone or something else needs to be revised. There needs to be an antecedent, general account—or a set of them. I would affirm the value of localized, revisionist histories, and yet I believe they have limited utility on their own. They may add nuance and complexity to larger or broader narratives: diving in, drilling down, wading into the depths. In a fundamental way, though, they therefore rely upon and perhaps even require generalized, background contextualizations: they dive *into something*, drill *into something*, wade *into something*.

Scholars engaged in writing localized histories, it seems to me, have understood the need for generalized histories as well as anyone. David Gold, for instance, argues that "rhetoric and composition historiography must not simply recover neglected writers, teachers, locations, and institutions, but must also demonstrate connections between these subjects and larger scholarly conversations" ("Remapping" 17). Indeed, writing in 2012, he lamented "the paucity of good general histories" while noting that "we are ripe for a reassessment of germinal moments of the last quarter century"—the very era I survey here (19, 29). In so doing, Gold echoed an earlier historiographical critique leveled by Janet Carey Eldred and Peter Mortensen. Despite its myriad benefits, they argue, the move toward smaller, narrower, localized histories could end up producing "a collection of fragmented histories read by an equally fragmented, narrowing audience." Though Eldred and Mortensen would acknowledge the "power in specialized histories," they also conceded, "We know that the flip side of this power is parochialism" ("Coming to Know" 754). The challenge they seem to raise, then, is to produce complementary narratives.

In my efforts to accept and fulfill that challenge, I made a basic historiographic assumption: elements hidden at certain levels of scale become visible at other levels. In temporal terms, consider: if you're only focused on today's weather, you might miss long-term changes in the climate. Or, in spatial terms, consider the merits of different perspectives: if you look in a microscope, you see otherwise unimaginable things, but you can't see the larger context. From thirty thousand feet, you can survey the landscape, but you can't make out anyone's face. Each scale has its own advantages and disadvantages. You can never account for everything by focusing on any given level. You can, however, provide a more robust account by toggling back and forth, by oscillating, and by acknowledging what you can and cannot see each time. Importantly, I will not pretend that this oscillation enables a more "complete" account. Completeness is an illusion, or at least an asymptote.

In optics, *resolution* is defined as the ability to separate or distinguish between closely spaced items. While consumers seem to desire higher and higher resolutions on their television screens, I would affirm that a historian doesn't always need a higher resolution, and sometimes it isn't even desirable. In an instructive example, Lance Massey has analyzed the reception history of Stephen North's *The Making of Knowledge in Composition* at different levels of resolution. As he points out, a "microscopic analysis" of "a relatively small set of texts published within a few years of [that text's] publication . . . enables [him] to reveal the complexities—the disorder—lurking within [its] reception" ("The [Dis]Order" 314). In other words, by zooming in, he can see that some early readers disagreed considerably over how to interpret and/or analyze North's work. But, quite importantly, Massey affirms that "this irregularity is a function of perspective, rather than essence" (314). Whether a difference of opinion is "large" and/or "obvious" and/or "important" depends entirely on *how* you look at it, on whether or not you wish to distinguish between adjacent or related phenomena. When Massey "decrease[s] the magnification of [his] analysis" by considering a wider array of scholarly texts, including those that don't cite *The Making of Knowledge* at all, "the wild tangle of discourses" among competing scholars "suddenly coalesces into a relatively smooth node. That is, the struggle among the various agents of *MKC*'s reception, themselves belonging to clusters of (very) broadly like-minded compositionists, emerges as one distinct part of a larger system of disciplinary activity" (315). At a lower resolution, fine-grained distinctions become invisible. But, sometimes, that invisibility is *useful*. In some cases, too much information produces conceptual static, unnecessary noise.

In writing this book, I have accepted and attempted to work from and through revisionist insights while still presenting a reasonably generalized historical account of a relatively under-documented past. Although a few chapters attend closely to coteries of scholars in specific locales, I have not written a local history here. Instead, I have attempted to account for the reasonably widespread history of (un-hyphenated) postprocess, a movement/theory/attitude about which there has been considerable scholarly disagreement in terms of (A) whether or not it ever existed at all; (B) whether it is best defined as a movement or theory or idea or concept or paradigm; (C) whether its impacts were beneficial or counter-productive; and (D) whether or not its insights even *should* be applied or practiced in the classroom, and if so how. In other words, there's been significant and prolonged disagreement at every level of stasis. To write the history of such a . . . *thing* may seem like a fool's errand. My hope is that it will prove not to have been. I have not attempted to resolve disciplinary disagreements about postprocess but to account for them and then to move past them—to tell other stories that are not simply the story of disagreement(s).

I recognize that I have not yet explained how I intend to use my key term, *postprocess*. I will in due time, to be sure. But, that ongoing omission is intentional, not accidental. To explain why I am delaying, I would like to turn to a relatively "minor" text Thomas Kent wrote before postprocess entered the discipline's discourse.

In his 1991 response to a *Journal of Advanced Composition* interview with Gayatri Chakravorty Spivak, Kent states, "Michel Foucault taught us to talk about history in terms of shifting discourses rather than in terms of transcendental master narratives. . . . Foucault asks us to think about history as changes in the way we employ vocabularies: once we talked like that; now we talk like this" (185). At first glance, this might seem like a conventional, postmodern rejection of historical teleology. Foucault suggests that what might commonly be called progress instead merely amounts to change—and a particular kind of change: one occurring at the level of vocabulary. People used to use one set of terms; now they use another; neither ought to be construed as inherently superior; they're just different. I will return to this argument in Chapter 2, inasmuch as it might help explain the transition from Process to postprocess. Here, though, I would focus on a less obvious conclusions that Kent draws from Foucault.

Working from this Foucaultian perspective, Kent reasons, "we can get rid of the notion that language mediates between us and the world," and thus "stop talking about a split world—a world possessing an intrinsic nature set apart from an internal realm of mental states." In short, he concludes, "We no longer need to worry about the Cartesian or what is now called the internalist problem of matching up our vocabularies to something that exists outside of our subjectivity" (185). One might, instead, recognize that language only attaches to "reality" in a provisional and contingent way; the bond between signifier and signified is conventional but arbitrary—and thus subject to revision. And, furthermore, language is not a neutral mediator; it does not enable one to describe the world as it really is. Rather, one's perception of the world is influenced by how one might describe the world, as well as how others have previously done so. From what Kent would call an externalist perspective, words offer tools for thinking, which means that they also shape what can and cannot be thought; they both enable and constrain. The contents of one's thoughts (or one's "mental states") are thus determined by factors outside of (i.e., external to) one's own head.

Kent frames Spivak as an exemplary externalist, and so he dwells on her response to a reasonably straightforward request: to "conceptualize" or define rhetoric. First, she resists this request. She claims that she is not qualified to define rhetoric because she is not a rhetorician and thus does not know how rhetoricians operate. When pressed, she quotes from Paul de Man, allowing that an essentialist (or internalist) definition might acknowledge rhetoric as "that which is the limit—that which escapes, that which is the residue of efforts at 'catching' things with systems." From Kent's perspective, this response demonstrates the insufficiency of internalist, transcendental categories. If we demand that "names correspond to things as they really are 'out there,' names will forever escape the systems we employ in order to pin down the meanings of names." One would be better served by talking as an externalist, as Spivak prefers to do; in such a light, rhetoric would be nothing more or less than "what rhetoricians do" (186).

If one were to apply this logic to the topic at hand, postprocess, one would stop seeking for a timeless, ahistorical definition of what it is in its essence, acting as though the name for the phenomenon could (or should) apply directly and unproblematically to one and only one thing. As a result, one might stop worrying quite so much—or, more to the point, in quite the same way—about identifying a singular, precise definition and then cementing it once and for all. One might instead track the term in its use by those who use or have used it, recognizing the ways that it has been applied, appropriated, extended, retracted. But, equally importantly, one would see postprocess itself—the conceptual constellation, the signified, not the signifier—as subject to redescription, acknowledging that it could enter into an entirely alternate vocabulary. In short, one might concede that what had been called postprocess might not continue to be called postprocess. One would then examine the tactics of those who have used different terms, attempting to decipher the logic behind their choices.

In my investigation, then, I took polysemy as a given—and, indeed, as a feature of postprocess' underlying theory of language, not some sort of "bug" to be "fixed." However, doing so presented me with a certain historiographic dilemma. I could not simply rely on usages of *postprocess* to tell me which sources were relevant. I couldn't just go to the nearest relevant database, type in a straightforward query for my keyword, read the items that query returned, and report back on my findings.

I also faced an additional layer of complexity. As I will discuss at length in this Introduction's next section, the homophonic but visibly discernible terms (hyphenated) *post-process* and (unhyphenated) *postprocess* entered widespread usage in the years after 1994. But, in that inaugural year, three different scholars, working from three different sets of assumptions, all employed the terms. Two, John Trimbur and Anthony Paré, hyphenated *post-process*. The third, Irene Ward, did not hyphenate *postprocess*. In Chapter 4, I will suggest that Paré's hyphenated vision of a post-process pedagogy shares many principles with what I will call (unhyphenated) postprocess, the designation introduced by Ward. In contrast, Trimbur's hyphenated form seems importantly different (if viewed at my own chosen level of resolution, of course).

For now, let me simply note that a fair amount of confusion arose over what *post-/postprocess* meant and how, if at all, the hyphenated term(s) related to the unhyphenated one. Let me also add a corollary caveat: while the unhyphenated term *postprocess* eventually became the commonplace signifier for a particular understanding of what writing is and how writing works, that convention took some time to develop. Several scholars who initially hyphenated *post-process* to refer to what I will call *postprocess*, including Kent, Sarah J. Arroyo, and Paul Lynch, would later drop it. Others, most notably Gary A. Olson, never (so far as I know) let go of the hyphen. Still others employed and discarded hyphens, apparently haphazardly, within the bodies of single texts (e.g., Ewald, "Tangled Web" 128–30; Petraglia, "Is There Life?" 50–53). In other words, the conceptual bifurcation between competing notions of post-/postprocess existed before scholars reached absolute consensus on a visible, typographic convention for separating them (i.e., the presence or absence of the hyphen). In this book, I have not silently altered any quotations to remove hyphens. For the sake of clarity, though, I have applied the (un-hyphenated) term *postprocess* when authors clearly seemed to be referencing the conceptions of communication I identify with that term.

Fixating on usages of the term(s) post-/postprocess seemed that it would produce more problems than it would solve. So, instead, I determined to focus on a core set of principles that, when combined, came to define postprocess. As I'll demonstrate, those principles circulated throughout the disciplinary discourse of composition studies well before 1994. Postprocess wasn't created ex nihilo in that year. Rather, at that time it received what would become (one of) its name(s). So, I attempted to determine when, where, and how its core principles entered the disciplinary discourse of composition studies. To do so involved a relatively simple initial step: I read texts that seemed indisputably postprocess, and I looked in their works cited entries, and I found out what texts were informing the ones with which I had started. If, as Spivak argues, rhetoric is what rhetoricians do, I assumed that postprocess is what postprocess scholars do, write, argue, teach. So, to give but one example, I turned to Kent's work. When Irene Ward introduced the unhyphenated term *postprocess*, she only applied it to Kent. He edited the first major collection on the topic, *Post-Process Theory* (1999), and he wrote the Preface to the second one, *Beyond Postprocess* (2011). So, analyzing his texts seemed a safe place to start.

I zoomed-in. In Kent's case, I couldn't find his CV online. So, I went to the databases at my disposal, and I queried them all, and I compiled an archive of his work. That archive included texts Kent published throughout the late 1970s and into the 1980s while still a literary scholar, including his first book *Interpretation and Genre*, which I'll examine in Chapter 2. Although some texts might have seemed irrelevant at first glance, I read all of them, and some proved to be quite relevant indeed. In the process, I found out whose ideas had influenced his own. Thus, I arrived at a second step, in which I zoomed out from Kent's work and examined the texts he had been citing. In effect, I moved against the flow of textual circulation, from newer texts to older ones.

From there, a third step followed. When charting the history of ideas, historians have typically begun near the most recent end of their historical timelines and worked backwards, as I was doing in step two. Given the affordances of print-based documents, which don't (because they can't) indicate the flow of their future circulation, the most straightforward way to know where and how ideas have flowed has been to consult one works cited list, then another, then another. However, the information-technological matrix now includes other possibilities, including the Google Scholar citation tracker. In my third basic step, I used that tool to identify textual circulation in the opposition direction. That is, I learned who had been citing Kent. I also took some of the texts that Kent had been citing, and I tried to determine which other composition scholars cited them. I did not pre-emptively restrict my purview. Rather, I presumed that postprocess was not a single, stable thing, and I acknowledged that I didn't yet know what it had been in various places and at various points in time. When I learned who had cited the same texts as Kent and/or who had cited Kent himself, I zoomed in on those authors. I tried to discern overlaps and points of agreement, as well as disjunctions and points of disagreement.

In simplified terms, my method involved zooming in and zooming out, moving forward and backward, in oscillating stages.

Stage One: Zoom in on the scholarship of Author A. Read their texts. Learn from them. For the purposes of different chapters, of course, different scholars filled the role of Author A.

Stage Two: Zoom out. Identify works cited by Author A. Move backwards along the path of textual circulation (from newer to older texts). Zoom in. Read those items that seem relevant. Learn from them. Compare and contrast the works of Author A with those now under consideration. Try to understand which concepts Author A adopted, which ones they dismissed, and which ones they transformed or revised.

Stage Three: Zoom out. Track citations of Author A's works and/or any relevant works identified in Stage Two. Move forward along the path of textual circulation (from older to newer texts). Zoom in. Read as much as possible. Learn things. Compare and contrast.

Then, I would repeat the process with Author B, Author C, and so on down the line, if necessary. Of course, there was no directly replicable formula here; each iteration followed its own path. And, certainly, my process was recursive and non-linear. But, as an approximation, this stage model will serve us well enough.

In analyzing textual circulation, I attempted to account for the formation of a postprocess *public* or a series of them. According to Michael Warner's stipulative definition, *a* public (rather than *the* public) is a "virtual" (or imagined) "relation among strangers," who have joined together inasmuch as they have extended their attention to a given text in the course of its circulation and have commented on it or responded to it, thereby producing a "concatenation of texts" addressing similar issues (50, 55, 61–62). Of course, to the extent that it can be said to exist, "the field" of composition and writing studies is, in Warner's terms, a public. As Kevin J. Porter argues, "the field" does not exist "apart from the fragile—and therefore necessarily continuous—efforts through literature reviews, taxonomies, citations, classroom instruction, doctoral programs, and so on, to manufacture and sustain links between researchers and texts and thereby to (re)constitute 'the field' as a normative ideal or myth" ("Literature Reviews" 365). Shrinking the scale, the same could be said of postprocess: it did not exist apart from the continuous efforts of scholars to "manufacture and sustain links" by discussing the texts and concepts they deemed relevant. And so, I understood the act of citation, or of inserting a given text in a literature review, "not as a way to acknowledge an antecedent community, but as a way to constitute or inaugurate, through a re-viewing of the past, an 'imagined community' [in Benedict Anderson's terms] or 'world' [in Heidegger's], however fleeting" (354).

As subsequent chapters will demonstrate, some of the publics I discovered contained relatively few members; they were akin to the groups studied in local histories in size but geographically dispersed. Even so, tracking citations (and scouring footnotes, and conducting all the other intricacies of scholarly research) allowed me to make sense of when they formed, roughly how long they lasted, and what (if anything) happened to the ideas they contemplated and debated after the initial public dissolved. Two of my chapters focus on publics that were geographically concentrated at first: one at St. Thomas University in Fredericton, New Brunswick, Canada; the other at Iowa State University in Ames, Iowa, United States of America. Each eventually grew its membership and dispersed across the physical landscape. Another public—this one advocating a postprocess model of rhetorical invention—ended up quite large; I will even argue that it has attained disciplinary dominance.

To make this methodological explanation more concrete, let us return to the example of Kent as Author A. I began by reading his work and thus observed his obvious and heavy citational debt to the analytic philosopher Donald Davidson (Author B). I employed the citation tracker and the search engines embedded in discipline-specific databases to find other examples of composition scholarship citing Davidson, including works by Reed Way Dasenbrock, Kevin J. Porter, Stephen R. Yarbrough, and William Duffy (Authors C, D, E, and F, respectively). I read the texts citing Davidson, along with any other texts by those scholars that seemed even remotely relevant.

I learned things. For instance, I found that Dasenbrock had reviewed Kent's *Paralogic Rhetoric* in *Rhetoric Society Quarterly* in 1994. From that text, I was able to learn how Kent's ideas were being interpreted and/or received at that time (before they were being called *postprocess*). Notably, Dasenbrock saw Kent's theories pointing in two primary directions: on one hand, toward a reintegration of theories of reading with theories of writing and, on the other, toward teaching writing in the disciplines ("Review" 103). Dasenbrock's claim struck me as a clear distillation of Kent's larger intellectual project. Having read Dasenbrock's other articles, I had come to admire his insights, especially regarding Davidson's work. And, via the citation tracker, I had already found and read two texts that made me even more inclined to trust him.

The first of these was a chapter entitled "The Social Perspective and Professional Communication," published in 1993 by two of Kent's colleagues at Iowa State, Charlotte Thralls and Nancy Roundy Blyler. That text, written before the terms post-process and postprocess were popularized, identified three primary "social perspectives" on writing research and explored how each might address four key concepts: "community, knowledge and consensus, discourse conventions, and collaboration" (Thralls and Blyler 6). Quite importantly, it distinguished social constructionism from what would become post-process (in Trimbur's parlance) and what would come to be called postprocess (in Ward's), naming the former "the ideologic approach" and the latter the "paralogic hermeneutic approach" (14, 22). In explaining the paralogic hermeneutic approach, Thralls and Blyler were forced to concede that only "a small number of writing theorists" had actually endorsed the position. In practice, however, they only referenced two: Kent and Dasenbrock. The second text inspiring confidence was Kent's highly congenial response to Dasenbrock's review of *Paralogic Rhetoric*, in which the book author assented to many of his critic's critiques and reformulated his assertions accordingly. If Kent was willing to defer to Dasenbrock, that seemed like a good sign for my budding research agenda.

So, I set off on two paths. In one direction, I examined texts from the 1980s and 1990s that aimed to reintegrate reading theories (especially reader-response theories, which Kent himself applied as a literary scholar) with writing theories. I queried the databases, employed the citation tracker, and so on. In sifting through that electronic archive, I focused especially on texts citing Kent or citing the texts he had also cited. That research eventually spawned two chapters. Chapter 3 examines a broad-based movement among scholars in the 1980s to reintegrate theories of reading with theories of writing. In effect, those scholars were formulating one of the three core premises of postprocess—writing is interpretive—before it was placed alongside the other two (writing is public and writing is situated) and their combination was named. One of them, Louise Wetherbee Phelps, even articulated a very strong argument for displacing Process as the single, central metaphor for composition theory. Chapter 4 focuses on three scholars from St. Thomas University: Russell Hunt and James Reither of the English department and Douglas Vipond of the psychology department. In a series of articles (often collaboratively written), those three theorized pedagogical methods that might account for the role of the reader in constructing textual meaning. As I will demonstrate, their work forms the foundation of the pedagogical methods Anthony Paré deemed *post-process* in his 1994 article.

Chapter 5, in contrast, follows Dasenbrock's other key insights: that postprocess points toward Writing in the Disciplines (WID). To explore that conceptual connection, I decided to return to some of Kent's texts from the 1980s, in which he was formulating his theories concerning writing instruction. If composition studies is defined narrowly by a preoccupation with first-year writing instruction, Kent published many of his proto-postprocess texts outside of its bounds, in journals focused on professional and/or technical communication. That is, before it was an approach to composition, (what came to be called) postprocess was an approach to other sorts of writing instruction. I suspected that this lineage mattered, and I set out to determine how postprocess tenets influenced that WID public. I found that several of Kent's colleagues at Iowa State University, including Thralls and Blyler, had advocated recognizably postprocess tenets in WID scholarship, as had several scholars they trained in graduate school. I traced the citations of their works, and interesting insights presented themselves. Foremost among them: the presently popular Writing about Writing approach, which amounts to teaching first-year writing courses as though they were Writing in the Disciplines courses, represents a point of convergence for the Iowa State postprocess public and the Canadian post-process one examined by Paré.

In tracking the circulation histories of postprocess texts, I tried to account for the formation of publics, for their scale, and for the influence of individual texts within them. However, I also tried to account for the reception histories of the most prominent individual texts—how they were interpreted at various points in time. Most large-scale histories of the discipline have focused on authors and their publications—saying, in effect, *in Year X Author Y wrote Text Z*—as though authors simply put texts into the world and those texts conveyed their messages perfectly, thereby achieving their intended goals. Here, in contrast, I assumed that any given text can be—and necessarily *is*—interpreted in a variety of ways, only some of which the author would endorse. I rejected the assumption that textual meanings remain static. Instead, I considered textual reception by asking what certain texts were understood to mean and/or allowed to mean at different stages—that is, how the meanings attributed to them have changed over time.

In Chapter 6, I will examine Marilyn Cooper's "The Ecology of Writing" (1986) as a conceptual precursor of postprocess inventional thought. Although that text only addresses invention obliquely, discernibly postprocess texts that do address something like invention commonly cite it, alongside canonical texts on invention. That is, I discovered "The Ecology" (and the other core texts I'll examine by Karen Burke LeFevre, James E. Porter, and Reither, respectively) circulating within an invention-related public. Janice Lauer has famously argued that 1986 marks the year when scholarship on rhetorical invention began to appear in a "diaspora of composition areas rather than in discussions labeled 'invention'" (2). My own account supplements hers by suggesting why that migration, which I would frame instead as a shift in vocabulary, might have occurred. As Foucault (and Kent, following him) might point out, invention is a concept better suited to an internalist vocabulary, inasmuch as it derives from Latin words meaning *come* and *in*. The inside/outside dichotomy embedded in the term is not particularly well suited toward an externalist conception of cognition that denies the distinction between mind and world. Indeed, as Steven Jeffrey Jones suggests in an excellent 1988 article, theorizing an externalist form of the first canon would require scholars to "rethink our terminology, speaking of 'assembling' or 'building' a text rather than 'expressing' a message as if it were some 'inner' happening which the text represents." In other words, "Rethinking the scene of writing . . . involves questioning the adequacy of idioms" ("Logic" 15). Thus, one might explain the alleged disappearance of inventional thinking after 1986 to a shift in word-choice (and an associated shift in thinking), rather than a decline in interest in associated issues.

In studying the circulation history and reception histories of Cooper's article, I drew two key insights. First, it has become much more commonly cited in recent years than it was at the time of its publication—a trend that calls out for an explanation. Second, at different points in time, it was examined within two very different publics, and it was interpreted to mean different things in each.

At a low level of resolution, let us begin by considering its citation history in quantitative terms, ignoring the myriad distinction between the works citing Cooper's article. In its first five years in print (1987–1991), "The Ecology" was cited 47 times. In its next five (1992–1996): 49. From ages ten to fifteen years (1997–2001), it dipped to a new low: only 28 citations. From that point, though, its growth shot up: 53 times from 2002–2006, 94 times from 2007–2011, and 174 times from 2012–2016. Thus, between 2011 and 2016 "The Ecology of Writing" received only three fewer citations than it had in its first twenty years in print *combined*. In short, Cooper's work has grown substantially more popular over time.

Now, one might argue that this increase in citations is the fate of many "classic" articles: they attain the sort of prestige that demands that everyone writing on a topic must cite them. But, such an argument can't account for a simple fact: in years eleven through fifteen, Cooper's article received far fewer citations than it had in years six through ten (roughly sixty percent of the previous total). It may now be a "classic," but it wasn't an "instant classic." Moreover, at one point, the text was starting to disappear slowly from "the" scholarly conversation. Its arguments were losing their "relevance"—until they weren't anymore.

To state the obvious: the text itself—conceived of as a set of stable markings on a page or screen—never changed. And yet, at one point in history, due to factors external to it, Cooper's article was considered to have less "value" than it is now credited with having. One might explain these developments in several ways. For instance, one might emphasize the role of *kairos* for academic scholarship—and not only at the moment of publication, but throughout the process of circulation. Or, per the economist Fritz Machlup's groundbreaking research in *The Production and Distribution of Knowledge in the United States*, one might deny the distinction between information distribution (and/or re-circulation) and information production. Moving information into a place where it can be useful is fundamentally an act of authorship. The text is re-newed, even re-produced, as it enters into a different textual and/or interpretive network. From this perspective, one might consider which other texts had re-interpreted, re-circulated, and/or re-newed Cooper's text during the late 1990s and early 2000s, teaching other scholars how to read it differently and/or filtering it into publics where it proved to be more useful. For what it's worth, I would primarily credit Cooper's own subsequent scholarship; Margaret Syverson's *The Wealth of Reality* (1999); two works edited and written, respectively, by Christian R. Weisser and Sidney I. Dobrin, *Ecocomposition* (2001) and *Natural Discourse* (2002); and Jenny Edbauer's "Unframing Models of Public Distribution: From Rhetorical Situation to Rhetorical Ecologies" (2005).

Or, as one final means of explaining the increasing "relevance" of "The Ecology," one might apply a transactional conception of textual meaning, drawing from the scholarship of Louise Rosenblatt (and some other scholars I'll discuss herein, including Louise Wetherbee Phelps, Russell Hunt, and Douglas Vipond). Rather than assuming that the meaning of the text exists independently of the readers who co-construct it and the contexts in which they do so, transactionality assumes that all of those elements are implicated in "a complex network or circuit of inter-relationships, with reciprocal interplay" (Rosenblatt, "Viewpoints" 101). One might then distinguish between the article-as-text, a set of static marks on a page, and what Rosenblatt might call the article-as-*poem*: "an occurrence, a coming-together, a compenetration, of a reader and a text," which "must be thought of as an event in time" ("Poem" 126).

Thus far, I've talked only about the quantitative elements of Cooper's citation history. But, knowing how many times "The Ecology" was cited is ultimately less important than understanding how it was interpreted, what those interpretations demonstrate about scholarly attitudes and assumptions, and what subsequent discourses were called into being via its circulation. Even if the same words appear on the same pages, textual meanings change over time, a point that transactional models help to explain. Cooper's text becomes notable in this regard because, in its earliest stages, it was very commonly understood as contributing to the dialogue on discourse communities and/or social-epistemic theories of rhetoric (c.f., Ewald "What We Could Tell"; Freed and Broadhead "Discourse Communities"; Killingsworth "Discourse Communities"; Reiff "Rereading Invoked"; David Foster "What Are We Talking About"). This pattern of reception quite clearly bothered Cooper. She begins her 1989 chapter "Why Are We Talking about Discourse Communities?" by opposing the underlying, foundationalist ideology of "many discussions of the notion of discourse communities," and she later notes, "I am concerned that the concept is easily co-opted to serve purposes that are directly opposed to what I feel to be the most productive way of thinking about discourse (*Writing as Social Action* 202, 204). She also ruminates, wistfully,

> Being cited is a pleasant experience. I suppose it's a sign that
> one has been accepted into a discourse community. It's also
> a learning experience of sorts: you learn all kinds of things
> about what you wrote. From a recent citation I learned that in

"The Ecology of Writing" I attempted "to describe a discourse community and the dialectic involved as discoursers and community each act upon the other and change each other." I didn't know I had done that. (203)

However, in a felicitous turn of events, the text has more recently found itself serving as a core document in the new-materialist or object-oriented criticism of human-centered, internalist conceptions of communication. To put matters plainly, "The Ecology of Writing" is now cited *to oppose* the very ideas it was previously cited *to uphold*.

To reaffirm an earlier point: of course, the stable markings of the text did not change as the text circulated. Instead, what changed was a set of broadly dispersed but nonetheless common (i.e., both ordinary and shared) scholarly assumptions, which readers brought to the text, and which informed their interpretations of it. Observing this hermeneutic transformation, one might conclude that contemporary scholars have seen the proverbial light: they finally understand what the text "always," "really" meant. In some sense, this may be true. But, I am less interested in construing some objective sense of interpretive correctness than I am with identifying widely dispersed interpretive conventions and considering what can be learned from them. At the time Cooper wrote, many readers did not—and perhaps *could not*—interpret the text as it is interpreted today. The contemporary impacts of the text—or what Kevin Porter would call its *consequences*—were not, at that time, being felt because its readers (i.e., its publics) so persistently connected up to the wrong concatenation(s) of texts and ideas. They interpreted by way of certain principles and premises, and those habits of mind blinded them to alternate interpretive possibilities, even ones suggested prominently and repeatedly by the marks on the page. Now, however, there's a textual archive that *author*izes readings of her article as a conceptual precursor of postprocess, one that enables readers to see how it works against the hegemony of Process and strives to articulate a complex model of writing not governed strictly or solely by human agency. There's also a public of scholarly readers who have accepted and absorbed such principles and who are struggling to develop them further.

Obviously, I don't want to lay too much weight on the fate of a single article. Still, I believe that reception histories can clearly indicate shifts in widespread conceptualizations or what, following Kent, I will later call *unformulated conventions*. In what follows, then, I'll apply similar methods of reading to other texts: attempting to determine what the text's author(s) may have intended at the time they wrote by reading as many of their other texts as possible, triangulating my interpretations against those of "early" respondents and critics, then tracking how responses and interpretations have changed over time. From those changing responses, I attempt to discern tacit or underlying premises, to account for modes of thinking and structures of feeling—only some of which are ever expressed in overt or direct ways.

THE HISTORICAL ORIGINS OF POST-PROCESS AND POSTPROCESS

"A word may never be precisely defined, exhausted, and, finally, put away," Kent argues in a postprocess ur-text, and thus it is often less productive to attempt to define terms than it is to "explain how we intend to employ them" (*Paralogic Rhetoric* 146). In this book, I have attempted to account for the history of what I will call (un-hyphenated) *postprocess*, not what I will call (hyphenated) *post-process*. I have tried to be rigorous in distinguishing between the two, so allow me to note my usage.

To make sense of how the hyphenated term *post-process* circulated in disciplinary conversations, it's useful to know its pre-history. Throughout the early-to-mid-1980s, several scholars, including James Berlin, Patricia Bizzell, Lester Faigley, Richard Fulkerson, and Steven Lynn, attempted to taxonomize the various sub-components of the Process movement. Demonstrating the difficulty of ever producing a "complete" or even "correct" classification scheme, three of those five (Berlin, Bizzell, and Fulkerson) would attempt the same task more than once. Without wading too deep into these waters, let us acknowledge that those taxonomies have proven quite durable, especially the tripartite division between expressivist, cognitivist, and social forms of composition posited by Bizzell and Faigley (and somewhat re-affirmed, though with different labels, by Fulkerson and Berlin). To be sure, each group evidenced internal disagreements. The term *social*, in particular, was employed to unify a number of tenuously connected theories (social constructionism, discourse communities, social-epistemic rhetoric, "academic writing," cultural studies) and pedagogical approaches (e.g., collaborative writing, peer editing, ideology critique). And so, the same sort of political factionalism that arose in the more famous expressivist-versus-social "theory wars" also arose among scholars committed to different social approaches.

This fact should not surprise us, of course. As the deconstructionists in English departments were demonstrating during those same years, an opposition between terms (say, *social* versus *expressivist*) often serves to mask the internal oppositions within each one. And, furthermore, ignoring those internal divisions is a necessary pre-condition for imagining each as a stable or unified "whole" in the first place. That which is presented as a natural and inevitable unit had to be *constructed* from an assemblage of unlike parts (Johnson, *Critical*

Difference x–xi). One might then de-construct each supposedly unified term, if one felt compelled to do so—showing, for instance, the disparate and competing elements of the social approach to composition during the Process period. Furthermore, and quite importantly, one can (almost) always shrink the scale and repeat the operation. Consider, for example, David Foster's critique of a single subset of the "social" grouping: social constructionism as presented by Kenneth Bruffee. Foster employs a vivid metaphor to prove his point:

> The difficulty is that Bruffee corrals the social constructionists
> in one well-marked pen, then rounds up what he variously
> calls "cognitive," "Cartesian," or "empirical" thinkers in a
> much larger pen on the other side of the ranch, hoping (one
> supposes) that their bawling and kicking won't be heard as
> they threaten to knock down the conceptual fences Bruffee
> drives them into. What undermines Bruffee's claims on behalf
> of social constructionism is his uncritical eagerness to herd
> together profoundly different thinkers on both sides. ("More
> Comments" 709)

In my estimation, Foster's critique is both fair and correct. And yet, there are better and worse ways to apply this rationale to other phenomena.

In many instances, deconstructive logics were applied nihilistically, to "prove" that nothing purported to be "real" actually exists. But, I think that's the wrong take-away. From my perspective, it's more important to acknowledge the underlying complexity and dissonance within each supposedly singular thing, and to admit that most conceptual "units" are the products of prior acts of *uni-fication*, that is, unit-making. *E Pluribus Unum*: out of many, one. Other units could have been made from the same plurality of "raw materials," and others can and will be. To make sense of this last point, consider Robert Hass' heavily anthologized poem "Meditation at Lagunitas" (1979). In its opening lines, Hass succinctly explains some central tenets of two conceptual units, Platonism and Post-Structuralism. The former sees objects in this world as corrupted versions of eternal Ideas; the latter demonstrates that there is no necessary correspondence between signifier and signified. Many commentators have framed Post-Structuralism as an attack on Platonism, and rightly so. Hass instead affirms their likeness: "All the new thinking is about loss. / In this it resembles all the old thinking." In other words, he *unifies* them. However, to affirm their resemblance isn't to suggest that the two discourses are identical; Hass himself shows how each focuses on a different sort of loss (and for different reasons). In suggesting their likeness, then, I think Hass aims at a larger point: the decision to unify or separate the two discourses always depends upon some arbitrarily selected, external criterion. Nothing inherent to either discourse determines that they should or should not be unified.

I note all of this because one could always find some basis by which to unify postprocess and Process, or post-process and Process, or post-process and postprocess, or All of the Above, for that matter. This is not to say that each hypothetical act of unification is as valid or conceptually useful as any other. It is, rather, to suggest that one should be prepared to defend any decision to join a multitude or to disperse a unit. In principle, I agree with Hannah J. Rule: "any efforts to definitively separate process approaches or ideas from postprocess ones should be interrogated" (*Situating* 51). She and I disagree, however, on how to apply that rationale. Whereas she collapses the distinction between the two, seeing the new as an extension of the old, I think one can examine the distinction carefully and still find good reason to uphold it.

For what it's worth, at the outset of this project, I chose to accept the story that postprocess scholars told about themselves—that their work should be distinguished from Process scholarship (and, yes, from post-process scholarship) on the basis of an underlying theory of mind and a belief in the uncodifiable and non-systematic nature of writing. I then asked what disciplinary narratives might emerge, if this distinction were considered to be meaningful. But, I will explain all of that in due time.

In his 1989 "Consensus and Difference in Collaborative Learning," John Trimbur critiques Bruffee's social constructionist, collaborative learning model of writing instruction. Trimbur gladly admits the progressive lineage of collaborative learning, which emerged during the Open Admissions program at the City University of New York. He also acknowledges that Bruffee pursued just ends—"democracy, shared decision-making, and non-authoritarian styles of leadership and group life"—and implemented conceptually consistent practices at the level of classroom management (605). Even so, Trimbur's article's examines two "left-wing" critiques of collaborative learning: first, that it represents "an inherently dangerous and potentially totalitarian practice that stifles individual voice and creativity, suppresses differences, and enforces conformity"; and second, that it "runs the risk of limiting its focus to the internal workings of discourse communities and of overlooking the wider social forces that structure the production of knowledge" (602-03). Then, Trimbur "extend[s] the left critique" by interrogating the metaphor of *conversation* and the end goal of *consensus* posited by other "social turn" collaborative-learning scholars (603, 606).

In a 1991 article, John Schilb offers a similar account. Within the "'social turn' of the eighties," he argues, "a new form of consensus [formed] around the notion of 'initiating' students into 'discourse communities.'" However, by Schilb's account, the theoretical foundation of that movement was offered by neopragmatist thinkers like Richard Rorty, Stanley Fish, and Kenneth Bruffee, who "scorned more radical critiques of the university and society at large." In response, during the late 1980s and early 1990s, "oppositional criticism . . . swept through the field," exemplified by "movements like feminism, Marxism, minority studies, post-colonial studies, and gay/lesbian studies. Separately and together they have brought up issues of difference, oppression, justice, power, and the academy's social responsibility" ("What's at Stake" 95).

With this preface aside, let us turn to "Taking the Social Turn: Teaching Writing Post-Process," Trimbur's 1994 review of three books, by C. H. Knoblauch and Lil Brannon, Kurt Spellmeyer, and Bizzell, respectively. The books in question, Trimbur suggests, "make their arguments not so much in terms of students' reading and writing processes but rather in terms of the cultural politics of literacy." Thus, he reasons, they

> can be read as statements that both reflect . . . and enact
> what has come to be called the "social turn" of the 1980s,
> a post-process, post-cognitivist theory and pedagogy that
> represents literacy as an ideological arena and composing as
> a cultural activity by which writers position and reposition
> themselves in relation to their own and others' subjectivities,
> discourses, practices, and institutions. ("Taking the Social
> Turn" 109)

The meaning of the *post* in post-/postprocess has been a considerable source of disagreement, with scholars debating whether it signals a rejection, or an extension, or an intensification of Process. To be direct: it has signaled each of those things, at one point or another, per the rhetorical needs of various scholars. This sentence, the only one in which Trimbur uses *post-process*, offers little clarity on what, exactly, he meant to indicate by the term at the time. Even so, I would draw attention to a few of his argument's key elements.

When it appears in Trimbur's text, the adjective *post-process* appears in an appositive position, syntactically equivalent to *post-cognitivist* but presumably not meaning the same thing, and modifying and/or explaining the social turn of the 1980s. That is, Trimbur initially indicates that the social turn itself was post-process. Given that social, expressivist, and cognitivist approaches tended to dominate the Process era, Trimbur appears to equate Process with expressivism and suggest that the social turn represented something separate both from it and from cognitivism. That is, I think, the simplest reading. Still, in the immediately following sentence, Trimbur suggests that the books under review "offer the opportunity . . . to take a look at . . . the leftwing trajectory of the social turn and its political commitments." So, drawing from Trimbur's review alone, one struggles to discern whether the entire social turn is to be considered post-process or only the left-wing critiques of it. He does, in any case, suggest that the works of Knoblauch and Brannon, Spellmeyer, and Bizzell "result from a crisis within the process paradigm and a growing disillusion with its limits and pressures" (109). So, I think there's at least some basic for seeing his "post" as signaling a rejection of Process, rather than intensification or even extension.

Trimbur is often credited with introducing *post-process* into the disciplinary lexicon, but that is not, strictly speaking, true. The term had been used a full decade earlier—by Judith Langer in an editor's introduction to the May 1984 issue of *Research in the Teaching of English*. However, so far as I can find, that fact has never been acknowledged within the discourse of so-called "high postprocess theory" (Sánchez, "First" 185). In addition, during the same winter of 1994 in which Trimbur's review article was published, Canadian writing scholar Anthony Paré published his own text using the same term: "Toward a Post-Process Pedagogy; or, What's Theory Got to Do with It?" I will address those texts extensively later, in Chapters 3 and 4, respectively. Here, let me note that neither Langer's nor Paré's usage became particularly influential (judging by their articles' citational histories). So, it's fair to say that Trimbur *popularized* the term.

Although scholars would use the (hyphenated) term *post-process* in a variety of ways, I believe that Alison Fraiberg aptly and concisely explains how it was most commonly employed throughout the 1990s and early 2000s. She writes,

> As a theoretical position, post-process argues that the theory of writing developed by the process movement over the past thirty years relied heavily on expressionism and, as such, did not attend to historical, social, and political circumstances of writers, readers, and texts . . . . Post-process thinkers rely heavily on critical theory's and cultural studies' critique of subjectivity to articulate a theory of writing based on discursive conditions. Writing, for the post-process composition scholar, is always social: subjectivity is multi-valenced and multi-voiced; writers and readers are always conditioned and interpolated by networks of social relations; and the goal of composition is in part about raising students' awareness of their own discursive formations. ("Houses Divided" 172)

Now, to be sure, one could argue with this definition on historical grounds: not all Process approaches were expressivist, for instance, and many expressivist approaches were more politically sophisticated than they're often credited with being. However, my purpose here is not to justify to the term's usage; instead, I want to describe it.

Throughout this book, then, I am using hyphenated term *post-process* to denote what Thralls and Blyer had called the "ideologic" social approach and what Trimbur called the "leftwing trajectory of the social turn": an exploration of how societal power dynamics affect individual writers and/or inform classroom-level pedagogical methods. From my perspective, post-process represents a rejection of Process (narrowly conceived of as expressivist and/or cognitivist) on leftist or progressive political/ideological grounds. Post-process theories also tend(ed) to focus on a series of (broadly defined) "social" concerns, particularly the connections between language, knowledge, and power, and they employ cultural-studies frameworks and/or the so-called hermeneutics of suspicion. Post-process pedagogies often entail(ed) or resemble(d) Freirean forms of liberatory or critical pedagogy.

In contrast, I am restricting the un-hyphenated term *postprocess* to refer to an externalist conception of the writer's mind and a paralogic conception of the writing act. I will explain my usage of those key terms—*externalist* and *paralogic* shortly—but, as with (hyphenated) *post-process*, to make sense of how the unhyphenated term *postprocess* circulated in disciplinary conversations, it's useful to investigate its earliest application. To my knowledge, Irene Ward was the first to use the unhyphenated term in her 1994 *Literacy, Ideology, and Dialogue*. However, for the sake of historical completeness, I would acknowledge that Raúl Sánchez seems to have used the hyphenated term *post-process* in his 1993 CCCC presentation to refer to what Ward would subsequently call un-hyphenated *postprocess* (Dobrin, *Constructing* 83–84).

At the outset of her book, Ward acknowledges a broad shift in composition scholars' thinking, away from sender-receiver (encoding/decoding) models of written communication and toward "a much more complex" one in which writing is seen as "a communicative, rhetorical, and, above all, dialogic process." This re-imagining, she notes, foregrounds collaboration and thus opposes the fiction of the solitary, autonomous author (2). Ward's book accounts for the dialogism evident in expressivist, social constructionist, "radical" (post-process), and "postmodern" theories of writing and/or writing instruction. By Ward's estimation, the first three "assume varying and sometimes contradictory notions of dialogism." But, they still differ from the fourth in one key way: expressivist, social constructionist, and radical dialogism "are considered part of composition's 'process paradigm.'" In contrast, she notes, "Recently, several compositionists have challenged the process paradigm, attempting to institute a postprocess, postmodern pedagogy. These compositionists have been heavily influenced by deconstruction and other poststructuralist theories" (129). More specifically, Ward refers to Gregory L. Ulmer, William A. Covino, and Kent.

Ward describes Ulmer as someone who "posits a rationale for a postmodern pedagogy in general," Covino as one who "has attempted to develop a postmodern composition pedagogy," and Kent as one "who through a sustained effort has worked to devise a postprocess, postmodern theory for composition studies" (130). Thus, while she calls each a postmodern thinker, she only directly applies the term *postprocess* to Kent. Repeating a gesture she had made the previous year in her *JAC* review of Kent's *Paralogic Rhetoric*, Ward identifies Kent's efforts to "move composition scholarship beyond the process paradigm" three times, using a slightly different phrase each time (Ward, *Literacy* 150, 146, 158; "Review" 183, 186). A few years later, a similar phrase, *Beyond the Writing-Process Paradigm*, would appear as the subtitle to the 1999 collection *Post-Process Theory*, which Kent edited.

Ward demonstrates why Kent might reject (left-wing or "radical") post-process approaches (based on their underlying internalism) and why post-process scholars might reject him (for failing to consider power relations).

Post-Process scholars critiqued social constructionism for failing to consider social power dynamics, but they generally still accepted its major premises: knowledge is socially constructed, discourse communities exist, and mastering the linguistic norms and/or knowledge-base of a discourse promotes success in subsequent acts of communication. Trimbur, for example, leads his students to question who is (and is not) empowered to construct knowledge and who benefits from stratified social relations. But, he leaves the basic logic of social construction otherwise intact. He writes, "One of the tasks of writing instruction, as I see it, is to help students learn how experts . . . make judgments and represent them in writing . . . [and] to examine . . . how professional monopolies of knowledge produce special interests, on the one hand, and deference to authority and public ignorance, on the other" ("Taking" 115).

Kent, in contrast, would level a "devastating critique" of those underlying social-constructionist premises (Ward, *Literacy* 150). He frames the "thick" version of social constructionism, which posits firm and fixed boundaries between discourse communities, as upholding untenable premises regarding the impossibility of communication across linguistic groups and/or the untranslatability of concepts across paradigms (Ward 150–51). From his perspective, a shared language is not a pre-requisite for communication because all communication invariably involves a form of on-the-spot interpretation or *hermeneutic guessing*. Nothing acquired prior to the act of communication can guarantee its success—certainly not knowledge of discourse conventions—but an examination of language-in-use shows that no such guarantees are necessary. Communicants (or, at least, those willing to do so) continually revise their expectations of each other's communicative conduct until they negotiate a good (enough) level of understanding. They start with *prior theories* about how fellow conversants will use language but each party continuously revises their assumptions until their respective *passing theories* align. In Kent's words, then, assimilating into the norms of a discourse community is not a pre-requisite for effective communication. Rather, he argues, "A knowledge of conventions—linguistic or otherwise—only helps make us better guessers" (*Paralogic Rhetoric* 31). Furthermore, Kent sees the "thin" version of social constructionism, which acknowledges the polyphony of voices within communities, as equally problematic: if the "thick" understanding of discourse communities does not hold, and members of various groups *can* communicate with one another, then "we no longer need the concept of discourse community" at all (Kent, "Very Idea" 428; qtd. in Ward 152).

At the same time, Ward demonstrates how one might critique Kent's social-interactionist approach by way of post-process principles. In her estimation, it does not consider power relations, especially gender-based ones, to an adequate degree (165–66).

Ward, an alumna of the University of South Florida, introduced the unhyphenated term *postprocess* into disciplinary circulation, and, so far as I can tell, her grad school peers were the next scholars to employ it. Julie Drew would do so in her 1995 review of Ward's book (161), and Sidney Dobrin likewise discussed postprocess theories and pedagogies in his 1997 *Constructing Knowledges*. As Ward had done, though to a lesser degree, Dobrin heavily restricts his usage of the term *postprocess*. He applies it to Kent's scholarship, to the theories Ward derived from it, and to the pedagogical theorizing of Sánchez, another USF alum. Notably, Dobrin alternately refers to Sánchez's theorizing as *postprocess* and *Kentian* (83–84). Subsequently, in his 1999 "Paralogic Hermeneutic Theories, Power, and the Possibility for Liberating Pedagogies," Dobrin would uphold the distinction I am making between post-process pedagogies and those derived from Kent's work. He begins that chapter by noting,

> In its most succinctly rudimentary definition, *post-process* in composition studies refers to the shift in scholarly attention from the process by which the individual writer produces text to the larger forces that affect that writer and of which that writer is a part. . . . The identification of larger influential structures afforded writing teachers the opportunities to teach definable, codifiable systems as conceptual schemes (Donald Davidson's phrase) that dominate discourse production. More recently, a few composition theorists have moved beyond this post-process inquiry and have begun to investigate ways in which the moment of communicative interaction supersedes

and possibly refutes the constructions of "systems." Thomas
Kent, for instance, has turned to the work of language philosophers Richard Rorty and Donald Davidson to propose
that every moment of communicative interaction is singularly
unique. (132)

In that text, Dobrin does broaden his collective of postprocess scholars—this
time adding to the mix Kent's Iowa State colleague David R. Russell and Anis
Bawarshi, who was a graduate student at the University of Kansas while Dobrin
worked there from 1995–1997 and who climbed the ranks at *JAC*—from editorial assistant to assistant editor to senior editor—during a period in which Kent
edited the journal and/or co-edited with Dobrin. But, this time around, Dobrin
exclusively refers to models derived from Kent as *paralogic hermeneutic* theories
and pedagogies, not as *postprocess* ones. Even so, when he theorizes a paralogic
hermeneutic approach to writing instruction (i.e., a postprocess one) that might
also attend to social power relations and employ methods of Freirean critical
pedagogy, he stacks one *post* on top of another, calling it *post-post-process* (133).

Postprocess as Externalist, Paralogic Mindset toward Writing

As I will use the term, postprocess *sans hyphen* implies an externalist and paralogic conception of writing. In simplified terms, *externalism* is a philosophy of
mind (or, a conception of what the mind *is*) that sees all thought as flowing from
and through the contributions of numerous factors outside one's own head: both
human and non-human others; material objects; languages and symbols and
virtual things. That is, it rejects the Cartesian (internalist) idea that one could
retreat into the solitude of one's own mind (and one's own mind alone) and still
produce thought. In place of *cogito ergo sum* it says something more like *Alii
sunt ergo cogito*: others exist; therefore, I think. For externalists, solitary thinking
is impossible. Thus, whenever one communicates, one does not do so "alone."
    Philosophers of mind commonly distinguish between two forms of external-
ism: *semantic externalism* (also called "content" or "what" externalism) and *vehicle
externalism* (also called "how externalism" and referred to as a component of the
"extended mind thesis"). As its name indicates, semantic externalism examines
the interplay between the meanings of the words and the environments in which
those words have been used. It also presumes that *what* people think—i.e., the
contents of their thoughts—is a function of the meanings of the words they know.
That is, unlike internalists who generally assume that thought precedes communication (or the translation of thought into language), semantic-externalists

suppose that languages both allow for and structure thought and that languages are functions of their environs and their histories of use; thus, they reason, environmental or external factors intrude into the thought process.

In its most basic sense, vehicle externalism assumes that (indefinitely many) objects outside the head drive cognitive processes. Words, which might be construed as cognitive tools, are counted among these things, but they are not alone. The list of cognition-extending objects includes high-tech gadgets like GPS systems, calculators, and search engines, but also relatively rudimentary devices like pencils and paper. Defining a "parity principle," cognitive philosophers Andy Clark and David Chalmers write, "If, as we confront some task, a part of the world functions as a process which *were it done in the head*, we would have no hesitation in recognizing as part of the cognitive process, then that part of the world *is* (so we claim) part of the cognitive process" (27). Or, to state matters differently, if those objects commonly employed to assist in thinking were removed, the cognitive process would deteriorate, just as if part of one's physiological brain were excised. Thus, vehicle externalists argue, it is reasonable to treat regularly accessible items with known functions as though they were a part of the ("extended") mind.

The human mind has always necessarily functioned via externalism, whether it was recognized as doing so or not. Even so, as high-speed internet connections, search engines, smart phones, and the like increasingly become sine qua nons of both contemporary labor and leisure, the externalist nature of human minds becomes more and more apparent. Clark suggests that the "ancient seepage" of mind into world, and vice versa, is "gathering momentum," such that the mind is located "less and less in the head" (4). For what it's worth, posthumanist theorists, who tend to be how-externalists, commonly voice similar claims. For instance, N. Katherine Hayles concludes *How We Became Posthuman* by asserting, "We have always been posthuman," by which she means that the Western notion of liberal, individualist humanism has never been philosophically tenable—and one did not necessarily need information technology to experience and respond to one's ecology (291, 288). Byron Hawk likewise argues: "Technology makes the fact that the body is immersed in networks of complexity much more immediate and harder to ignore" (*Counter-History* 234).

For what it's worth, early postprocess scholarship, especially in the work of Kent, presupposed semantic externalism but only gestured very tentatively toward vehicle externalism. Later critiques of his work, especially by Byron Hawk, Thomas Rickert and Collin Gifford Brooke, and Jennifer Rae Talbot, have faulted it for being insufficiently vehicle-externalist.

By presupposing externalism, I will argue, postprocess also necessarily presupposes paralogy. In one of his first texts on the subject, Kent defines a *paralogic* rhetoric as one "that treats the production and the analysis of discourse as open-ended dialogic activities and not as codifiable systems" ("Paralogic Hermeneu-tics" 25). To simplify heavily: Kent and postprocess theorists following him see writers as being at least as engaged in hermeneutics (i.e., interpretation) as readers. In their eyes, "successful" communication (that arrives at something like "shared" meaning or agreement) flows from a non-systematic and non-systematizable set of guesses that communicants make about each other's inter-pretations of language and the world. In foregrounding the necessity of guessing, postprocess scholars suggest that nothing that is known or done in advance of communication can guarantee the success of that communication. Instead, to the extent that communicative interactions (i.e., conversations or textual inter-changes) may be said to succeed, their success derives from the ability of com-municants to align their interpretive strategies during the process of communi-cation itself (31).

In this book, I have followed other postprocess thinkers in dividing move-ments within composition scholarship according to their underlying philoso-phies of mind. Kent may have been the first to do so, but Joe Marshall Hardin states the case most pointedly: "Even the most social of process theories . . . are internalist philosophies masquerading as externalist," whereas, from his vantage, a "radical externalism . . . undergirds postprocess theory" ("Putting" 71, 65). Hardin asserts a clear division between Process and postprocess theories accord-ing to their respective internalism and externalism, but I would temper this claim slightly. Considering Process to designate a (very broadly defined) theoret-ical and/or pedagogical approach, as well as a temporal era, I would acknowledge externalist outliers during the period, including Richard Coe, Robert Zoellner, and the difficult-to-categorize Ann E. Berthoff. Even so, if one were to follow the commonplace tripartite taxonomy of major Process approaches—cognitiv-ist, expressivist, and social—one could illustrate the internalism of each sub-field's leading theorists.

Internalist suppositions are most evident in the early cognitivist models of Linda S. Flower, John R. Hayes, and their followers—one thinks here of their attention to the student writer (singular) and to their characteristic method of studying physically quarantined students. But, they appear equally in the expres-sivist call to express oneself, to take ideas that (allegedly) found their origins internally and move them outward. As Lisa Ede and Andrea Lunsford rightly demonstrate, many of the expressivist theorists most commonly associated with student-centered instruction, including James Moffett, Donald Murray, Peter Elbow and Ken Macrorie, quite ironically avowed "traditional concepts of autonomous individualism, authorship, and authority for texts" (*Singular Texts* 113). Though I might situate them in a historical interregnum, as those providing a conceptual bridge between internalism and externalism, or between Process and postprocess, Kenneth Bruffee and other social constructionists/ social-epistemic rhetoricians did ultimately avow internalist principles, as well (Kent, *Paralogic Rhetoric* 98–104). Bruffean collaborative learning, for instance, supposes that individuals can, if they so choose, operate alone. In contrast to these Process-era approaches, the externalist theories emerging since the dawn of postprocess suggest that such aloneness is an ontological impossibility, forbidden by the very fact of one's being in the world. All writing is always already over-written by other people and, crucially, other stuff. Or, to give one final illustration: while analyzing the socio-economic and/or cultural factors "conditioning" or otherwise influencing subject-formation, Marxist and/or left-wing social-turn scholars typically presupposed the prior existence (if only at birth) of a "pure" or "unsullied" mental core. Externalists would dispense with these metaphors of purity and pollution, of conditioning and influence; for them, the inside-outside logic that presumes a separation between the (interior) mind and the (external) world cannot hold. Mind is smeared or distributed across world and entangled with it.

At the same time, the break between Process and postprocess is "clean" only to the extent that one privileges philosophy of mind as a disciplinary movement's or epoch's defining trait. Those who have preferred to ground their taxonomic schemes on separate criteria have often argued that postprocess continues the legacy of Process rather than stepping out from it. By Kevin Porter's account, Process and postprocess share an underlying theory of meaning ("Literature" 369–70). Raúl Sánchez sees the two connected by a "subject-oriented, representational writing system ("First" 187–88). Following Diane Davis, who sees postprocess hermeneutics as failing to attend adequately to the otherness of the other ("Finitude"), Byron Hawk argues that postprocess is, like Process, still oriented toward "the goal of communication and understanding," rather than "an ever-new invention that breaks out of dialectic and into multiplicity" (*Counter-History* 222). And, Collin Brooke and Thomas Rickert have faulted postprocess for retaining humanist assumptions, rather than fully accepting posthumanism ("Being Delicious" 163–66). The viewpoint from which and the (conceptual) apparatus through which one observes the phenomenon shapes the phenomenon itself, and so I would acknowledge the validity of those alternate viewpoints, even if I do not personally endorse them. There's no necessary reason why any criterion should prove superior to any other; each is ultimately arbitrary. Still, I have attempted to narrate the history of postprocess from its own perspective, which means that I'm privileging externalism and paralogy here—and also producing a certain version of postprocess in the process.

CHAPTER 2.

THE VOCABULARY OF POSTPROCESS; POSTPROCESS AS VOCABULARY

In the last chapter, I occasionally referred to postprocess as a movement/theory/attitude—a cumbersome appellation that may seem to punt on the scholarly obligation to classify phenomena precisely. In the rest of this book, I primarily refer to postprocess as a noun, rather than applying the term adjectivally to some other thing (e.g., "the postprocess movement"). My decision to do so is deliberate, not accidental, and it reflects an important truth: critiques of Process have shown that several of the best and most obvious categorizations applied to it were, ultimately, untenable.

POSTPROCESS AS PARADIGM? A VERY BRIEF REJOINDER

If there wasn't a Process paradigm—and there wasn't—then there certainly wasn't a postprocess one, either. What Robert Connors wrote nearly forty years ago strikes me as equally true today: "[Thomas] Kuhn's terms, applied analogically as a claim for the essentially scientific or prescientific nature of the discipline [of composition], lead us only to blind alleys or to unrealistic expectations" ("Composition Studies and Science" 17). The methods and procedures of experimental sciences that allow for paradigm-formation simply do not exist in composition and/or writing studies. Although this distinction is often framed as demonstrating an inherent deficit in writing research, I would caution against such a conclusion. Rather, I would follow Gesa E. Kirsch in affirming that "as scholarship in composition expands and diversifies, it becomes more insightful and valuable (133).

THE TROUBLE WITH MOVEMENTS AND THEORIES

Of course, many scholars imagined themselves as belonging to the Process movement. Chris Anson recounts being "transformed by" and even undergoing "a kind of metamorphosis" after his exposure to it (214). Similarly, Nancy DeJoy's chapter in *Post-Process Theory* is entitled "I Was a Process-Model Baby." Process was a term for self-identification with strong affective dimensions; it offered a sense of progress and of belonging. But, one might rightly ask whether scholars' self-identification with a given banner provides sufficient justification for historians to consider them to have been unified under it. In some obvious sense, the answer to such a question would be yes. However, any answer would ultimately be a function of the resolution of one's conceptual apparatus, the extent to which one distinguishes between closely related items.

Although many scholars identified with Process, they didn't always identify their work with one another's. Despite extensively demonstrating the existence of a discernible group of "supporters of writing as a process," Richard Fulkerson agrees that the term *movement* should not apply to them. Instead, he conceives of them "as a political party (the WAP), with members frequently willing to vote together for the same candidates, and more or less united around certain slogans lacking in nuance and short enough for bumper stickers" ("Pre- and Post-Process" 98). Lisa Ede notes, "At the level of scholarship, the term 'movement' was certainly elastic enough to allow for what in retrospect seems to be considerable diversity" among Process approaches (*Situating Composition* 70). And she continues,

> Though there was broad support for and interest in process-based research in the 1970s and early 1980s, it is important to remember that there were many scholarly and curricular projects—many "movements"—on-going in the composition during this time. It's certainly true that few of the scholars involved with these projects saw themselves as working in opposition to the writing process. But it is equally true that research on the writing process was not central—and in some cases not relevant—to their efforts. (71)

Thus, she ultimately concludes, "Depending on where and how you look, there both was and was not a writing process movement" (*Situating Composition* 64). This is no small point—one worth applying to classifications of Process as a theory or even as a set of theories.

Depending on where and how you look—depending on your conceptual resolution—there was and wasn't such a thing as Process theory. This ambiguity is fundamentally related to how words work. As Friedrich Nietzsche carefully demonstrates: "every word . . . has to fit countless more or less similar cases—which means, purely and simply, cases which are never equal and thus altogether unequal. Every concept arises from the equation of unequal things." Any given word—*Process*, for instance, or *postprocess* or *leaf*, which is Nietzsche's example—"is formed by arbitrarily discarding these individual differences and by forgetting the distinguishing aspects" ("On Truth" 83). This truth was infrequently applied to Process, though.

In her 1978 response to Sharon Crowley's "Components of the Composing Process," Nancy Sommers castigates Crowley for failing to define her central term, *process*. However Sommers' primary quarrel isn't with Crowley but with a broader tendency among composition scholars: "The word process exists in such a terminological thicket and has become so much jargon, so maligned and misunderstood, that the more the term is used, the less we seem to understand what is meant by the idea that composing is a process" (209). I would affirm that Sommers was, in all likelihood, correct on this point. Yet, I would also affirm that any other, single term would, eventually, have suffered the same fate.

Although the term *Process* was applied extensively and enthusiastically, Process tenets did not impact all areas of collegiate writing instruction simultaneously or in the same ways. As scholars of L2 writing themselves admit, Process entered their domain well after it had begun to affect L1 writing pedagogy and research. In a 1995 article, Tim Caudery surveys the impacts of Process on L2 writing scholars, ultimately hoping to validate the movement. In doing so, he also provides what I believe is the best and most straightforward explanation of how the term *Process* proliferated. "As teaching approaches become more widespread," Caudery observes, three trends tend to emerge. The first of these is diversification: "different people interpret ideas in different ways." Second is simplification, which implies a sub-element of distortion: "as ideas spread from one teacher to another, it is the strongest and most distinctive elements of the original approach that tend to survive." And third, selection: "while some teachers may use, say, a particular teaching method in its 'pure' form, others come to incorporate bits and pieces of it into their teaching." Thus, for Caudery, Process could not help but mean different things to different people—and the same would be true for any other pedagogical approach. But, he suggests, the evolution of the term (Process) might be seen as demonstrating the strength of the movement in question, not a fault within it.

In a 1986 reply to Daniel Horowitz, Joann Liebman-Kleine similarly praises the polysemy of *Process*. In her estimation, to attempt to fix the meaning of the term, or to affix only one set of associations to it, is to do violence to Process itself. Only its critics, acting in bad faith, would do so. She writes,

> People who criticize the process approach seem to treat it
> as some sort of monolithic entity, complete with canon and
> commandments. Horowitz says it has been "miscast as a com-
> plete theory of writing." If so, the casting agents are not the
> advocates of process, but its detractors. The process approach
> is not *an* approach; it is many approaches. There will never be
> *a* process approach because writing—the process of writing—
> is such a complicated and rich process. . . . The process per-
> spective will inevitably encompass many different approaches,

for a key assumption of all process theory, research, and
pedagogy is of difference: Writers have different processes.
("In Defense" 785)

As Liebman-Kleine's response demonstrates, Process was sometimes understood
as an umbrella term, even by those who self-identified with it, and the accusation that it meant one and only one thing was seen (by some) as an outright
attack on it.

Postprocess was not granted the same level of terminological flexibility, in
contrast. I will gladly grant that the clean-cut linguistic distinction I am employing here—separating politically oriented, "social" post-process from paralogic,
externalist postprocess—was not always so clear in earlier scholarship. But, even
granting the confusions that these homophones produced, *post-/postprocess* was
never so generalized a term as *Process*. It never grouped together phenomena
so different as cognitivism and expressivism and social-epistemicism. Even so,
from its early stages, terminological clarity and consistency were demanded of
it in ways not initially demanded of its predecessor. Its semantic indeterminacy
was used as a bludgeon against it, typically as evidence that it did not exist at all.

In concluding this section, I would offer one final, crucial remark. Even
in demonstrating that Process was a highly disparate phenomenon and that
Process theory only exists as a very generalized abstraction, I would still resist
assuming that *postprocess* (as an adjective) should modify the noun *theory*—at
least as theories are commonly conceived. That is, I am rather dubious about
calling postprocess a *theory*—except as a "theory with a very small *t*"—and I
have consciously avoided doing so in this book, given the baggage that the term
theory has been made to carry (Kent, "Preface" xvi). I prefer to see postprocess as
describing a state of affairs regarding the limits of what is conventionally called
(capital-T) Theory: something that can stand outside of practice and guide
it. To make a broad-scale distinction, Process scholars generally believed that
learning more about writing processes and then teaching that knowledge would
enable students to produce texts better and/or to produce better texts. In contrast, postprocess scholars have tended to assume that "an appeal to theory—an
attempt to construct a theory of writing, whether process or some other—is mis-
guided, because theory simply does not guide or govern our practice." Rather,
as Gary A. Olson affirms, "Practices arise instead out of the very specific, local
conditions that generate them" ("Why Distrust?" 426). Just as knowing that one
is in a rhetorical situation provides one with little guidance for how to act within
that actually existing situation, knowing that one has a writing process (or even
several writing processes) offers almost no direction in terms of how to approach
any specific writing task (Olson, "Fish Tales" 253–54).

Though I hesitate to acknowledge the existence of postprocess theory, I do believe that postprocess has functioned as a theory, if *theory* is understood in a constrained and specific way: as a form of practice itself—in Kory Lawson Ching's words, "a way of seeing, a vehicle, a momentary rest stop, an instrument with which to think otherwise" ("Theory" 452). Ching offers a rigorously externalist conception of theory, one that recognizes that words and concepts are not merely neutral media for thought; rather, they alternately enable and constrain it. Elaborating on this conception, Karen Kopelson affirms the value of theoretical *relexicalization*: offering a different lexicon, an alternate vocabulary. She argues, "One of theory's most indispensable, urgent tasks is the work—or *play* . . . —it does on and in language. Theory works against received grammar so that we might exceed the constraints language imposes upon the thinkable itself, so that we might uncover, resist, explode, and enter into what is foreclosed by the habitual" ("Back" 602). Scholars who lament the "difficulty" of theoretical language are thus not entirely wrong to do so. Theoretical language does demand that one expend cognitive effort not normally spent when using what Nietzsche might call "the usual metaphors," those constructions that have been attributed by convention the force of truth—statements like *writing is a process* ("On Truth" 84). I will have more to say about relexicalization at the chapter's close, when I consider the value of framing postprocess as a *vocabulary*.

A BRIEF DIGRESSION ON DOUBLE STANDARDS

Before proceeding onward, I want to pause briefly to consider two common criticisms of postprocess. First, several scholars, including Bruce McComiskey, Helen Foster, Richard Fulkerson, and John Whicker, have attempted to undermine the existence of postprocess by demonstrating the ambiguity of the category *postprocess* (Foster 5; Fulkerson, "Of Pre- and Post-Process" 107; McComiskey, *Teaching* 47; Whicker 499). Even scholars sympathetic to postprocess and hoping to extend its rationale have felt compelled to address their key term's inherent polysemy before proceeding onward (e.g., Breuch 121; Heard 285). Second, several have accused postprocess of caricaturing its predecessor in order to validate its own existence (Ede 75, 85; Fulkerson, "Twenty-First Century" 670; Hawk, *Resounding* 48; Matsuda 74; Sánchez, "First" 186). I hope I have already demonstrated that the first of these criticisms could have been—and often was—leveled at Process. The second also could have been—and occasionally was, as well. I would note here a historical irony: in theory, at least, postprocess was better suited to absorb criticisms concerning semantic ambiguity than Process. It is a vision of language which does not demand that terms have clear and stable referents.

Bemoaning the homophonic status and/or the linguistic indeterminacy of *post-process* and *postprocess* entails applying a criterion that postprocess, at least, fundamentally works to undo or reject. To assume that words have clear and static definitions and that those words (can or should) carry those meanings in(to) every new context is to deny that language-in-use constructs language-as-system and to deny likewise the inevitability of hermeneutic guessing and radical interpretation. In my estimation, criticisms of postprocess that fixate on terminological indeterminacy betray a failure to understand or—per the principle of charity—even to try to understand what postprocess scholars worked so hard to convey.

To approach postprocess on its own terms is to approach those writing about it as though they are ethical and intelligent actors making true statements about the world. It does not demand that one (i.e., the reader) understand in advance what those authors mean by their terms. Rather, a central postprocess premise is that arriving at a "proper" or "correct" interpretation is not a function of knowing a language. Instead, postprocess would seem to request that readers work with authors (and the textual traces they have provided) to negotiate workable meanings by considering whole utterances, rather than individual statements or passages.

The underlying logic of postprocess implies that the term *postprocess* could not help but have multiple meanings, as it would be employed by an indeterminate number of writers/speakers in an indeterminate number of settings for a relatively wide array of uses. In this way, postprocess offers a large-scale critique of language use as it had come to be conceptualized by Process-era compositionists. Indeed, Olson distinguishes postprocess from Process on precisely these grounds: the term itself (i.e., *postprocess*, which Olson notably hyphenates as *post-process)* cannot have just one meaning because the upshot of the theory is that words neither have nor need to have just one meaning. He admits, "Post-process does *not* refer to any readily identifiable configuration of commonly agreed-on assumptions, concepts, values, and practices that would constitute a paradigm." But, immediately thereafter, he hastens to add, "Neither does 'process'—it only seems to refer to something specific and identifiable to those caught in process's thrall" ("Why Distrust" 424). When Olson refers to "those caught in process's thrall," I believe he references scholars working from internalist suppositions who accept and even demand ahistorical, prescriptive definitions. To distinguish a Process vision of language from a postprocess one, Olson refers to the meaning of the word *writing.* He argues, "Despite attempts to deny that they are doing so, process theorists always return to a language"— by which he probably means a vocabulary, but by which he might also mean an understanding of language—"that assumes that writing and the activities that comprise it can somehow be filled with a content, can somehow be specified and made stable." That is, they want the word *writing* to mean something consistent and predictable, regardless of the context in which it appears. The trouble here, of course, is that writing (the act or object, i.e., the signified) differs so wildly from one instance to the next that no single signifier (e.g., *writing*) could adequately address or describe each instance. From Olson's perspective, then, specifying and stabilizing the definition of writing represents "an impossible goal, for it assumes that writing can be untethered from specific contexts, that somehow we can describe writing detached from specific acts of writing, specific attempts to communicate particular messages to particular audiences for particular reasons." Postprocess, in contrast, rejects this impossible goal at the outset. It focuses on particulars, especially those that cannot be captured or conveyed by generalized theories or generalized terms. "So," Olson concludes, "to say that 'post-process' doesn't have a specific referent is to pay it a compliment. It's to say that the message has gotten through that no such specificity is possible—and never was" (425). Many readers either did not understand this critique or failed to accept it, though. As a result, they assessed postprocess according to their conventional methods for scholarly argumentation. In Thorstein Veblen's (and later Kenneth Burke's) terms, they may have had a trained incapacity for engaging differently with postprocess.

To undermine postprocess—even to deny its claim to exist—its opponents have also demonstrated its (alleged) tendency to create a straw man or caricature out of Process. By Sánchez's account, without this caricature, postprocess would have been "unidentifiable, unimaginable" ("First" 186). According to Fulkerson, post-process actually "commits the straw-character fallacy twice over," by suggesting that Process emphasizes linear rigidity (i.e., a singular, non-recursive writing process) and in portraying Process as solely expressivist and cognitivist and thus not also social ("Twenty-First Century" 670). It's worth remembering three points, though.

First, those various scholars who benefited from operating under the Process umbrella were also disregarding just how very different their work was from some other Process scholars. That is, each of them, in their own way, also made a caricature of Process, accentuating some features and diminishing others. In Caudery's terms, they selected and distorted. In this light, I would suggest, Process was always a caricature, even long before postprocess.

Second, Process has also been accused of caricaturing current-traditionalism in order to validate its own existence (Matsuda, "Process" 71; Miller, *Textual Carnivals* 110; Tobin, "Introduction" 4). George Pullman, for example, demonstrates the "oversimplifications and obfuscations" within commonplace histories of Process, and he argues that "the Process movement first constructed and then dismissed current-traditional rhetoric in order to valorize itself" ("Stepping"

16). If anything, I find the logic of this critique more persuasive when applied to Process than to postprocess. Postprocess simply did not invent Process in the same way that Process invented current-traditionalism. As I've already demonstrated, many, many scholars self-identified with Process of their own accord, well before the terms *post-process* and *postprocess* entered the discipline's conversation. In contrast, as Pullman convincingly argues, current-traditionalism, as it's often discussed these days, "did not exist as a theory except to the extent one could extrapolate a theory from the textbooks current at the time" (22). In an important sense, current-traditionalism (as a unified theory, a noun) never existed, except as an argumentative straw-man. From one tenable perspective, then, Process did not invalidate current-traditionalism, given that it could not: current-traditionalism had never really existed previously. Instead, current-traditionalism was invented to validate Process by contrast (Pullman, "Stepping" 23).

Third, current-traditionalism was internally variegated, in the same ways as Process, and for the same reasons. In a 1981 article, Robert Connors identifies current-traditional rhetoric as "a palimpsest of theories and assumptions stretching back to classical antiquity," and he argues, "C-T rhetoric is not, as is sometimes supposed, a coherent, static whole. In actuality, it is a dynamic entity forever in flux, dropping used-up or discredited theories and assumptions and gradually absorbing new ones" ("Current-Traditional Rhetoric" 208). Notably, Connors concludes his article by affirming, "C-T rhetoric will never, <u>can</u> never, merely 'wither away' or be overthrown as many of us dreamed it might be in the sixties and the early seventies. C-T methods will always be the armature upon which change is shaped" (220). In his "Discursive History" of Process and post-process, Paul Kei Matsuda similarly suggests that "the popular history of the Process movement . . . oversimplifies the multiplicity of perspectives that have always been present throughout the twentieth century," that is, during the time in which current-traditionalism purportedly reigned ("Process" 67). Current-traditionalism was far from monolithic, he argues, and Process was not the first critique of it, only the most successful (68).

Postprocess, we are told, called forth its own being by creating a straw man out of Process. The force of this accusation is clear: postprocess doesn't exist—and never existed—because its existence was justified on false premises. But, if one were to trace out the underlying logic of this accusation, one would have to say that postprocess doesn't (or didn't) exist because Process didn't exist because current-traditionalism didn't exist, either. For what it's worth, Ede presents this argument concisely: "Just as scholars arguing for the writing process movement established a strawman they termed current-traditional rhetoric, so too have those who have critiqued this movement, for they have reified and essentialized a loosely held affiliation of projects" (Situating 75).

On one level, I completely agree with her reasoning: critics of prior models have often selected and distorted features to build their own cases in opposition.

And yet, I worry about one possible, logical extension of her argument. If one were to call each movement an imaginary, unreal strawman, thereby undermining the existence of each, in turn, one would end up with an oddly flattened and conceptually undifferentiated vision of the history of the field. Claiming that postprocess doesn't exist because it differentiated itself against something else that did not exist may produce one benefit—a "better" acknowledgement of the variegated qualities of each historical epoch. But, that benefit would necessarily come at a very high cost in terms of being able to differentiate periods from one another. To argue that nothing has changed in one hundred years would be absurd. That gesture would also ignore something fundamental about how language works: it always produces certain distinctions and flattens others. But, the flattening that's so commonly lamented is offset by—and worth it for—the benefit of being able to construct knowledge at all.

On top of all that, I'm not convinced that this strawman argument actually disproves the existence of postprocess in the way that its proponents contend. As Olson has been very direct in demonstrating, postprocess is very much a critique of (one particular vision of) Process ("Why Distrust?" 424). But, it isn't simply or solely a function of a reductive characterization of its predecessor. Regardless of how one feels about its characterizations of Process, it also differs in important ways, particularly in its emphases on paralogy and externalism. Postprocess has "positive" content (i.e., it affirms things); it is, as Reed Way Dasenbrock once described Kent's *Paralogic Rhetoric*, "far from being purely a negative critique" ("Forum" 103). Any characterization of postprocess as simply a continuation of Process (according to some necessarily and yet still arbitrarily selected category) would thereby do a sort of reductive violence to it.

Ede emphasizes that scholars "would do well to develop some healthy suspicions" of disciplinary taxonomies, "particularly when they are used primarily to establish hierarchies and create opposing theoretical camps that suggest that teachers can and should enact 'purified' theoretical positions." I strongly support that reasoning, and yet, because that argument has proven so persuasive, I want to affirm her immediately prior point: "Scholars need terms and taxonomies to help organize our thinking" (*Situating* 97). Yes, whenever one generalizes, one always risks over-generalizing. But, every word is, in some sense, a generality, a concept, "aris[ing] from the equation of unequal things"—and we haven't dispensed with words yet. Therefore, in the same way that we have learned to use words, despite the dangers incumbent in doing so, I would argue that we ought not dispense with taxonomies—say, current-traditional versus Process versus post-process versus postprocess.

On Not Over-Extending Process

In the previous section, I demonstrated that two of the most common criticisms of postprocess could have been (and sometimes were) leveled equally at Process. And yet, *Process* became and has remained a conceptually and theoretically necessary category for theorists and historians of composition, so much so that they have found themselves unable to dispense with it, even after admitting all its faults and perils. There's now a general agreement that theories of Process (Process theory, Process pedagogy, the Process movement, and so forth) reduced the complexity and diversity of underlying phenomena. But, whereas there's now a (generally unspoken) moratorium on discussing current-traditionalism and postprocess for those exact reasons, Process has remained oddly insulated. It rests on unsteady but still hallowed ground. As a result, Process comes to absorb everything, if only by default. The tendency to leave Process intact doesn't just occur in the works of postprocess opponents, though. And it isn't simply an effect of theoretical naïveté, either. It also arises in theoretically sophisticated texts by those who have shown themselves sympathetic to and/or respectful of postprocess. Consider, for example, Byron Hawk's *Resounding the Rhetorical* (2018).

In that text, Hawk attempts to produce "a more expansive sense of composition, one based on new materialist ontologies that see composition as a larger material process in constant modes of transformation" (36). Composition as a practice is and should be understood as being more expansive than just writing, and so the discipline that studies it must also be understood as fundamentally dynamic and emergent. To develop his argument, Hawk categorizes composition as a "quasi-object," something "primarily relational . . . constituted via social relation and circulation" (22). However, as Hawk also notes, quasi-objects are not entirely relational; they have certain objective properties that exist, regardless of what viewers attribute to them; they are also "part material specificity. They aren't simply static or preexistent—they are partially moving, emergent, composed events that are slowed down and partially stabilized by relations" (28). That is, composition is an ongoing and inherently dynamic historical entity that is constantly re-made as it (re-)circulates and (re-)connects with other nodes in an expansive and proliferating conceptual network.

Now, notably, in the course of *Resounding*, Hawk attempts to reimagine the meaning of several key disciplinary terms: "composition, process, research, collaboration, publics, and rhetoric" (12). In a gesture reminiscent of Stuart Hall's work, he plays upon the dual nature of articulation: as both a saying and a form of joining. He uses words in relatively novel ways so as to join them to different concepts, thereby transforming both the terms themselves and the intellectual networks through which they circulate and which they co-construct. This method also accords with one of his long-standing approaches to historiography, which he elaborated in *A Counter-History of Composition* (2007): "Writing affirmatively by using categories to open up possibilities rather than exclude them" (270). That is, he focuses less on what a word *has been taken to mean* and more on what it *might come to mean*. In each chapter, he aims to "produce a reorientation of the field through the iteration of the key term" in question (*Resounding* 12). This is very high-level, impressive theorization.

Hawk's second chapter, "Process as Refrain," re-works his entry in *Beyond Postprocess* (2011), which I will apply for my own purposes in Chapter 6. In both of his texts, Hawk attempts to "reassemble" postprocess by connecting it to Deleuzian, Heideggerian, and Latourian concepts. In his earlier text, he aimed to do so by "articulat[ing] a posthuman world of open invention through the expression of worlds" ("Reassembling" 77). In the latter case, he writes, "Reassembling postprocess theory articulates a parahuman world of the refrain, open invention through the expression of worlds where the quasi-object of composition is the network that inscribes the subject as the subject scribes the network" (*Resounding* 53). As even this sentence alone shows, his latter text is considerably more complicated than its earlier iteration.

But, more to the point, the latter text is considerably less affirmative toward postprocess. In it Hawk draws heavily from Ede's *Situating Composition* in order to articulate a different vision of Process—one that, in my estimation, arrives at the expense of postprocess. Hawk begins with some arguments that might seem to undermine Process: it was never as coherent a paradigm as it has sometimes been credited with being; its existence as some sort of coherent entity was "far from obvious"; and "its history has largely never been written in a way that accounts for its large body of scholars, its wide array of practices and institutional locations, its wide array of agents, and its more complex chronology" (47–48). I agree with each of these claims but disagree with the conclusion Hawk draws from them. Rather than disintegrate Process, he aims to extend and entangle it in novel ways—to treat it as a quasi-object.

Even if he might explain the operation in more complex terms, Hawk's basic argumentative operation involves subsuming postprocess back into Process, framing it as an extension of its predecessor rather than a departure. In this way, his work aligns with continuationist appraisals offered elsewhere by Bruce McComiskey (*Teaching* 47) and Helen Foster. In *Networked Process: Dissolving Boundaries of Process and Post-Process* (2007), Foster writes, "My primary purpose is to (re)acclimate our sensibility to the historical richness of writing process discourse and to bring into relief those aspects of process against which post-process situates itself" (31). As Lance Massey notes, Foster "finds a 'rebuttal' to post-process in the sheer diversity of process approaches" ("Book

Review" 158). Hawk seem to do something quite similar, though his argument also rests on the continued application of Process pedagogies within individual classrooms.

Per Ede, Hawk endorses a turn toward the local, the "material sites of practice where theory gets used and produced, such as the classroom." Focusing on localized concerns would, by this account, "keep scholars from making overly general paradigmatic claims about the field, such as a movement into postprocess, that cover over practices such as the continued use of writing process pedagogies" (48). To my mind, this sort of attention to only one level of scale (i.e., the local) presents its own problems. Historical transformations don't occur all-at-once. As the science-fiction writer William Gibson notes, "The future is already here—it's just not very evenly distributed." The same, of course, could be said of the past: it is still here—just not very evenly distributed. A residual regime can continue to exist alongside the emergence of its replacement, and many do. But, pointing toward the residue of the residual in one's own classroom does not, *ipso facto*, deny the existence of that replacement. Of course instructors would continue to employ writing process pedagogies even as the theories and methods underlying them were slowly rejected. Many aspects of current-traditionalism remain with us, after all. I would also note another objection: here Hawk posits a movement into postprocess as a problematic, "overly general paradigmatic claim" (48). One is left to wonder, then: why not apply the same logic to Process? And, perhaps even more: why continue to absorb more and more things into Process when its internal diversity already presents incumbent conceptual challenges? Why generalize an already-too-generalized phenomenon further still?

Hawk admits that "the concept of process allowed the works of many people to be collected together even as their projects and practices varied widely." Even so, he credits Ede with "looking at the ways past practices continue under present theories" and being able to see "writing processes, social processes, and postprocesses as blurring together and evading clear breaks." From Ede's perspective, which Hawk seems to endorse here, "postprocess is a continuation of process, not a break" (51). By this account, it did not produce a rupture because Process was always itself dynamic and emergent; at most, Hawk suggests, "postprocess rearticulated process through the social turn" (53).

At the start of his chapter, as I've noted, Hawk claimed to be reassembling postprocess theory. But, by its end, postprocess has been absorbed back into Process. Again the differences between the *Beyond Postprocess* and *Resounding the Rhetorical* versions of his text are illuminating. In his former entry, Hawk offers not "a refutation of Kent's model of postprocess but an extension of his position beyond the limits of his passing hermeneutical theory," arguing that "the theory itself has to change and evolve. It has to move beyond itself as it rearticulates with new situations, new assemblages, new expressions, new publics, new worlds" ("Reassembling" 92). The underlying logic here is not so very different from what he re-presents in his updated account. But, there, Kent's work is no longer classified *as postprocess*. In *Resounding*, Hawk claims that a reconfiguration of Kent's key terms (situated, interpretive, and public) "extends Kent's model *of process* beyond the limits of his passing hermeneutical theory and into a version *of process* that shifts it from the social turn into the material turn" (*Resounding* 73; emphasis added). Indeed, the three terms that Kent had used to differentiate postprocess approaches from process ones "ultimately collapse into a model for processes of material composition, which builds, invents, coproduces associations with highly localized sets of practices, agencies, and mediators" (75).

I think that Hawk correctly conceives of Process as a "quasi-object" with a "variable ontology," that is, "a network of multiplicities, multiples, and swirls that materially entangle pasts, presents, and futures" (53). Although I have tried to state my case in less dense language, I am conceiving of postprocess (and, for that matter, Process and current-traditionalism) in very similar ways: as something that transforms as it connects with other concepts, an internally variegated thing—that is, an assemblage or multitude—with (at minimum) spatial, temporal, and relational dimensions. However, I disagree with the conclusion that Hawk derives from this premise. After defining Process as a quasi-object, he states, "The move, then, is not to oppose process but to extend and entangle it—produce other versions through particular compositions or locations" (52). There isn't one and only one move one could make here, though.

The decision to privilege Process is *a decision*, one with both benefits and costs. And, at the risk of redundancy, I would repeat myself: there is no reason why Process would need to be the preferred or privileged term in his or anyone else's analysis, especially given the problems incumbent in constituting it as an object in the first place. If anything, I might suggest, postprocess actually has less conceptual baggage, if for no other reason than that fewer things were ever connected up to it. Furthermore, even if Process is a quasi-object, surely other quasi-objects must exist, as well, each with its own bounds and limits.

In justifying its own existence, postprocess faced a stronger burden of proof than Process ever did. Hawk's chapter, I would argue, serves as a strong example of this tendency. Within his argument, Process remains a useful and even necessary analytic category, despite its dubious claims to existence, whereas postprocess is deemed merely an extension or variant of Process. However, if one is willing to concede the existence of the one, there is no *a priori* reason to deny the existence of the other. If one is willing to conceptualize Process as a quasi-object, I see no reason why one couldn't conceptualize postprocess as a quasi-object, too.

To be clear, though, I am not chiefly concerned with which term Hawk has chosen to privilege. The term is ultimately arbitrary. Instead, I want to point out that he could not conduct such an analysis without *some term* to fill the argumentative slot. His argument requires historical periodization, even if periodization is complicated and messy. In continuing to employ the term *Process*, and in arguing that it should be continuously articulated and entangled anew, Hawk applies standards to one term (*Process)* that he cannot, by extension, apply to the other (*postprocess*). Within the structure of his argument, there could never be something like postprocess (i.e., a replacement for Process) because it would always already be some newly entangled, emergent form of Process itself. In the end, Hawk is willing to differentiate Process from current-traditionalism, if only by implication. But, he ends up unwilling to differentiate postprocess *from it.*

POSTPROCESS AS *PERIOD*

Having contemplated the dangers of characterizing postprocess as a paradigm, a movement, and a theory, I'd like to consider the merits of treating it as a temporal indicator, a period or an era. To do so, I'd like to turn to a text that seems to have everything and nothing to do with postprocess: Kent's *Interpretation and Genre: The Role of Generic Perception in the Study of Narrative Texts*, a work of literary criticism that has its roots in the author's dissertation at Purdue University. As its name indicates, *Interpretation and Genre* is chiefly concerned with the "clear relation" between how readers conceptualize genres and how they interpret literary texts (9).

Throughout the book, Kent attempts to formulate a "systematic, reader-centered theory of genre" that would account for both its synchronic (i.e., "static and rule-bound") and diachronic ("dynamic and culturally dependent") elements (9, 15). He presents these various aspects as "interact[ing] in a continuous dialectical activity," and therefore concludes, "A genre is a changing perception within the human mind just as much as it is a fixed set of things" (33). In Kent's model, then, "each literary text should be viewed simultaneously as an unchanging body of words and as a continually developing cultural artifact" (27). William Styron's *The Confessions of Nat Turner* both was and wasn't the same text in 1967 and 2017, after all, and so on. One can know the conventional, formal elements of a Petrarchan sonnet and even how contemporary poets are re-appropriating the form and yet not know in advance how to interpret a given instance of the genre—nor how it will be interpreted in the future. Because genres change over time, so do the meanings of texts. Thus, even if it isn't postprocess per se, *Interpretation and Genre* still closely connects to his later work on communicative interaction and paralogic hermeneutics. Rather than focus on writers whose work will be interpreted, though, it focuses on readers who will do the interpreting. It asks similar questions but from the opposite angle.

Given its concern with the dynamic and evolving (diachronic) elements of genre, *Interpretation and Genre* requires a theory of historical change, which will be my primary concern here. Importantly, within Kent's genre model, many diachronic elements of genre remain tacit. They are, in his words, "unformulated conventions" (38). Those who write at a given time may share a set of core assumptions, even if they are not consciously aware that they share them, and a careful reader can derive those premises or strategies or rules. However, those unformulated conventions are not fixed, either. Because these unformulated conventions achieve an unspoken commonality in the absence of direct negotiation and/or prescription, they "always ha[ve] something to do with change and a culture's inconstant sense of what is significant and important" (40).

To account for the evolution(s) of unformulated conventions, Kent turns to Leonard Meyer's *Music, the Arts, and Ideas*, extrapolating several historical principles. First, in its cultural-determinedness, history is hierarchic: some phenomena are considered to be more important than others, and those important elements hold a longer "reverberation time," thereby outlasting less important elements and remaining in "the present" longer (40). Furthermore, events can become important by being associated with other important events. Second, only when the (alleged) "full significance of an event is known" is it "closed out," thus entering into "the past" (40). Third, periodization schemes function like genres for historical narration. On this last point, Kent quotes (and I will repeat) Meyer at length:

> Periodization is not . . . merely a convenient way of dividing up the past. It follows from the hierarchic character of history. Periodization is a necessity, if the succession of particular events in the past is to be understood as being something more than chronicle—that is, as being more than a series of events strung like beads upon the slender thread of sequence. Were it not hierarchically articulated into reigns, epochs, style periods, movements, and the like, the past would lose immeasurably both in understandability and in richness. . . . Our conceptual classification of an event influences the way in which we perceive and understand it. (43)

That is, just as genre-perceptions guide literary interpretations, so to do periodization schemes guide historical interpretations. Thus, one cannot simply dispense with periodization; periodizing events endows them with meanings and makes them understandable.

In Kent's framework, periods are understood to hold some sort of internal consistency and to differ from other periods. However, their boundaries are "fuzzy and indistinct" and "characterized by turmoil" (44). The work of the literary historian, then, entails describing the emergence and disintegration of periods, which Kent comes surprisingly close to equating with unformulated conventions:

> One of the literary historian's projects is to provide a description of the disintegration of unformulated conventions and the emergence of new ones. Or stated another way, part of the literary historian's task is the description of periodization, how periods develop and how they collapse. (*Interpretation and Genre* 44)

While describing historical periods, however, the historian must remain mindful of her own historical positioning, the present in which she exists (44). From his analysis of unformulated conventions, then, Kent identifies "three independent sets of hierarchic structures" that the historian must contemplate: first, periodicity, the traits that "differentiate one set of events from another; second, the unusual or unconventional events that have affected the author, given that authors often compose texts that do not "reflect the unformulated conventions of [their] time"; and, third, the unformulated conventions that affect the historian's own writing (44).

In terms of its relevance to literary study, I am not qualified to assess Kent's assertion that periods can be (and perhaps are) defined by their unformulated conventions. However, this insight strikes me as quite useful to the disciplinary historian of rhetoric and composition and/or writing studies. As I demonstrate in Chapter 5, the vast majority of inventional strategies during the Process era relied upon an internalist conception of the mind. To my knowledge, nobody within the discipline ever said outright: this is what the mind is, and therefore this is what invention ought to look like. Nobody needed to. Internalism was an unformulated convention. However, its status as a convention seems to me to be beyond dispute. One could find (externalist) historical outliers, if one were really willing to dig, but one would struggle to do so. Given the centrality of the unformulated convention, when externalist models of invention began to appear within composition scholarship, they were un-recognizable as theories of invention. Some were dismissed; some were ignored; some were absorbed into the exact (internalist) conversations they had intended to critique.

Because the unformulated conventional—invention is internalist—held such sway, no less a scholar than Janice Lauer ("Rhetorical Invention: The Diaspora") could only express puzzlement at the apparent absence of new scholarship on invention in the 1990s. She couldn't find other inventional work because she couldn't accept that externalist scholarship *was* inventional scholarship. To be clear: I don't fault her for this inability. That work was, functionally speaking, invisible to her. Rather, I use Lauer as an example because her work has been so obviously admirable.

At some point, though, the unformulated convention switched over; (what was once called) invention became externalist. Again, nobody announced that a transition was occurring, but the transition did occur. These days, one would be hard-pressed to find a reasonably current article or book on invention that doesn't (at minimum) gesture toward posthumanist or ecological, externalist conceptions of the mind.

One might also consider this same issue—the invisibility of externalist invention—from a separate perspective. Throughout this book, I've argued that postprocess differs from Process inasmuch as it foregrounds (i.e., formulates conventions regarding) externalism and paralogy. In contrast, as Joe Marshall Hardin argues, "Even the most social of process theories . . . are internalist philosophies masquerading as externalist" ("Putting Process into Circulation" 71). Following the transitive property, then, one might say that inventional scholarship had presupposed internalism and thus presupposed a Process approach. Turning once more to Lauer's scholarship, one can observe how an unformulated convention—invention is internalist—can attach itself to a formulated, explicit convention: invention requires Process.

In "Composition Studies: Dappled Discipline" (1984), Lauer famously celebrates the existence of multiple modes of inquiry and suggests that composition does not require paradigmatic unity. Even so, she identifies one research branch that (in her estimation) does require conceptual consensus: invention. She writes, "Social fields like composition studies depend on attributions of consensus that act as preconditions for arguing the validity of any theory. For example, in composition studies, those who advance new theories of invention must presuppose consensus in the scholarly community about the conception of writing as a process" ("Composition" 23). Here, Lauer implies that "writing as process" is so central to invention that there can be no inventional scholarship apart from it. If one were to reject Process, by this logic, one would find oneself unable to study invention.

So far as I know, this invention-requires-Process convention had been unformulated prior to Lauer's statement, even if the converse claim—that Process depended upon inventional research—had been previously expressed (Harrington; Lauer, "Heuristics"; Young and Becker). But, her reasoning helps explain why so few externalist conceptions of invention were considered to be theories of invention at their moments of emergence: they weren't Process approaches.

Rather, sometimes even overtly (e.g., Reither "Writing and Knowing), those scholars forwarding an externalist vision of invention expressed frustrations with the limit(ation)s of Process. Because I'll spend an entire chapter expanding on this claim, though, let me turn now to some separate issues here.

In particular, I want to assess (by applying) Kent's assertion that the historian's task is to describe "the disintegration of unformulated conventions and the emergence of new ones," or, stated differently, "how periods develop and how they collapse" (*Interpretation* 44). To do so, I want to examine a text that existed along the borderline between eras, asking how different periodization schemes impact what contemporary readers might understand it to mean or to be saying.

In 1986 Gary A. Olson published "Extending Our Awareness of the Writing Process" in *The Journal of Teaching Writing*. Since that time, the article has only ever been cited once. I am less concerned here in hypothesizing reasons for that silence than I am in periodizing and thereby interpreting the document. Throughout the rest of this book, I've tried to triangulate my interpretations of texts against other scholars' interpretations—especially the most immediate responses. Olson's text becomes useful here, though, because triangulation isn't possible. The other texts that I might triangulate my interpretation against simply do not exist.

I should note, at the outset, my reason for selecting this article: I think there are compelling reasons for considering it to be an example of Process scholarship and also of postprocess scholarship. In that light, I plan to analyze the text twice: first as though it were a Process-era document, second as though it were a postprocess-era document. To do so, I'll need to repeat some passages—but for a reason: as Kent points out, readers interpret texts based off of their genre expectations, such that different categorizations produce different meanings. Ultimately, then, what I do with the text may also justify Kent's assertion that a text remains in the present to the extent that it is associated with other, important events, thereby "reverberating" historically.

Much like Kent's early works, which may appear to be surprisingly "practical" compared to his later theoretical texts, many of Olson's articles in the early-to-mid 1980s are surprisingly "empirical." At the outset of "Extending Our Awareness" he recounts overhearing an excellent student writer confess to having written an essay while "sky high" on marijuana (227). Intrigued by this insight and curious about its generality, Olson created a questionnaire that included "one open-ended and 19 multiple-choice questions" (228). The first few questions included therein ask students to assess their ability as writers. However, the rest ask about elements of the students' writing environments and/or their somatic experiences of/while writing: their preferred times of day and locations for writing, whether they listen to music or keep the television on while writing, whether they consume alcohol or smoke marijuana while writing, and whether they believe that consuming "euphorics" is helpful or harmful to their writing (229–31). He distributed the questionnaire to instructors at seven institutions throughout the southeast United States and received 1,021 anonymous replies.

I think there's a strong case to be made for characterizing this article as a Process-era document. Considered in this light, Olson is arguing for—as the title indicates—extending scholarly examinations to previously un- or under-examined aspects of the writing process. In his initial framing, he states, "Throughout the last two decades, scholars and educators have become increasingly more sensitive to the fact that composition involves a series of complex, integrated activities and is more than a simple matter of generating a product according to rigid, preestablished strictures" (227). Thus, by Olson's account Process-era research does not depict writing as narrow or linear. However, he admits that students "introduce elements into the composing process that many of us as educators and scholars might not have considered previously." And, while acknowledging some foregoing research on "the writer's composing environment," he asserts that "no one, to [his] knowledge, has asked questions beyond those related to 'writing atmosphere,'" that is, the affective mood in the room (228). Even at the close of the document, Olson never quite makes the kind of turn one might expect (based on his later, theoretical work). Drawing insights from his survey responses, he states, "Certainly, the writing process is much more than prewriting, arrangement, revision and the other activities and techniques we have been studying for over two decades," and, "if this study reveals anything, it is that our present conception of the writing process is limited" (235–36). But, he doesn't use those insights to ground any grand theoretical pronouncement or even to provide practical applications. Thus, both in terms of his empirical approach and his continuationist framing, Olson appears to be engaging in Process research. The phrase "the writing process" (singular) appears frequently, and, even if the results of his survey show that students' processes actually differ dramatically from one another, he doesn't attempt to problematize the idea of the (singular) writing process. The closest he gets is an admission on the article's first page:

> We have failed to remember perhaps the most important
> fact about the composing process: all writing originates from
> *human beings*, each with unique writing habits. Studying only
> the *mechanics* of how writers compose tends to make us forget
> that writers, particularly the student writers with whom we
> are most concerned, bring to the composing process a bewildering assortment of personal writing habits that are certain
> to influence that process, often in complex ways. (227)

When considered as a Process-era article, Olson does present an intriguing new direction for empirical research—learning more about the roles of embodiment and environment on writing—but his work may have relatively limited appeal. When he offers practical applications for his insights, they're relatively mundane: for instructors "to spend the first few class periods of each semester covering proper study habits" and to invite "study skills specialists" to their classes (235) And, besides, I can understand why other scholars did not immediately follow him in asking students about their recreational drug use.

On the other hand, as even the mere presence of this discussion in this book indicates, I think there's a compelling case to be made for "Extending Our Awareness" as a postprocess text. It presents Olson as a scholar colliding with the limits of an internalist Process approach and struggling to conceptualize an externalist approach to writing. After all, the boundaries between periods are not only "fuzzy and indistinct," but also "characterized by turmoil." When read in a (proto-)postprocess light, Olson's text takes on a new meaning. The opening sentence, for instance, now seems mildly disdainful: "Lately it has become almost a cliché to speak at professional conferences and in journal articles about the 'writing process.'" In the paragraph that follows, Olson admits that Process scholars have become "increasingly sensitive to the fact that composition involves a series of complex, integrated activities and is more than a simple matter of generating a product according to rigid, preestablished strictures." However, in calling the complex recursivity and non-rule-bound (paralogic?) nature of writing a "fact," and in noting that scholars have become "more sensitive to it," he doesn't voice much confidence in his peers. He can be read as saying, "I'm glad the rest of you finally noticed this obvious point." Olson then provides an extensive list of conceptual improvements in Process research, but he frames some other scholars as "studying only the mechanics of how writers compose." In doing so, he argues, they "fail to remember . . . [that] all writing originates from human beings, each with unique writing habits" and "forget that writers . . . bring to the composing process a bewildering assortment of personal writing habits that are certain to influence that process, often in complex ways" (227). These things, he seems to be saying again, are and should be obvious. But, occupational psychoses produce distortions.

As I'll explore later, complexity has become a key term in ecological and posthuman, postprocess theories of writing, especially in the works of Byron Hawk and Sidney Dobrin. While I don't assume that Olson intends to use the term in precisely the same way, he does use *complex* twice on his article's first page. In both instances, he contrasts a complex model of composing, which he prefers, to a mechanistic one, which he opposes. Again, he never arrives at a fully complex or externalist or ecological approach and he even seems somewhat dubious about its possibility, but he also moves toward it. After rather mildly acknowledging that "marijuana users believe that use of the drug while writing should not be considered to be a problem," he follows with a stronger claim: several well-known authors famously wrote "under the influence of various euphorics" and "perhaps [the effects of euphorics on the writing process] should be a matter of great concern (231–32). Similarly, after discussing the widespread use of background media, especially music, while writing, Olson asks, "Is it possible that they can contribute to a writer's composing process?" In the sentences that follow, he indicates his own answer: yes. He quotes from Dr. Darwin Nelson, Director of Counseling and Testing at the University of North Carolina at Wilmington, who claims, "Background music . . . can even help some students concentrate" (233). And Olson also quotes an anonymous survey respondent who concedes, "I can't write without music" (235).

Thus, Olson ultimately concludes, "The writing process is much more than prewriting, arrangement, revision and the other activities and techniques we have been studying for over two decades." It is less mechanical, and it's less governed by the autonomous wills of internalist minds: "writers perform under the influence of external elements such as euphorics and stereos. . . . It may even be possible that the factors discussed in this study can help individual writers compose more effective prose," even if, Olson admits, "such an assumption seems doubtful." In any case, he suggests, scholars ought to acknowledge that their "present conception of the writing process is limited," and they should no longer "restrict [their] investigations to academic and procedural elements of the process of writing" (236). In terms of pedagogical applications, then, "students need to know . . . that their writing environment can affect their performance and that they must, therefore, choose such an environment carefully" (235).

I've spent a fair amount of time on "Extending Our Awareness," which is obscure in multiple senses: unknown, difficult to periodize, and thus difficult to interpret. At this stage, I'd like to turn away from it and back toward Kent's principles for historical narration. "Extending Our Awareness" has neither been nor yet become an important work in the history of composition and/or writing studies. But, the hierarchical nature of history can help to account for its status as such. Despite having a well-known author, it was not published in a particularly well-known journal. Furthermore, if—as I want to argue—it stands at the end of one (Process) tradition of scholarship, and if it considers aspects of the writing process that other scholars were not at the time interested in contemplating, then one should not be surprised that it did not become associated with "important" events or ideas that might have elevated it, in turn. Quote/unquote disciplinary "importance" is often a measure of a text's afterlife, its circulation, rather than anything immanent to the text itself or its delivery.

Responses produce importance. And, this article has, to date, represented a historical dead-end, though its status as a precursor to contemporary, ecological models of composing may endow it with relevance and thus citations and thus importance. In this way, it may eventually have an afterlife akin to Richard Coe's 1975 "Eco-Logic for Composition," which was only cited twice before the year 2000 but which, at the time of my writing, has been cited more than forty-five times since the turn of the millennium. To the extent that Coe's article has returned to the scholarly conversation, it is as a result of (not because it was a cause of) renewed interest in ecological perspectives on composing.

In addition, Olson published his text in the Fall 1986 issue of *The Journal of Teaching Writing*. As the title of Chapter 6, "Around 1986," makes clear, I want to argue that this is a crucial year in the history of postprocess. While Process-era scholarship had been trending toward increasingly "social," quasi-externalist-but-still-internalist conceptions of "mind" for quite some time, this is the year when the transformation becomes clear and identifiable. When I published an earlier version of that chapter (Lotier, "Around 1986"), I was unaware of "Extending Our Awareness." But, even if I had known of it, I may not have included it. Still, I cannot help but note its resonance here. And, this sort of resonance—not necessarily a harmonization, but not an echo, either—strikes me as an important but relatively under-explored element of history and thus historical narration. Unformulated conventions still exist despite their unformulatedness, and historians can recover them.

In "Around 1986," I focus on three articles (by James A. Reither, James E. Porter, and Marilyn Cooper, respectively) and a book (by Karen Burke LeFevre) published between 1985 and 1987. Those texts, I argue, present an externalist conception of the mind while examining ideas directly relevant to (what had previously been called) invention. However, in cross-referencing the works cited by those documents, I found only one shared work: Stanley Fish's *Is There a Text in This Class?* Only eight authors are cited by three of the four documents in question: Patricia Bizzell; Thomas Kuhn; Elaine Maimon, et al.; Roland Barthes; Kenneth Bruffee; Jonathan Culler; Linda Flower (sometimes solo, sometimes with John Hayes); and James Kinneavy. And, from that small sample, only three individual texts are shared: Bizzell's "Cognition, Convention, and Certainty"; Kuhn's *The Structure of Scientific Revolutions*; and Maimon, et al.'s *Readings in the Arts and Sciences*. LeFevre cites Reither. Reither cites one of Cooper's articles, and she returns the favor by citing his work. Certainly, there's a social constructionist bent to these shared texts and many of them assert perspectives drawn from post-structuralist and/or deconstructionist and/or reader-response-theory. But, I think it's fair to say that Cooper, Lefevre, Porter, and Reither approached an externalist position circa 1986 from (at least somewhat) different paths.

Of course, scholars interact with each other in non-textual ways, and so my focus on citations here is somewhat misleading. The relationship between LeFevre and Reither provides a case-in-point. Though LeFevre does cite "Writing and Knowing," she provides a much more extensive thank-you to him and two other Canadian scholars (Anthony Paré and Richard Coe) in her book's acknowledgements, noting, "By debating points, suggesting readings, and directing me to other people with like interests, each has helped me test ideas and bring this work to completion" (*Invention* xiv). Furthermore, *Invention as a Social Act* was published in 1987. However, LeFevre gave a presentation of the same name at the 1986 Inkshed conference, which carried the theme "The Social Context of Reading and Writing," which Reither organized and attended, and at which he also presented (*Inkshed* 5.2, page 2; *Inkshed* 5.5, page 1). Notably, only one presentation would occur at Inkshed at a time (i.e., it did not feature concurrent sessions). Thus, Reither may have had access to LeFevre's ideas before their publication in book form. LeFevre, Reither, and Coe also led a full-day, pre-CCCC workshop on "Teaching Writing as a Social Process" in Atlanta on March 18, 1987 (*Inkshed* 5.6, page 9). Finally, as a demonstration of the reciprocal bonds of this relationship: in the acknowledgments section of their 1989 "Writing as Collaboration," Reither and his co-author, Douglas Vipond, thank LeFevre for helping workshop their paper. Furthermore, they write, "Those who know LeFevre's *Invention as a Social Act* will recognize in this paper an intertextual debt which is but poorly acknowledged in our few direct allusions to that fine book" (866).

Let us return to the textual record for a few more moments, though. As I'll explore more fully in the next chapter, whatever else it may be, postprocess represents the incorporation of theories of reading into theories of writing. Reader-zresponse literary theories, as embodied by Fish, and deconstructive literary criticism, as embodied by Culler, strongly influenced externalist approaches to invention. And, of course, Kent was himself a reader-response literary critic, as evidenced by his first monograph, *Interpretation and Genre*. This genealogy has remained largely un-accounted-for in histories of postprocess, although Dwight Atkinson does point toward it, obliquely, in a footnote to his "L2 Writing in the Post-Process Era: Introduction." Atkinson states, "Another way of looking at what I am calling the 'post-process' era in L2 writing would be to think of it as an unpacking and reconceptualization of the 'coherence' concept" (5). I find Atkinson's proposition intriguing and historically tenable, although I believe it applies even better to (what I am calling) postprocess than to post-process. As I note in Chapter 5, Thomas Kent's proto-postprocess scholarship in the 1980s was generally concerned with cohesion strategies (e.g., the given-new contract). Likewise, Russell Hunt and Douglas Vipond, whom I discuss in Chapter 4, were then researching how readers construct a sense of coherence within texts through "point-driven reading." Marilyn Cooper, who figures strongly in Chapter 6, was similarly concerned with coherence (e.g., "Context as Vehicle") at the time. So were scholars engaged in lateral, but not necessarily post-process research, including the subjects of Chapter 3, Louise Wetherbee Phelps and Martin Nystrand. All of this is to say: though Atkinson provides no documentation for his genealogical claim, I would affirm its validity.

But, I do not think that theories of reading and/or theories of cohesion can fully account for the genealogy of postprocess. Instead, I think another alternative suggests itself as equally plausible: by the mid-1980s, externalist ideas had become or were becoming broadly distributed, perhaps even widely shared. However, before the closing months of 1985, they had been either tacit or nascent. Then, all of a sudden, they weren't. All of a sudden, there they were: stated, explicit, circulating.

We have now arrived, I suppose, at the contentious portion of this chapter. But I hope that the foregoing analysis has prepared those who might otherwise recoil to reconsider the position I'll forward. As I've mentioned previously, Kent quotes Meyer to argue that "periodization is not . . . merely a convenient way of dividing up the past" but also "a necessity, if the succession of particular events in the past is to be understood as being something more than chronicle." Were it not for periodization "the past would lose immeasurably both in understandability and in richness," inasmuch as periodization schemes inform interpretations of historical events (*Interpretation and Genre* 43). As I've demonstrated by way of Olson's article—which has essentially no citational history, and which is thus as close to a disciplinary "blank slate" as one could hope to find—slotting the text into different historical periods produces very different textual meanings.

In affirming the importance of periods, I am all too aware of the predictable objections; however, I would note here an underlying assumption of many of them: that a convention must be formulated or explicitly stated in order to be real or demonstrable. Even Richard Young, who did as much to popularize the term *current-traditionalism* as any other, was forced to remark on this point: "The main difficulty in discussing the current-traditional paradigm, or even in recognizing its existence, is that so much of our theoretical knowledge about it is tacit" ("Paradigms and Problems" 30). Because scholars of the "current-traditional era" didn't talk about current-traditionalism (under that name) or necessarily always apply its insights uniformly, some critics argue that it did not exist. However, according to the analysis I have been running here, unformulated conventions and periods are closely intertwined. Furthermore, in line with Kent's work in *Interpretation and Genre,* I have been conceiving of unformulated conventions as the diachronic (i.e., dynamic and culturally determined) elements of historical narration. However, diachronic elements are no less important than synchronic (static, formal[ized]) genre elements in Kent's estimation.

Although unformulated conventions are extraordinarily difficult to prove in a definitive or empirical sense, I would argue that disciplinary historians of composition have tended to be more comfortable, though still reluctant, to talk about a/the Process period, as opposed to either current-traditionalism or post-process. This predilection, I suspect, stems from a simple fact: nearly from its outset, self-identified Process scholars attempted to formulate rules and models and methods for a Process approach to writing. They created check-lists of criteria for inclusion. In "Teach Writing as a Process, Not Product" (1972), Donald Murray offers ten implications of his pedagogical model. In "The Winds of Change" (1982), Maxine Hairston offers twelve "principal features" of what she had come to call the Process "paradigm." For those who espoused it, Process wasn't (supposed to be) tacit or unformulated. But the various prescriptive formulations were, if anything, remarkably unsuccessful in gaining widespread assent. Because it was institutionally and disciplinarily expedient to be seen as doing Process work, an extremely wide variety of theories and pedagogical practices came to be called Process approaches, some of which seemed eerily similar to those current-traditional ones they had aimed to expel. As a result, for a time, producing taxonomies of Process became an intellectual fad—and, seemingly, one of the easier ways to get published in *College English* or *College Composition and Communication*. One only needed to explain how these various elements were somehow alike yet importantly different. Calling something a "Process" approach came to mean *this is something that people are doing now*. Those who employed what would come to be called "current-traditional" methods did not acknowledge themselves to be doing so, and those employing quote/unquote "Process" approaches did. But, the distinction of one period (Process) relying on a set of formulated "rules" that could not and did not hold and the other (current-traditionalism) relying on unformulated ones that also could not and did not hold strikes me as more or less meaningless in terms of demonstrating that one period did (or did not) exist and the other did not (or did).

To be clear, I am not interested in trying to establish the historical veracity of the existence of current-traditionalism or, for that matter, Process in any sort of objective sense.

I could not be less interested in trying to do so.

What I do want to suggest, though, is a commonsense claim: members of any number of cultures or groups or organizations agree to follow—or, at minimum, submit to—rules and orders that they are never directly taught; norms emerge and evolve without centralized planning.

But, Kent does not merely say that periods exist, or even that periodization schemes inform interpretations. He argues that they are necessary for interpretation. He suggests that they are more than useful; they are essential. Unless one wants to present history as entirely non-hierarchical and undifferentiated—every event of equal importance—one needs to allow that periods exist. And, of course, the disciplinary history of composition and/or writing studies is itself hierarchical. At any given moment, some texts are being cited more than others, and those that were once cited very heavily continue to be cited frequently, even well into the future. Such texts reverberate, remaining within the "present." But, just as crucially, some texts come back to life or gain new life.

Consider this: every one of the four key texts I will examine in Chapter 7 ("Around 1986") was cited less frequently in its second full decade in print than in its first, as one might expect. The laws of physics at work: loss, entropy, decay.

But, also consider this: each was cited more frequently in its third full decade than in its second—or even in its first. For two of the four texts, the increase in citations has been massive. To be precise, Cooper's article was cited ninety-three times in its first decade, seventy-three times in its second, and 261 times in its third. Porter's was cited seventy-eight times in its first decade, seventy-seven times in its second, and 213 in its third. (Given publication lag-times, I have exempted the year in which each article was published from consideration. Thus, since Cooper's article was published in 1986, her decades run from XXX7–XXX6, and so on.) Thirty years after publication, each has become increasingly important within the scholarly conversation(s) in which it finds itself. Scholarly readers, I would therefore argue, have come to rely on a new set of unformulated conventions in conducting their own work.

As a corollary, I would suggest that contemporary scholars have come to periodize those 1985–1987 texts and their own scholarly practices differently—whether or not they are aware of doing so. One could trifle over what to call this new period, in which we currently find ourselves—whether *postprocess* is indeed the best term, for instance—and one might likewise argue over its boundaries or borders or defining traits. Those are productive discussions, and I hope that readers will engage with me over precisely these points. But, I hope that readers will agree with me that periods exist because they need to—even if they are social constructions and thus only real in their (reified) effects, not in their essences. And, if periods exist in this virtual sense, then there is no a priori reason to argue against the existence of a postprocess period.

POSTPROCESS AS *VOCABULARY*

To conclude this chapter, I want to present one other possibility for how to characterize postprocess (and, for that matter, Process, and current-traditionalism, and a host of smaller conceptual enterprises). As I mentioned, Kent wrote *Interpretation and Genre* while still, in effect, a literary scholar. Although it exemplifies an important phase in his thinking about historical interpretation, that text emerged well before he made any concerted turn toward (what would come to be called) postprocess writing theory. While he was developing his externalist, paralogic approach, Kent preferred to talk about disciplinary formations as "vocabularies."

To my mind, this approach holds considerable merits. First, as compared to a *movement* or *group*, the existence of a vocabulary does not imply common cause or unity. It does not require a shared set of motivations nor a shared set of goals. It doesn't even directly gesture at a group of people—but rather a group of words. At most, the existence of a vocabulary indicates a collective willingness to communicate with the same terms. Second, unlike a period, a vocabulary doesn't imply temporal boundaries. A vocabulary need not have a clearly defined origin or end-point. Third, one can distinguish between vocabularies without arranging them into a hierarchy. Fourth, vocabularies are highly flexible and they lack numerical limits. We continuously add new words to our vocabularies and, although most of us gradually alter our word choices as we age, there's no zero-sum logic of addition and subtraction. New words don't *replace* older ones; old and new can and do exist alongside one another.

In a text that I've quoted previously, his 1991 response to a *JAC* interview with Gayatri Chakravorty Spivak, Kent states, "Michel Foucault taught us to talk about history in terms of shifting discourses rather than in terms of transcendental master narratives. . . . Foucault asks us to think about history as changes in the way we employ vocabularies: once we talked like that; now we talk like this" (185). A few years later, he makes the same basic argument but attributes it to another philosopher, Richard Rorty. In *Paralogic Rhetoric*, Kent conceives of shifts (if not necessarily "advances" or "progressions") in knowledge "in the Rortyian sense of a redescription—a new vocabulary that breaks with an established vocabulary" (67).

In *Contingency, Irony, and Solidarity*, Rorty explains the logic of redescription in concise and direct terms. Opposing correspondence theories of truth, he suggests that no vocabulary ever more fully or more adequately captures (what might conventionally be called) the truth or the real nature of a phenomenon. In contrast, at best, a given vocabulary represents a tenuous social consensus. A group of people has reached a reasonable level of agreement about the usefulness of a given set of words and phrases—whatever minimum level is needed to accept and employ particular terms. But, even if demonstrating the arbitrariness of any given vocabulary is relatively simple, arguing against its continued usage is comparatively harder. Rorty notes,

> The trouble with arguments against the use of a familiar
> and time-honored vocabulary is that they are expected to be

> phrased in that very vocabulary. They are expected to show
> that central elements in that vocabulary are "inconsistent in
> their own terms" or that they "deconstruct themselves." But
> that can *never* be shown. . . . For such use is, after all, the
> paradigm of coherent, meaningful, literal, speech. (8–9)

To replace an old way of speaking, then, one cannot merely argue against its usefulness. Instead, one can only replace the old vocabulary with the new one by making the latter "look attractive by showing how it may be used to describe a variety of topics." At its most basic level, the method of redescription is simple: "to redescribe lots and lots of things in new ways, until you have created a pattern of linguistic behavior which will tempt the rising generation to adopt it, thereby causing them to look for appropriate new forms of nonlinguistic behavior" to investigate. Quite importantly, this new vocabulary will not present itself as "a better candidate for doing the same old things which we did when we spoke in the old way. Rather, it suggests that we might want to stop doing those things and do something else" (9).

Notably, Rorty suggests that redescription can succeed, but it is most likely to do so among "the rising generation," rather than among those accustomed to employing certain terms and thus thinking in certain ways and investigating certain phenomena. Applied to society-at-large, this observation is common sense: kids use new "slang" terms far more often than adults do, and they're willing to cycle through redescription after redescription, seeking out apt vocabularies to account for the subtleties of their experiences. But, I would argue, the same basic phenomenon applies to scholars. Whether the tendency represents a "trained incapacity" or an "occupational psychosis" or something else altogether, academics absorb certain ways of communicating during their training and their early years as researchers, and they prove resistant toward subsequent transitions in vocabulary. So, if you want to gauge the effectiveness of a scholarly effort in redescription, you might not want to look at what happens in the immediate aftermath of an article or book's publication. Instead, you might want to look at texts written, say, ten or twenty years later.

In his texts from the early 1990s, Kent is quite careful to refer to prior approaches to writing instruction as vocabularies, rather than movements or camps or schools or even theories—a tendency also evident, though somewhat less pronounced, in the works of Olson ("Toward" 8) and Dobrin (*Constructing Knowledges* 23, 67–69). In *Paralogic Rhetoric*, Kent states, "Nowadays, we usually talk about discourse production by employing either an expressivist vocabulary, a cognitivist vocabulary, or a social constructionist vocabulary" (98). He also repeatedly refers to his own "paralogic stance" as a "vocabulary," noting,

"When we combine Bakhtin's formulations of genre and open-ended dialogue with Davidson's conceptions of triangulation and the passing theory, we possess, I believe a powerful vocabulary to describe the activities of reading and writing (66, 156). In "Externalism and the Production of Discourse," he critiques the assumptions of the "internalism [that] dominates current research in rhetoric" and offers "an alternative vocabulary . . . that allows us to talk about the production of discourse without getting caught up in the old Cartesian dualisms and paradoxes" ("Externalism" 62). In that text's final section, Kent suggests that externalism will move the field "beyond a Process-oriented vocabulary," a phrase notably similar to—and yet importantly different from—the subtitle of the 1999 collection he edited, *Post-Process Theory: Beyond the Writing-Process Paradigm* (69). And he closes that article with some prescient claims,

> In fact, we are beginning already (albeit slowly) to talk differently about language, about the production and reception of discourse, and about rhetoric, too, although no one would deny that internalist vocabularies—in the forms of expressivism, cognitivism, and social construction—still dominate the discourse in our discipline. Such a shift toward an externalist vocabulary may not take a Davidsonian turn, and it may not resemble the brand of externalism that I have promoted here. However, I believe that the discipline is nonetheless moving steadfastly toward the rejection of a vocabulary that posits a split between the human subject and the world. (Kent, "Externalism" 70)

In what remains of this book, I hope to show that Kent was correct in each of these three assertions. By the early 1990s, scholars were "beginning already (albeit slowly) to talk differently about language, especially by eschewing internalist vocabularies. But, the Davidsonian terms that Kent employed never quite caught-on. And yet, a longer historical view of the field would demonstrate that scholars eventually did reject "a vocabulary that posits a split between the human subject and the world" (Kent, "Externalism" 70).

As they moved in this direction, though, subsequent scholars tended to avoid talking about *prior theories* and *passing theories* and *triangulation* and *the principle of charity* and instead discussed *ecologies* and *networks* and *new materialism* and *posthumanism* and *embodiment*. Indicating a sense similar to Kent's—namely, that how we talk about writing will shape how we perceive it—Laura Micciche has recently offered another phrase for consideration. At the conclusion of *Acknowledging Writing Partners*, she states, "I hope this book generates a change in thinking and vocabulary from 'writing about' to 'writing with' to reflect that partnerships abound in relation to writing activity" (111).

Indeed, in the early 2020s, one might profitably consider externalist approaches to writing theory and/or pedagogy a broad (if seldom directly acknowledged) umbrella category. Drawing from the prior insights of Jay Lemke, Jody Shipka presents such a case, although the term *externalism* itself never appears in her *Toward a Composition Made Whole*. Shipka acknowledges that scholars applying insights from actor-network theory; situated, distributed, or social cognition; ecologies or ecosocial semiotics; and mediated activity "all tend to share" two primary insights. "First," she notes, they accept "a belief that human behavior is social in origin and 'mediated by complex networks of tools'" (Russell, "Looking" 66; qtd. in Shipka 41). That is, they are how-externalists (and perhaps also what-externalists). Furthermore, Shipka states,

> Second, they share a desire to rethink the "person-proper,"
> to dissolve the boundary between "inside and outside" and
> "individual and context," thereby troubling the artificial
> boundaries separating "the mental and the material, the indi-
> vidual and the social aspects of people and things interacting
> physically and semiotically with other people and things."
> (*Toward a Composition* 41)

In other words, they use their insights about how (externalist) cognition occurs or arises to rethink their notions of what the mind—and thus the person—is or may become. Their externalism leads them toward posthumanism. Writing in the early 2010s, Shipka cited five composition and/or writing studies scholars applying these insights: Clay Spinuzzi, Margaret Syverson, Charles Bazerman, Paul Prior, and David R. Russell (41). These days, one could add many, many more to the list—the authors collected in *Thinking with Bruno Latour in Rhetoric and Composition* (2015), who variously apply actor-network approaches, to give but one obvious example. Because I will discuss those externalist positions, particularly as they pertain to what was once called invention, in Chapter 6, I will lay them aside here.

In this book, I am identifying postprocess as an externalist, paralogic approach to writing instruction. I would note, then, that the same sort of linguistic transformation that Kent prophesied regarding externalism has also transpired regarding paralogy. Subsequent scholars have increasingly accepted that writing (as a form of communicative interaction) is so situation-specific as to be uncodifiable, though they haven't necessarily employed the noun *paralogy* and/or the adjective *paralogic* to describe their views. This migration occurred slowly, as subsequent scholars re-stated and re-stated each other's claims. In the course of that transference (and as disciplinary "common sense" has shifted), though, a claim that was once received as heresy has come to appear banal.

To prove my case, let me begin with Kent's assertion that "writing and reading—conceived broadly as processes or bodies of knowledge—cannot be taught, for nothing exists to teach" (*Paralogic Rhetoric* 161). That proposition, which Kent himself would subsequently characterize as "a contentious and underdeveloped position," may be the single most famous (and most controversial, and most misunderstood) claim in the history of postprocess ("Response to Dasenbrock" 106). To be fair, Kent precedes it by explicitly and carefully delineating six fundamental premises that inform his definitions of writing and reading. In short, he identifies reading and writing as uncodifiable (paralogic) forms of communicative interaction that invariably and unavoidably entail guesswork. In other words, his affirmation that reading and writing cannot be taught emerges as the conclusion of an extensive deductive chain. (Really, all of *Paralogic Rhetoric* builds up to it.) Thus, the famously controversial sentence is itself very, very poorly suited for quotation and the decontextualization that it invariably produces. Indeed, Kent follows his assertion about the un-teachability of writing and reading by stating, "In order to be understood on this point . . ." (*Paralogic Rhetoric* 161). Then, he issues a statement that has been very commonly disregarded by his critics.

By Kent's estimation, his argument that writing and reading cannot be taught—given that they are paralogic hermeneutic activities—should not be separated from a related "commonsense observation." He states, "Clearly some of the background knowledge useful for writing—like grammar, sentence structure, paragraph cohesion, and so forth—can be codified and reduced to a system" (*Paralogic Rhetoric* 161). Elsewhere, elaborating on this point, he acknowledges that instructors "certainly may teach systematically and rigorously subjects dealing with how texts operate, how texts shape understanding, and how texts function within different social contexts" ("Principled Pedagogy" 432). However, knowledge of those items cannot guarantee subsequent communicative success; it can, at most, prepare one to become a "better guesser" (*Paralogic Rhetoric* 31). But, becoming a better guesser does, for him, represent an improvement in communicative capacity. So, he accepts the merits of courses in (what is now called) writing studies, or what he himself preferred to call *composition* (as opposed to *writing*).

Though he uses reasonably complex philosophical language to do so, Kent means to indicate a relatively simple point: even mastery of those writing-related matters that *can* be taught (grammar, sentence structure, paragraph cohesion, and so forth) does not guarantee communicative success. Many "fully grammatical" and "perfectly coherent" texts that employ the terminology and discourse norms of a given community still fail to achieve their ends—for any number of reasons. The success or failure of any given act of writing is ultimately a function of situation-dependent considerations that cannot be prescribed by a generalized theory or model. Thus, on the last page of *Paralogic Rhetoric*, he concludes, "We cannot instruct students to become *good writers* or *good readers* because *good writing* and *good reading*, as transcendental categories, do not exist" (170). Rather, he reasons, "*Good writing* and *good reading* can only mean something like 'utterances that make good sense in some particular situation'" (170). Even if he doubts that writing, as a generalizable or transferable ability, can be taught once and for all, Kent does still endorse what has come to be called Writing in the Disciplines, an effort to "decenter" writing instruction within the undergraduate curriculum (164).

A few years later, Joseph Petraglia would re-brand what Kent had called *writing classes* with a "freshly minted" acronym, GWSI, or General Writing Skills Instruction, an educational enterprise that "sets for itself the objective of teaching students 'to write,' to give them skills that transcend any particular content and context" ("Introduction" xi–xii). Petraglia likewise eschews Kent's Davidsonian language of hermeneutic guessing and paralogy, and he replaces it with the cognitivist vocabulary of *ill-structured problem-solving*, in which "contingency permeates the task environment and solutions are always equivocal." Even so, he follows Kent in emphasizing the challenge of generalizing methods across situations. Where Kent expresses doubt that a passing theory can simply or straightforwardly inform a subsequent prior theory, Petraglia instead reasons, "Ill-structuredness means that problems that appear to share salient characteristics and might thus be categorized as similar 'problem types' are, at root, fundamentally and unpredictably different" ("Writing" 83). But, even if the verbiage is different, the ideas overlap strongly. Even situations that might seem the same may prove not to be, and you can't know how they differ until you're (with)in one. The best you can do is guess and proceed.

Finally, Petraglia follows Kent's affirmation that composition (or writing studies) can be taught, even if writing cannot. Although, once more, his vocabulary diverges considerably from Kent's. He concedes, "Nothing I have suggested is intended to deny the importance of teaching the building blocks of literacy," and yet he concludes, "If we genuinely accept the premise that writing is ill-structured problem-solving, we will be dissuaded from insisting that rhetorical skills can be taught as a generative set of axioms or procedures that can be induced within the confines of the writing classroom" (97–98). Or, stated differently: you cannot teach students to write, once and for all, in a first-year writing class. This is, more or less, Kent's argument, even if it doesn't sound like it.

At present, neither Kent's Davidsonian terminology nor Petraglia's social-scientific, cognitivist terminology pervades mainstream composition research. But, the fundamental ideas they examined—that writing is not a single, stable, or generalizable thing; that prior knowledge about The Writing Process is only vaguely useful for directing individual acts of writing; that readers co-construct meaning alongside writers; that communication involves something like guessing or risk-taking—have attained disciplinary centrality. Thus, by my estimation, what Kent could foresee concerning his externalist vocabulary has proven true with reference to his paralogic one: scholars have shifted their vocabularies so as to avow the underlying concept, even if their chosen phrases are not those he initially proposed. To prove this case, I would point to two recent collections.

First, let us consider the 2017 textbook *Bad Ideas about Writing*, which officially declares a series of commonplace Process-era assumptions to be Bad and often presents postprocess ones in their place. Among the category of Bad Ideas, we find the following statements: *you can learn to write in general; reading and writing are not connected; and the more writing process, the better.* In contrast to the Bad Idea that writing-in-general exists, Elizabeth Wardle affirms, "There is no such thing"; rather, "writing is always in particular" ("You" 30). And, she continues onward, "A better notion of how writing works is one that recognizes that after learning scribal skills (letters, basic grammatical constructions), everything a writer does is impacted by the situation in which she is writing. And thus she is going to have to learn again in each new situation" (31). This formulation, I would affirm, follows Kent's ideas very closely: you can teach background skills, but the success or failure of a subsequent act of writing depends upon decisions negotiated in the act of writing. One must revise prior knowledge (or, in Davidsonian terms, one's *prior theory*) in light of new information gathered while writing (i.e., one must formulate *a passing theory*). In Wardle's words, this idea becomes *to write well is "to learn again in each new situation."*

In contrast to the Bad Idea that reading are writing are disconnected, Ellen C. Carillo directly avows an interpretive conception of communication, one of the three central tenets of postprocess: "To read and to write is to create, to interpret" ("Reading" 41). As I will demonstrate further in the next chapter, postprocess can be construed as an effort to re-incorporate reading theories into writing theories, even if it is seldom construed as such.

In his chapter, which very directly critiques Process approaches to writing, Jimmy Butts presents the ideas avowed by Kent and Petraglia as though they were common sense: "Of course, the idea of following a formula to write a perfect draft is a false construction. We write for specific situations, each unique. A certain set of cognitive steps are involved in writing anything—from academic papers to tweets; however, the set of steps used to compose one thing isn't necessarily a learnable and reproducible set of steps. We cannot follow a writing process, because writing is messier than that" ("More" 111). In other (Kentian) words: writing is interpretive and situated and thus it cannot help but be paralogic.

Though the particular words and phrases adopted by Kent and Petraglia remain largely absent, their way of talking about writing also appears repeatedly in *Naming What We Know: Threshold Concepts in Writing Studies* (2015), a text overtly aiming to canonize a particular vision of writing and concomitant approach to writing instruction. Editors Linda Adler-Kassner and Wardle make Kent's writing/composition distinction in referring to writing as "an activity and a subject of study," and they indicate that writing is not a "'basic skill' that a person can learn once and for all and not think about again" ("Metaconcept" 15). Kevin Roozen begins Chapter One with a series of externalist claims, highlighting both semantic-externalist propositions ("No matter how isolated a writer may seem . . . she is always drawing upon the ideas and experiences of countless others") and vehicle-externalist ones ("The social nature of writing . . . also encompasses the countless people who have shaped the genres, tools, artifacts, technologies, and places writers act with as they address the needs of their audiences") (Roozen, et al., "Writing" 17–18). Shortly thereafter, Charles Bazerman identifies the inexorably interactive, negotiated nature of textual meaning: "writing expresses and shares meaning to be reconstructed by the reader." Though not employing the language of guessing, he still foregrounds the author's fundamental uncertainty: "We may not be sure others will respond well to our thoughts or will evaluate us and our words favorably. Therefore, every expression shared contains risk and can evoke anxiety" (22). And Dylan B. Dryer similarly affirms that even an author's best efforts to define terms clearly "will not guarantee perfect understanding." Rather, at most "they can help increase the chances that readers will produce the particular meaning the writer intended" (25). And, to reaffirm: all of this happens *just within the confines of Chapter 1*.

Chapter 4, which carries the title *All Writers Have More to Learn* is even more directly invested in paralogic principles. In its opening sentences, Shirley Rose attacks the commonly held assumption (implicitly cultivated by some Process pedagogies, I might argue) that "writing abilities can be learned once and for always." Two paragraphs later, she notes the difficulty of *transferring* skills across contexts. She also suggests that nothing a writer does nor any knowledge that a writer acquires prior to the act of writing can guarantee that act's success: "Even when strategies work"—that is, in the best case scenario—"writers still struggle to figure out what they want to say and how to say it . . . thus a writer never becomes a perfect writer who already knows how to write anything and everything" (Rose, et al., "All Writers" 59). Indeed, one page later, Rose concludes, "There is no such thing as 'writing in general'; therefore, there is no one lesson about writing that can make writing good in all contexts" (60). In a subsequent section of that same chapter, Collin Brooke and Allison Carr avoid the vocabulary of *hermeneutic guessing* and writing's *paralogic* uncodifiability, but they nonetheless affirm that "there is no way we can expect [students] to be able to intuit [the] shifting conditions" that would grant them success in any and all writing tasks. As a result, then, "they must have the opportunity to try, to fail, and to learn from those failures" (63). And, two sections later, Doug Downs issues a similar refrain: "In the same way that writing is not perfectible, writing also is not in the category of things that are often right the first time" (66). That chapter ends with some very postprocess-sounding assertions from Paul Kei Matsuda. Matsuda frames "the negotiation of language as an integral part of all writing activities." Though he eschews the verbiage of *prior theories*, he notes that "writers strive to use a shared code that allows for effective communication," and he acknowledges the role of readers in co-constructing negotiated meaning. Matsuda also suggest that communicants might need to forego their expectations (i.e., *eschew prior* theories for *passing theories*) in the act of communication itself (69).

All of this is not to say that *Bad Ideas about Writing* and *Naming What We Know* are postprocess texts, exactly. Indeed, both include numerous statements that postprocess thinkers might criticize, even some offered by the scholars just listed. And, furthermore, some of the scholars just listed—most notably Matsuda and Wardle—have expressed their skepticisms toward postprocess publicly. If one wished to know what postprocess has been and might become, *Bad Ideas* and *Naming What We Know* would not be very good places to turn. (Instead, one could keep reading this book.) All of this is to say, though, that a way of talking about writing that traces its roots back through discernibly postprocess texts pervades those books, even if original phrases posited by Kent, Petraglia, and their ilk have been replaced with others conforming more closely to contemporary needs and demands. What was once the source of intense controversy and even scorn—Kent's claim that you cannot teach writing—has been re-phrased and re-phrased until it achieved palatability, even something like dominance.

CHAPTER 3.

WHEN EVERYONE WAS WRITING ABOUT READING (AND WRITING)

Postprocess emerged in a sporadic and discontinuous fashion. Eventually, its three central tenets—writing is interpretive; writing is public; and writing is situated—coalesced into a reasonably coherent conceptual formation, a "three-part mantra" with "poster-ready brevity" (Lynch, *After Pedagogy* 32). Before that convergence, though, the three principles circulated through different branches of composition and/or writing research, relatively independent of one another. In this chapter, I explore 1980s scholarship on what might now be called the *interpretive* dimensions of writing but which were, at the time, more commonly called its *interactive* and/or *transactive* dimensions.

In the Introduction to *Post-Process Theory*, Thomas Kent argues that "to interpret means to enter into a relation of understanding with other language users. So, understood in this way, interpretation enters into both the reception and the production of discourse" (2). Postprocess "interpretation" is, in short, the conceptual space in which theories of reading converge with and/or inform theories of writing. In his review of Kent's *Paralogic Rhetoric*, Reed Way Dasenbrock effectively elucidates this point. By Dasenbrock's account, "Kent's theories move in two directions simultaneously." At the level of pedagogy and/or writing program administration, they point toward writing in the disciplines. On a conceptual plane, they advocate "a greater integration of reading and writing, since the hermeneutic act of interpretation is central to finding the available means of persuasion" ("Forum" 103). In retrospect, one can see some of Kent's texts in the early-to-mid 1980s as trending toward paralogic hermeneutics and communicative interaction inasmuch as they focus on the textual means by which authors and readers negotiate meanings. At the same time, many other scholars were also considering this integration of reading and writing, the inevitable hermeneutics of communication, although few would arrive at precisely the same implications. Even during its own time, what came to be called postprocess (paralogic hermeneutic) writing instruction was certainly not the only and not necessarily the best approach to certain intellectual questions. It may have had the best branding, though, and thus the most extensive afterlife.

To demonstrate just how prevalent this *writing is interpretive* notion was during the 1980s, I will focus on the works of Louise Wetherbee Phelps and Martin Nystrand, both of whom claimed a synecdochal relationship to scholars of composition, and by extension writing, and by extension communication as a whole. That is, they rightly presented themselves as representative examples, engaged in a common intellectual task, not as solitary geniuses. Although their works are undoubtedly impressive in terms of rigor and depth, the subject matter of their investigations was hardly unusual. While discussing Nystrand and Phelps, I'll focus primarily on how they re-integrated reading and writing research. Still, I hope the reader will notice how many other common postprocess themes they also endorsed: questioning the viability of generalized models of The Writing Process; emphasizing situational and/or contextual dynamics of text-production; criticizing the non-interactive qualities of much "academic writing"; advocating discipline-specific forms of writing instruction. And yet, despite these strong conceptual overlaps, neither Nystrand's nor Phelps' scholarship has been assimilated into or absorbed by postprocess discourse. Thus, an important corollary follows: the more you read, the less dramatic, radical, or revolutionary postprocess seems to be. To write an honest history, not a hagiography, is to admit as much.

During the period before postprocess coalesced, no term or category existed that might have summoned its disparate elements—its theoretical tenets, its pedagogical principles, its insights toward writing program administration—into a unified constellation. But, the ideas that came to be associated with postprocess predated that naming. And so, it's important to affirm that scholars developing (proto-)postprocess tenets did not understand their work to be contributing to such an endeavor, *per se*. To borrow a line from Lin-Manuel Miranda's *Hamilton*, they "wrote [their] way out" of one thing without knowing what, precisely, they were writing their way into (Miranda, "Hurricane"). This last claim may strike some readers as overly obvious, hardly worth stating; however, I am not simply engaging in hypotheticals. Although John Trimbur is commonly credited with introducing the term *post-process* into composition scholarship in 1994, the term had been employed a full decade prior. Phelps was aware of that usage (c.f., *Composition* 80). But, although she opposed the status of *process* as the central term or metaphor for the field, she did not advocate replacing it with *post-process* or any other single term.

In *Networked Process*, Helen Foster characterizes postprocess as a particular "sensibility, one that inexplicably yearns for rupture" from Process (180). She also argues, "Not only was there no break with process during [the 1980s], there was also never a serious suggestion that there ought to be. No such suggestion was seriously made until the 1990s" (38). In contrast to Foster's first point: I believe this yearning for rupture was explicable and even justifiable, and I hope this chapter many demonstrate why. Regarding the second: in my estimation, the historical record proves otherwise.

At least four scholars that I will consider in this book—Marilyn Cooper, James Reither, Judith Langer, and Phelps—overtly called for reforming Process theories and/or rejecting Process as the primary model for writing during the 1980s. From their perspective, understanding writing solely or even primarily *as a process*, rather than associating it with a broader set of terms or ideas, was producing intellectually deleterious effects. As Cooper noted at the time, "Theoretical models even as they stimulate new insights blind us to some aspects of the phenomena we are studying"; each one, invariably "projects an ideal image" and thus "influences our attitudes and the attitudes of our students toward writing" ("Ecology" 365). By her account, the "dominant model," built on the assumption that *writing is a process* had "become too confining" (366). Imagining writing as an *ecology*, rather than a *process*, would allow for a more expansive view and enable interesting, new research trajectories.

In his 1985 article "Writing and Knowing," Reither demonstrates a "tendency in composition studies to think of writing as a process which begins with an impulse to put words on paper" and asks whether "our thinking is not being severely limited by a concept of process that explains only the cognitive processes that occur as people write" ("Writing and Knowing" 621). By his account, scholarship on writing processes had "bewitched and beguiled" scholars "into thinking of writing as a self-contained process that evolves essentially out of a relationship between writers and their emerging texts (622). Thus, he suggests, "The 'micro-theory' of process now current in composition studies needs to be expanded into a 'macro-theory' encompassing activities, processes, and kinds of knowing that come into play long before the impulse to write is even possible" (623).

Of course, under one viewpoint, Reither and Cooper did not reject Process *per se* so much as the dominant, narrow instantiation of it. According to Hannah Rule, they "do not turn away from processes as much as them make much, much bigger" by employing "the language of infinite extension" in their work (*Situating* 59–60). I find this argument apt when applied to Reither's work but less so when applied to Cooper's. In "The Ecology of Writing," Cooper repeatedly stresses that models shape and/or distort the phenomena they purportedly represent (365–70). Models are, she reasons, "ways of thinking about, or ways of seeing, complex situations" (370). To conceive of writing *as a process* is to circumscribe the boundaries of what writing is, what it does, and what it conceivably could do. To conceive of it *as an ecology* would not offer a more complete or correct perspective, precisely. But, it would nonetheless allow scholars to "reformulate" their research questions "in a way that helps us to find new answers" (370). Thus, I believe Paul Lynch is correct in affirming that "Cooper explicitly offers ecology as a replacement for process" (*After Pedagogy* 85). As we shall see, Langer and Phelps presented similar arguments. By their account, the scale of the process was not the primary problem with conceiving of writing as one. Rather, from their perspective, the binary opposition between Process and Product had too narrowly defined what each could mean. Phelps would extend this logic farther still, faulting the conceptual constriction that occurs when writing is equated with *any* single term.

When they took over the editorship of *Research in the Teaching of English,* Judith Langer and Arthur Applebee began to include a brief editor's introduction at the start of each issue, which they called "Musings." The two, and particularly Langer, seem to have been disturbed by the focus or scope of the Process movement, and to a lesser extent by the connection between research on writing processes and purportedly Process-based pedagogy. Conventional disciplinary histories suggest that scholars in the Process Movement shifted their focus from the products of writing toward the process(es) involved in the act(s) of writing. Langer and Applebee support this assessment, noting that "such a shift was necessary to correct previous imbalances"; however, they hasten to add, "The pendulum may have swung too far." They argue, in short, that processes are oriented toward producing products; they are purpose-driven. Therefore, to study one (i.e., process) without the other (i.e., product) "may severely limit our understanding of both" (6).

In the following (May 1984) issue, Langer picks up and extends this argument. In particular, she presents *process versus product* as an "unproductive" binary or a "false dualism." Focusing on process had caused some scholars to "los[e] sight of the enterprise in which the process is engaged." While Langer understood that new research often defines itself in opposition to older research by rejecting central tenets and/or objects of inquiry, she suggests that exploring a new idea would eventually cause scholars to see "not only its strengths but also its limitations" (117). The strengths of Process had been numerous and obvious, but its limitations were "beginning to be clear" (118). Whether considering "reading, writing, or spoken language," separating process from product had produced negative effects. In dividing the two, Langer suggests, "we lose the essence of the process itself. Process does not consist of isolated behaviors that operate willy-nilly, but of purposeful activities that lead toward some end for the person who has chosen to engage in them." From her viewpoint as the editor of a major venue, Langer therefore cautions that "process studies in both reading and writing are approaching a theoretical dead-end" (118).

Because process models could no longer answer the questions that needed to be asked of them, Langer imagined a "post-process paradigm . . . one in which process models were built and process activities examined with explicit intent to relate the processes observed to the resulting products." In this post-process paradigm, scholars would reject generalized notions of good or bad reading and writing behaviors in favor of situationally contingent definitions. Without such a post-process turn, Langer worried that some actions might come to be "regarded as generally 'helpful' or 'unproductive'" and that (supposedly) process-oriented pedagogy might promote "a range of activities never examined in terms of their usefulness toward *particular* instructional ends." That is, something like *the* writing process (or even several acceptable writing processes or approaches) might be reified through scholarship. In contrast, to construct genuinely useful classroom activities and/or exercises, instructors would need "a clear sense of the purposes in which we are enlisting them, and of the complexities attendant upon those purposes." Ultimately, a new vision of process that might also attend to products would be one in which "all processing behaviors" would "be looked at interactively" (118).

As we shall see, Phelps advocated reintegrating a focus on products into Process approaches well before Langer's post-process proclamation. For now, though, let us turn briefly to her arguments against conceptualizing writing solely or primarily as a *process*. In her 1982 "The Dance of Discourse" Phelps argues that "terminology" offers "a point of entry to any conceptual framework": "any nomenclature, whether deliberately chosen or spontaneous, acts as a 'terministic screen' through which reality is selectively perceived" (31). Thus, both perceptions of the phenomena under investigation—say, writing—and subsequent analyses of it are shaped and directed by the words one uses to describe and discuss it. In her 1985 "Dialectics of Coherence," Phelps picks up on this logic. She begins her work by heralding *Process*, as both a movement and a term. In line with Susanne Langer's *Philosophy in a New Key*, Phelps identifies it as one of those "great generative ideas that periodically arise to transform our intellectual enterprises by changing the very terms in which we frame our questions and conceive our purposes." However, she argues, because such key terms "possess" or transfix us, they are not immediately critiqued or questioned. One only arrives at the "critical distance" necessary to "refine and correct" such key terms over time, "as a paradigm matures" (12). *Process* had offered just such a key change, presenting and/or enabling many notable advances. Even so, she writes, "In the next stage of our development as a discipline, we need to take up a more critical attitude toward process theory, to probe its limits and to articulate and address some of the conceptual problems it leaves unresolved" (12). One such limit of Process is its (relative) inability to "account for the role of texts in discourse events"—that is, in the emplaced and temporally specific interactions between readers and writers via texts. In other words, because Process (the movement itself, but also the term as employed within the movement) had been "constituted initially by a contrastive opposition between composing (dynamic process) and texts (inert product)," scholars within the movement tended to avoid studying texts themselves directly (12). The mantra *study process, not product* entailed a way of not-seeing particular phenomena: the products themselves. As Phelps acknowledges, this was a "'logological' problem, a consequence of the terms in which the key concept was originally framed." The primary issue to be addressed in subsequent research, then, was "the conceptual reach or stretch of the language of process"—whether or not it could be re-oriented to accommodate a more robust, interactive vision of writing (13). Notably, even while admitting the problems with doing so, Phelps would continue to employ a writing-as-process vocabulary throughout the late 1980s. However, as we shall see, she changed course by the start of the 1990s, making use of a broader set of concepts while interrogating the utility of each as a metaphor or model for writing.

RELEGATED REPRESENTATIVES: PHELPS AND NYSTRAND AS UNDER-EXAMINED SCHOLARLY SYNECDOCHES

In "Written Text as Social Interaction" (1984), Nystrand and his co-author Margaret Himley allow that "interactive views of language and meaning are by no means universal and are indeed uncommon in writing research" (198). Even so, they present a numbered list of scholars in other domains who have examined the "joint 'contract' between producer and receiver," including psycholinguists and co-authors Herbert H. Clark and Susan E. Haviland, philosopher H. Paul Grice, psychologists (but not co-authors) Ragnar Rommetveit and Lev Vygotsky, linguist M. A. K. Halliday, and social phenomenologist Alfred Schutz (199). A few years later, Nystrand opens *The Structure of Written Communication* (1986) by noting, "In the last decade, writing and reading researchers have increasingly drawn closer together" and later states, "Since 1970 writing and reading researchers have increasingly echoed each other" (ix, 13). During the "Social 1980s," he would explain in a 2006 retrospective, "Increasingly the nature of writing, like all language, was viewed as inherently social and interactive. Each act of writing began to be viewed as an episode of interaction, a dialogic utterance, ideally exhibiting intertextuality within a particular scholarly community or discipline" ("Social and Historical Context" 20–21). Thus, per Nystrand's evolving accounts, interactive approaches gradually entered and then attained centrality within writing research.

To understand how Nystrand conceptualized his own disciplinary positioning, one benefits from examining a history that he himself wrote. In "Where Did Composition Studies Come From?" (1992), he and his co-authors, Stuart Greene and Jeffrey Wiemelt, knock earlier histories by Faigley and Bizzell for treating various phases in the discipline's history (e.g., the shift from "text to individual/cognitive to social") as independent or unrelated phenomena, instead of demonstrating their connections to one another and to their "general intellectual context" (271–72). Notably, for our purposes, Nystrand et al. suggest that "the story of composition studies has a much broader and more penetrating scope than has heretofore been examined," but when they want to justify their own approach to historical narration, they turn to Phelps' work (272).

They had good reason to do so.

In the preface to her book *Composition as a Human Science*, Phelps states, "Theory is autobiography" and acknowledges the "reciprocity of biographies— myself and field" that animates her work (vii, ix). Ever attentive to widespread shifts in disciplinary thinking, though, she positions herself as "a synecdoche for the ways composition theorists have encountered the limits of their concepts and attempted to revise and surpass them ("Audience" 172). While positioning her own growth within an evolving academic field, she also positions the field's evolution as a function of changing material conditions. Rejecting the solitary author and dissolving the boundary between audience and writer are "not just the abstruse speculations of theorists," she argues. Instead, concepts and theories were forced to evolve "under the pressure of new social and technological conditions," including novel forms of collaboration, the affordances of hypertext and multi-media textuality, and various copying technologies ("photocopying, facsimile, and videotaping") that would "allow anyone to reproduce anything regardless of copyright" (162).

To summarize: Nystrand and Phelps positioned themselves within a circulatory ecology of other ideas, texts, and scholars. They understood their own ideas to spring from this ecology, rather than from anything innate within their own free-floating minds. These are, to be sure, prototypically postprocess gestures. But, postprocess did not invent them. In addition, judging from the subsequent circulation of their own work, neither Nystrand's nor Phelps' made a direct or appreciable impact on scholarship in quote/unquote "High Postprocess Theory"—though, I would argue, for almost exactly opposite reasons.

I suspect that Nystrand's scholarship—given its positioning within literacy studies and English education—has remained isolated from the spheres that postprocess theorists tend to frequent. Of course, there's nothing insidious about this distancing. Given the insularity of academic niches, the scholars who read and publish in *Written Communication* and *Research in the Teaching of English* are not always those who also read *JAC* or *Enculturation*, and vice versa. However, I also imagine that Nystrand's work has also been dismissed out-of-hand by many postprocess theorists as a-theoretical, as having nothing at all to say to (purportedly) "more theoretical" work in the field. Of course, from the viewpoint of many theorists, there is a fate worse than conducting a-theoretical research—doing *empirical* work. And, as Charles Schuster notes in his review of *The Structure of Written Communication*, within Nystrand's book "control and experimental groups abound, chi square tests worm their way into arguments, graphs and tables appear with alarming frequency" (89). Though he allows that Nystrand's "heavily parallel style . . . thick with nominalism . . . is itself a form of argument," Schuster still concludes that "its ultimate effect is to alienate many of the readers who most need to share in his knowledge" (91). To state the obvious, I imagine that this alienation has indeed occurred. Although, in fairness to Nystrand, Stephen P. Witte and David Elias, two considerably more sympathetic readers, would call *The Structure* "an excitingly ambitious attempt—perhaps the most exciting and the most ambitious to appear to date" to discuss "the complex interactions among the textual, contextual, and ideational components" that allow for written communication ("Review" 676). One person's utter lack of "theory" is another person's theoretical bombshell.

Phelps' work, in contrast, seems to have suffered the fate of many other purportedly "theoretical" texts both within composition studies and abroad. As Daniel Smith notes, "One of the most common criticisms leveled against 'postmodern theory' is that its often hard-to-read and jargon-laden prose functions to hide the vacuity of its ideas or to imbue the author's writing with an air of importance and substance that it does not have" ("Ethics" 525). And these seem to have been the unfair—Smith might even suggest *unethical*—objections to Phelps' work. Even in a *College Composition and Communication* review that begins, "Every serious scholar in the field of composition must read Louise Phelps's *Composition as a Human Science*," Jasper Neel still characterizes Phelps as "utterly, militantly theoretical throughout" (94). Neel also presents a series of common anti-theory arguments, some of which seem to conflict with one another: the book tries to achieve too much; it moves too quickly and yet it also gets bogged down in minutiae; it presents a "dead-earnest seriousness" without sufficient "play or humor or lightheartedness or joy" (94–95). The end result of all of this, he suggests, is that "Phelps has written a book that most composition professionals will have to work very hard to read" (96). Reading Neel's review in the early 2020s, I cannot help but remark on its gendered aspects: he criticizes Phelps for writing too much like Derrida and Chomsky and not enough like Mina Shaughnessy. Women are commonly expected to perform emotional labor in ways that men aren't, and Phelps isn't working hard enough to make her reader happy; *she needs to smile more.* And, of the two major reviews of *Composition as a Human Science*, Neel's is the less theory-antagonistic. (I won't repeat any phrases from John Schilb's review in *Rhetoric Review*, which seems oddly gleeful in denouncing the alleged difficulty of Phelps' vocabulary.)

All of this is quite ironic. *Composition as a Human Science* was one of the earliest texts to diagnose the "strong undertow of anti-intellectual feeling" that resides "deep in the disciplinary unconscious" of composition and "that resists the dominance of theory in every institutional context of the field" (*Composition* 206). And, furthermore, Phelps actively formulated a "context-sensitive form of application" that might bypass an all-too-common but false dilemma: to either "naively accept" theory or "reject it as impractical, overly abstract, and irrelevant" (220). She presented theory "as plastic, not an indigestible lump but a heterogeneous, multiplistic text or open system of meanings capable of entering into a communicative relation with other knowledge systems" (214). That is, she understood that her ideas were complex and that they wouldn't appeal or apply to all teacher-scholars equally, and she tried to preemptively account for possible resistances.

Determining the fate of Phelps' articles is obviously harder than accounting for the reception of her book, of course, given that there's no equivalent of the book review for articles. However, she herself has commented directly on the after-life of "The Dance of Discourse." In the collection *Pre/Text: The First Decade,* she acknowledges the irony of her task: "Writing a retrospective on 'Dance'—an essay on how readers and disciplines intersubjectively create textual and institutional meanings over time—in the absence of substantive response from the composition community" (59). This statement is not self-pitying hyperbole; according to the Google Scholar citation tracker, "The Dance of Discourse" was cited six times during its first decade in print (1982–1992)—with Phelps herself accounting for two of those citations.

AN ALLEGEDLY A-THEORETICAL ALTERNATIVE: NYSTRAND'S INTERACTIVE APPROACH

Martin Nystrand has had an extremely prolific career as an instructor, an academic author, and an editor. He helped to found the Rhetoric and Composition Ph.D. program at the University of Wisconsin-Madison, and he served as an editor of *Written Communication* from 1994–2002. In addition, he is the author or co-author of more than seventy-five peer-reviewed journal articles and the author, editor, or co-editor of eight books (Nystrand Personal Webpage). According to Google Scholar, his works have been cited more than 7,000 times. All of this is to say: within certain branches of composition and/or writing studies, the idea that he might need an introduction would seem ridiculous. And yet, his work has remained largely invisible from the scholarly conversation(s) surrounding postprocess. He isn't cited at all in Kent's *Paralogic Rhetoric* (1994), Dobrin's *Constructing Knowledges* (1997), McComiskey's *Teaching Composition as a Social Process* (2000), Foster's *Networked Process* (2007), Hawk's *A Counter-History of Composition* (2007), Dobrin's *Postcomposition* (2011), Arroyo's *Participatory Composition* (2013), Lynch's *After Pedagogy* (2013), Jensen's *Reimagining Process* (2015), or in any of the chapters of the *Beyond Postprocess* collection (2011). Helen Rothschild Ewald cites one of his co-authored pieces in her contribution to *Post-Process Theory* (1999). But, that's it. Now, as I hope should be obvious, I don't mention Nystrand's absence to shame these prior scholars, upon whose work I am entirely reliant. I only mention it to show just how distant his work has been from postprocess in citational terms even as it brushes against postprocess conceptually. Nystrand and Kent, in particular, pursued a very similar scholarly trajectory along a very similar timeline, even though the two rarely cite one another.

Much like Kent, Nystrand distinguishes between Social approaches to writing instruction and clearly differentiates the social constructionism of Bizzell, Bruffee, Faigley, et al. from his own "social interactionist" approach. By Nystrand's account, social constructionists focus on "the large-scale processes of writers and readers as members of discourse and interpretive communities" and emphasize the normative and shared elements of discourse. In contrast, he presents himself as interested in "the dyadic interactions of particular writers and readers," understanding discourse to be "ordinarily varied and heteroglossic" ("Sharing Words" 4, 9). Whereas social constructionists' approach is "top-down," focused on the canon, his own is "bottom-up," focused on individual texts (8). Because this is the place where Nystrand's work most resembles Kent's, I'd like to dwell on their respective approaches to social interaction(ism).

Throughout the 1980s, Kent frequently examined how readers interact with texts, most notably in his first book, *Interpretation and Genre*. But, during this same period, he also analyzed writer-reader interactions in his texts on writing instruction. In the first of his eponymous "Six Suggestions for Teaching Paragraph Cohesion" (1983) Kent advises instructors to "stress the reader's role in the communication process" (270). His 1984 article "Paragraph Production and the Given-New Contract" extends Grice's cooperative principle, "the dictum that speakers and listeners must cooperate with one another in the quantity, quality, relation, and manner of their communications" (46). Likewise, he begins his 1987 "Schema Theory and Technical Communication" by defining writing as "a communicative *process* where writer and reader work together" (244). In his closing remarks to that text, Kent suggests that instructional guidelines for writing might be better defined as "descriptions of how readers read" and he suggests that "writers must continually seek out the common ground, the contracts, the cooperative agreements, the mental representations shared between writer and reader" (249). In a separate article published that same year, Kent argues that both reading *and writing* proceed "generically": the elements that a writer chooses to include in her text should correspond to "expectations that both the reader and writer hold in common" ("Genre Theory" 237). Kent, of course, draws many of his terms from Donald Davidson: triangulation, prior and passing theories, the principle of charity. Because Nystrand does not derive his own concepts from Davidson, he tends to use different terms, which, of course, have different inflections. Even so, his insistence on communicative interaction between writers and readers is abundantly clear.

In a 1984 article Nystrand and his co-author Margaret Himley outline their sense of interaction: "Language generally is interactive," they write, "in the sense that all discourse presumes a joint 'contract' between producer and receiver, both of whom must abide by its terms if they are to understand one another" (199). The key term in this contract is a "reciprocity principle"—akin to the principle of charity—in which the communicants pre-suppose that they can and will understand one another (200). The authors then outline two crucial moments in textual production when reciprocity is threatened—at the outset and whenever new (i.e., un-shared) information is inserted—and they explain authorial strategies and textual means by which reciprocity can be maintained (200–201).

In his 1986 *The Structure of Written Communication*, Nystrand elaborates on reciprocity, noting that it "is not knowledge at all" but instead "the principle that governs how people share knowledge" (53). For Kent, the principle of charity "constitutes the opening move in all communication," one that conceives of "communicative interaction as a public act and not as a subjective private act of the mind" (*Paralogic Rhetoric* 107). Along these lines, Nystrand argues, "Without a contract between writer and reader, both meaning and purpose are unfathomable at best and untenable at worst" (*Structure* 48). Furthermore, once they have established reciprocity, those who wish to communicate must still act accordingly, negotiating a shared understanding. As a result, "all elements of a text" should be designed to balance the writer's "expressive needs" against the reader's "comprehension needs" (47).

Nystrand understood this interactive conception of writing to have profound ramifications. Unlike the scholars mentioned at the outset of this chapter, he did not (so far as I know) directly suggest that scholars move away from *Process* as a metaphor or model of writing, but he did present an alternative model in its place. In "A Social-Interactive Model of Writing" (1989), he states, "If we conceptualize writing *not as the process of translating writing purpose and meaning into text* but rather as *the writer's negotiation of meaning between herself and her reader*, we radically alter our conceptions of writing, text, and text meaning, and of the relationship of the composing process to the text" (76; emphasis added). By his estimation, the framing of Process versus Product—what Phelps had called their "contrastive opposition"—had led scholars to see written texts as solely as "the result of composing" (75). To be fair, that is, of course, one thing that texts are. But, within Nystrand's negotiated, social-interactive approach, the text would also be recognized as "a medium of communication mediating the respective purposes of the writer and reader." Therefore, it would only be credited with having meaning to the extent that its "potential for meaning is realized by the reader." Meaning, in other words, would be construed "not in terms of the text's *semantic content* but rather in terms of its *semantic potential*" (76). And, as an important corollary, this negotiated conception of meaning would demonstrate "that more than writer variables—notably the reader and the text—figure integrally and not just ancillarily into the composing process" (82). That is, even at the point of textual creation (i.e., invention), writers do not solely act; they are also acted upon.

Whatever disagreements they may have, most postprocess scholars strenuously deny the existence of The Writing Process a singular or generalizable entity, and they agree that writing is not a masterable ability that transfers unproblematically from situation to situation. Nystrand supports very similar positions. Because he conceives of communication—even in written form—as being inexorably interactive, he sets himself apart from those scholars "interested almost exclusively in the composing process in some generic sense" ("Social-Interactive" 67). Indeed, he argues that any "decontextualized" or "exemplar Composing Process," inevitably elides the "very character of writing as a language system" (*Structure* 26). Therefore, Nystrand contends, "Writing is not a straightforward skill like eating or swimming or typing," and "no one learns to write fluently once and for all" (18). Writing is simply too variegated, too situation dependent. The skills a writer learns in one instance *may* prove useful in some others, but those skills cannot guarantee success in all cases. Near the end of a chapter entitled "Notes toward a Reciprocity-Based Text Grammar," Nystrand states,

> It might seem . . . that certainly there are no descriptive rules or principles which might be said to characterize, if not govern, the matter of generating and elaborating text; that indeed composing is a new enterprise every time, always requiring the writer to find appropriate forms to fit given occasions, subjects, and individual purposes. (*Structure* 71)

In all of this, to be sure, he sounds very much like a postprocess theorist. However, at the moment he seems closest to Kent, he immediately departs—though perhaps not so very far. "But," Nystrand asserts, despite the joys of iconoclasm, the foregoing analysis is not quite true: "Every written text is not wholly idiosyncratic." He therefore frames his purpose as a researcher in terms of salvaging order amid chaos, much like Paul Lynch has done in *After Pedagogy* and Rule has done in

Situating Writing Processes. At minimum, he writes, "The constant in the equation of discourse is reciprocity, the underlying premise that the text generated must result in shared knowledge between writer and reader" (*Structure* 71).

The foregoing paragraphs should, I hope, demonstrate that Nystrand conceived of writing as an interpretive or interactive phenomenon; however, his ideas also align with those later endorsed by postprocess scholars in subtler ways. So far as I know, Nystrand never frames his own work as being *paralogic* and his references to *hermeneutics* are infrequent. Even so, he clearly applies a (semantic) externalist framework. He draws from Hilary Putnam to suggest that a term's reference is established in and through use, rather than existing as some "unequivocal aspect of reality" (*Structure* 44). Similarly, he argues that "the resources of discourse are not ancillary to cognition but actually shape the possibilities for and hence the conduct of discourse itself" ("Rhetoric's 'Audience'" 7). He also gestures toward a conception of the extended mind (i.e., vehicle externalism) in his suggestion that "writing systems assist and extend the limits of natural memory" (16). Nystrand commonly cites Bakhtin and Vygotsky; unsurprisingly, then, he conceives of writing as a form of *activity* and understands textual meaning to be *negotiated* between reader and writer.

When Nystrand explains the practical implications of his theoretical positions, these also resemble the approaches endorsed by self-identified postprocess thinkers, who frame writing as an activity oriented toward practical ends. As a pragmatist, he defines language as "an activity motivated by users' needs to make things known in particular ways for particular purposes and to establish and maintain common understandings with other conversants." For him, then, language is as valuable for what it can accomplish (in a functional sense) as what it can express. Nystrand also understands the formal (generic) features of texts to arise as much from their functions as their contents ("Rhetoric's 'Audience'" 10). A genre, from that perspective, is defined by what it accomplishes within an activity system. In all of this, he sounds quite a lot like David R. Russell and Joseph Petraglia, among others.

Like Russell and Petraglia, Nystrand understands writing to be fundamentally interactive—except in one peculiar instance. "Aside from school writing," he argues, "writers and readers meet each other more or less half way—each bringing her respective purposes to bear on the text and each proceeding in terms of what she assumes about the other" ("Sharing Words" 8). Unsurprisingly, then, he condemns what Petraglia would call pseudo-transactional academic genres, stating, "Writing in the absence of a rhetorical context is not really discourse; it is the bloodless, academic exercise of essay-making, dummy runs and pedagogical artifacts such as the five-paragraph theme—in short, a degeneration of rhetoric" ("Rhetoric's 'Audience'" 5).

TRANSACTIVE MODIFICATIONS: PHELPS' GENERATIVE TERMS FOR COMPOSITION

For those interested in postprocess, I suspect that Louise Wetherbee Phelps may require less introduction than Nystrand. She was the founding director of the stand-alone Writing Program at Syracuse University, whose doctorate in Composition and Cultural Rhetoric was the first rhet/comp Ph.D. in the United States offered outside of an English department. She also co-founded the graduate consortium of Doctoral Programs in Composition and Rhetoric. More to the point: while reflecting an uncommonly, even shockingly broad knowledge base, her work often engages with the sorts of (continental philosophy) texts that are commonly considered *to be theoretical*. She solo-authored one book and co-edited several more. She has published more than twenty book chapters and at least twenty peer-reviewed articles, many of which appear in the most "mainstream" of composition journals: *College English, College Composition and Communication, Rhetoric Review, JAC*, and so on down the line (Rodrigue, "Portrait").

As I noted earlier, the first known usage of the term *post-process* in composition and/or writing studies scholarship arises in a brief 1984 text by Judith Langer. For Langer, current-traditionalism represented a focus on the "products" of writing (i.e., static, finished texts) and Process represented an alternate focus on the dynamic acts that might bring written products into being. In the forthcoming "post-process paradigm," though, Langer believed that scholars would eschew the "false binary" of product versus process. She also believed that scholars would stop searching for the features of (generically) Good Writing or the generalizable strategies and methods that might lead writers to produce it. Instead, they would investigate the particular, situated processes employed to produce specific texts for practical functions.

Phelps was aware of Langer's arguments, and she is one of the very few scholars to cite the particular "Musing" in which the word *post-process* appears. More importantly, though, Phelps had begun reintegrating product and process well before Langer issued her own call for scholars to do so. While proving that case here, I also want to demonstrate two central points. First, much like Nystrand, Phelps developed an interpretive (and/or interactive or transactive) vision of writing during the 1980s, and she consistently affirmed her placement alongside other scholars engaged in a shared project. But, despite the simultaneity and conceptual overlap of her work and Kent's, her work has not been assimilated under the rubric of postprocess. Second, in my estimation, Phelps presents the strongest and clearest and most sustained case against presenting any single term (*Process* or *postprocess* or any other) as a central metaphor for writing research. In discussing Phelps, I'll primarily address three of her articles, which she would retrospectively figure as a sort of trilogy: "The Dance of Discourse" (1982), "Dialectics of Coherence" (1985) and "Audience and Authorship: The Disappearing Boundary" (1990). I'd also like to examine her book *Composition as a Human Science* (1988), which would re-configure and/or re-present portions of the first two of those articles.

In the last of these texts, "Audience and Authorship," Phelps acknowledges her prolonged efforts "to surpass a process/product dichotomy" by "modify[ing] the concept of process . . . to refer more inclusively to the cooperative enterprise whereby writers and readers construct meaning together" (154). The textual record clearly evidences this sustained preoccupation. Phelps had begun the work of (re-)integrating process and product as early as 1976. In her master's thesis from Cleveland State University, *The Development of a Discourse Model for Composition*, she writes,

> In the theory I outline below, there are elements of, on
> the one hand, the progressive emphasis on expression, the
> composing process, and affective values; on the other, of the
> traditional interest in the rhetorical nature of language, the
> interaction of writer and audience, the structure of discourse,
> convention and form, and cognitive values. It is my purpose
> to reconcile these elements in a view of composition as an
> organic whole of process and product. (27)

Here, to an astonishing degree, Phelps places the major pre-occupations of 1970s composition scholarship (the composing process, expression, rhetoric) alongside what would come to be the field's central pre-occupations for the next several decades (cognition, interaction, affect). And, of course, she also suggests reconciling product and process.

Phelps hoped to (re-)integrate studies of process and product(s) and thereby "to build up a unified theory of composition," and she believed that it could be achieved through a "relatively simple step" ("Dialectics" 14). Her solution: "to extend the dynamic of meaning-construction from the composing process to the interpretive acts of readers." Phelps' efforts here appear deconstructive to me, inasmuch as she would not simply invert the terms of the binary but attempt to reinscribe them in an altogether different economy of meaning. She writes, therefore,

> What this means is that the process/product relations change
> and each acquires new reference. Before, "process" referred to
> the writer's act of composing written thought and "product"
> to the text encapsulating that meaning. Now, the overarching
> "process" is the cooperative enterprise whereby writers and
> readers construct meanings together, through the dialectical

> tension between their interactive and interdependent pro-
> cesses. . . . In this view the composing and reading processes
> are no longer distinct. The reader's perspective is bound up in
> the writing process itself. (14)

While Phelps would admit having "limited" goals for her article, she maintained that "articulating a working vocabulary in which to formulate questions
and carry out observations" might "lay a foundation for studying actual processes of coherent discourse in context" (15).

In Phelps' account, a (re-)integrated, cooperative vision of the meaning-
making process would produce "momentous consequences because it changes
the root metaphor of composition from that of creation to one of symbolic
interaction" (14). Inasmuch as *Paralogic Rhetoric* (subtitled *A Theory of Communicative Interaction*) would likewise advocate such a reintegration, and likewise
prophesy its discipline-shaking impact, it seems to me that Phelps anticipates
Kent here. She argues that reinscribing *process* and *product* according to her stipulations would move beyond a simple accounting for "writing as social action,"
and instead recognize that "written thought—thought which emerges through
writing into situational contexts—is radically social and intersubjective through
its very constitution as a discourse" (14). In other words, just as Kent would
eventually adopt the term *public* to indicate a form of sociality more social than
that which had come to be called *social* (constructionism), Phelps seems to drive
sociality not merely into writing as *action* but into writing as *thinking*.

Despite their discipline-shaking potential, though, Phelps would not claim
these insights as her own or attempt to take credit for discovering them. Instead,
she frames them as a collective achievement. She writes, "This metaphoric shift
toward a more intersubjective and deeply contextualized view of written language is, I think, the point of convergence toward which much important work
in the profession is moving, from very different initial perspectives, sources, and
modes of inquiry" (14). Or, stated differently, a large portion of the field had
already begun to see the limit(ation)s of one view of writing as *process* and had
moved toward a different set of metaphors. Writing in 1986, Phelps would note
that "this transactionalist perspective dominates the May, 1983, issue of *Language Arts* devoted to reading and writing relationships," highlighting works by
Robert J. Tierney and P. David Pearson. She would also name eight other scholars—plus herself—as people engaged in similar work ("Domain" 193).

To this point, I have focused on the middle text in Phelps' article trilogy.
But, in examining the opening and closing texts, one sees her prolonged efforts
to dissolve many of the binaries—not merely process/product—on which Process theories had depended. In "The Dance of Discourse," she argues that "the

dualism itself" is the problem, not "the way the [product/process] polarity is construed" (58, 35). She sought, therefore, to displace a Cartesian-Newtonian ontology with an Einsteinian one that would "merg[e] subject and object, structure and process," offering "an interactive conception of the relation between ourselves and reality (36, 44). Though she doesn't use the same language here, Phelps advocates externalist, anti-Cartesian principles. Thus, it's worth recalling Kent's stated purpose in writing *Paralogic Rhetoric:* to interrogate and ultimately displace "the ubiquitous influence of Cartesianism or . . . *internalism* on certain contemporary accounts of reading and writing" ("Response" 106, 105). To achieve a similar end, Phelps would reverse the tendency to privilege linguistic system (*langue*) over discourse event (*parole*) (46). Although "emphatically" avoiding any effort "to prescribe practice or even give advice," Phelps would ultimately posit a "reconstruction" of discourse as "essentially dance, event, or pattern of symbolic energies in which the discourser participates, ordered or structure with the aid of cues laid down by the writer in the text for himself and the reader (54–55).

By 1990, Phelps was no longer trying to dissolve the subject-object distinction; instead, she would present that dissolution as a *fait accompli.* She opens "Audience and Authorship" by noting that "theory and research," as well as composition pedagogy were already "carrying us beyond the concept of 'dialogic interaction' between writer and reader" by "break[ing] down the barriers and boundaries that allowed us to distinguish audience from writer, text, and context" (154). To the extent that a disciplinary shift had occurred, though, Phelps saw "process theory generat[ing] its own critique," shifting away from "isolated writing process studies" in order "to reconnect writing to reading within a transactive discourse act" (154, 155). At the same time, though, Phelps acknowledged the limitations of recent studies on audience. "They don't go far enough," she would write, characterizing them as "radically incomplete if taken to account comprehensively for the social dimensions of writing," insofar as they did not "collapse" the distinction between audience and author (156, 158).

Before proceeding, some terminological clarification may be in order. In instances that I've quoted above, Phelps sometimes refers to her scholarship as being *interactionist* and other times as *transactionalist.* Importantly, though, she did not consider *interaction* and *transaction* to be synonyms. Rather, following Louise Rosenblatt, she understood *interaction* to indicate "the impact of separate, already-defined entities acting on one another" (Rosenblatt, "Transaction vs. Interaction" 97). In contrast, in a *transaction,* "instead of breaking the subject matter into fragments in advance of inquiry, the observer, the observing, and the observed were to be seen as aspects of a total situation" (98).

In this light, then, one can better understand Phelps' proclamation that conceptions of dialogic interaction would be replaced by more thoroughgoing models of transactionality. She prophesies

> the imminent replacement of dialogic interaction (an exclusive, cooperative relation between writer and reader, mediated by text) with a more fully contextualized, polyphonic, contentious model of transactionality that encompasses multiple participants and voices along with situation, setting, institutions, and language itself—and finds it hard to maintain firm boundaries between self and other. ("Audience and Authorship" 156)

By 1990, Phelps had concluded, it would no longer be sufficient to conceptualize a dialogue between author and reader, mediated by text. Nor would it be enough to consider the text as dialogic, a pastiche. To do so would be to imply that each element was (or could be) separated out from the others. Instead, in a transactional model, all elements would be seen as mutually implicated: author, reader, text, context. In this light, the author might be considered a construction or composite, no longer "distinct from reader and other voices of the intertext (158, 161). With the disintegration of "every boundary that formerly separated (however permeably) mind from mind, mind from text, mind from material world, text from other text, text from talk . . . and so on," scholars might re-direct their attention. Under such conditions, Phelps argues, "Audience is no longer the problem, but the given . . . It is authorship we cannot take for granted" (163). Of course, inasmuch as composition "teach[es] authoring," this new view of authorship posed problems. She would therefore formulate a theoretically rigorous approach that might still "account for the fact that we do experience ourselves as authors" (163). To do so, she would turn to Bakhtin, a "thoroughly contextualist theorist" who still "preserves heuristic"—that is, "simplified and limited" but also useful—"boundaries between authorship and audience" (170, 169, 165).

Phelps' work presents a strong and abiding sense of a scholar (and, synecdochally, a scholarly field) continuously wrestling with the relations between subject and object, reading and writing, writer and audience. By 1990, Phelps sounded very much like an externalist. But, then again, so did she in 1982. The difference: by 1990 a sizable group of "composition theorists [had] now begun to argue various broader notions of the social element in composing . . . (as political ideology, as ecology, as genre)" (161).

In the foregoing paragraphs, I have focused primarily on Phelps' article trilogy, which critiques the Process movement forcefully and presents a fairly radical reimagining of it. By 1990 she would distinguish between "isolated writing process studies" and a "modification of process theory" that "reconnect[ed] writing to reading within a transactive discourse act" ("Audience" 155). Even so, she would continue to refer to a *process* approach or movement within those works, despite acknowledging the logological problems incumbent in doing so. In the terms of continental philosophers, she used the term *under erasure*. However, she presents a different approach in *Composition as a Human Science*.

In *Composition*, Phelps seems perfectly willing to eschew the term *process*, though at once hesitant to adopt any other, single term (or "totalizing mechanism") to take its place (46, 52). She suggests that *process* is "too frail" to continue supporting serious scholarly investigations. It is, she argues, "deeply flawed, being burdened by scientism, psychologism, dichotomization, severely restricted scope, and ecological blindness" (45–46). She even wonders whether it ought to be "rule[d] out . . . as a generative term for composition" because "it just carries too much baggage that needs to be cleared away before we can perceive the contextualist possibilities [that] it evokes only partially and distortedly" (46). I'll have more to say about those contextualist possibilities in a moment. Here, though, I would note Phelps' longing for a "productive abstraction," a term or concept that scholars might "treat . . . as trope," so as to "exploit the associations evoked" by it. This productive abstraction, she suggests, would "not simply designate phenomena but describe them," enabling scholars to "reconceiv[e] facts in fresh and surprising ways" and "assign negotiable meanings to vague but important terms like audience, coherence," and so on (47).

Phelps admits that, for the sake of the discipline she would prefer to inhabit, several terms might be preferable to *process*, including "event, act, activity, interaction, transaction, open system, relation, ecology" (46). At the same time, she concludes that each is, in its own way, both "too powerful" and "too unspecific" to be a "generative term for composition." In her estimation, whatever term(s) might replace *process* would need to "spring directly from our subject matter," and scholars would do well to "proliferate what Peirce calls 'interpretants'—signs that refigure and resymbolize the key term in a process of 'unlimited semiosis'" (46). Ultimately, she also recognizes the "personal nature of such [terminological and conceptual] choices," and so she admits that others would need to be extended the right to (and would *need* to) champion their own "values and attitudes." At the same time, this proliferation of perspectives would offer one further benefit: other compositionists' "copresent values" would "criticize and limit" her own, and hers would do the same to theirs in turn (52)

Throughout Part One of her book, Phelps refers to what she calls "the process decades" using past tense verbs (47; c.f. 42–46). Though she doesn't directly state as much, she subtly implies that the Process movement may have already reached its limit, even if scholars hadn't yet come to terms with that terminus.

Thus, it would need to be reconfigured or revitalized. Importantly, though, she figures Process as "pluralistic" and "not really a theory at all, but the common ground among many theories and practices that encompasses highly diverse and frequently conflicting emphases, beliefs, values, and treatments of texts" (161). She also criticizes Maxine Hairston for claiming that Process represented an "emerging paradigm" or a sort of "scholarly consensus." To her mind, any generalized "agreement [concerning Process] depends on not trying to go beyond a list of features, which conceals profound conflicts and leaves open the question of how these principles might be coherently related" (180). That is, Process was internally diverse, even if that diversity was commonly ignored—even by its proponents. Given its variegated nature, then, one could not dismiss the whole formation simply by dismissing one of its components. And yet, Phelps genuinely did see faults with Process—both the term and the movement.

Although Phelps refuses to dismiss or directly replace the term *Process* with any other, single term, she does signal her preference for a particular conception of writing instruction: a contextualist one, which might join together and/or operate through that aforementioned string of concepts: "event, act, activity, interaction, transaction, open system, relation, ecology." Crucially, contextualism is understood here as the Quantum Relativistic (i.e., Einsteinian) form of process that Phelps had addressed in "The Dance" (43). But, whereas her comparison between a Newtonian-Cartesian process and a Quantum Relativistic one would seem to imply that the former preceded the latter historically, Phelps denies this suggestion. Instead, she argues that "contextualist themes are latent in the very origins of process," even if the Newtonian model "dominated conceptions of process" in its early stages (44). She comes dangerously close to suggesting that contextualism has overtaken its "linear, deterministic" opponent in the 1980s, but she stops just short. Rather than trumpet the intrinsic superiority of one approach to another, she historicizes. Contextualism, she suggests, "shares, or perhaps comprehensively articulates, the peculiar reflexivity of postmodern thought" (32). Therefore, it is valuable to compositionists to the extent that it adds to Process "a dimension . . . that clarifies certain radical possibilities in postmodern themes" (30).

This appraisal aligns with (what I take to be) Phelps' overall purpose in *Composition*. Throughout her book, but particularly in its opening pages, she places rhetoric at the point of convergence of "the positive directions of postmodern culture" and argues that composition is uniquely suited to help "articulate and realize this paradigm," insofar as it provides a site for working in/out/through the relations between theory and praxis (6). Or, stated in the simplest terms I can offer, Phelps believes that a lot of smart people in a lot of disciplines—including composition—are coming to recognize the inseparability of subjects (e.g., people) and their environments. She admits that conceptual overlaps may be difficult to see, but she affirms that composition provides as good a place as any in which to see them. She thinks that composition has been, is, and will increasingly be *contextualist*.

Phelps borrows her notion of contextualism from Stephen Pepper's *World Hypotheses: A Study in Evidence* (1942). To simplify Pepper's work heavily: any given philosophical system will intertwine with a "world hypothesis" or world-view, which will itself rely upon a "root metaphor" that provides an explanatory key or interpretive frame (akin to a Burkean terministic screen) and also a "truth criterion" through which one makes sense of the world. For Pepper, the root metaphor for contextualism is difficult to define "even to a first approximation by well-known common-sense concepts." But, he allows that the best available term "is probably the historic event"—an event that he defines as "alive in its present," and which he calls a "dynamic dramatic active event" (Pepper 232). The event in this sense is an act—one that is best described by "us[ing] only verbs." The event happens in time (i.e., it is *historical*) but it is also ongoing: it reverberates, and it is probably better figured in terms of *change* than *growth* (which is central to a separate worldview: organicism). Furthermore, the event must be understood as "an act in and with its setting, an act in its context." In this way, contextualism opposes convenient or simple dichotomies. It focuses on both the quality of an event—its "intuited wholeness or total character"—and also to its texture, "the details and reactions which make up that character or quality" (238). Importantly, though, it denies that either quality or texture is an "absolute element," apart from the other. It does not allow for the common conception of a whole as merely the sum of its parts, nor does it allow that a whole might be "a sort of added part like a clamp that holds together a number of blocks." Rather, the whole is "immanent in an event" and thus Pepper calls contextualism "the only theory that takes fusion seriously" (238, 245). Fusion, within this framework, implies that "the qualities of the [purportedly individual] details are completely merged in the quality of the whole," and in this sense it does amount to a form of "sheering" or "qualitative simplification and organization" (243–44, 249). Unlike any other philosophical system, contextualism provides fusion with a "cosmic dignity" (245).

Finally, for our purposes, contextualist analysis differs from other varieties in that it never bottoms-out or arrives at definitive answers: "there is no final or complete analysis of anything" (249, 250). For any given event, one might always analyze different textures (i.e., elements), even pulling at the "strands" of those textures, and thereby arriving at different conclusions (250). Any meaningful analysis must therefore be conducted "in reference to the end" in sight—that is, for and in acknowledgment of its practical or pragmatic purposes (250–51). Parsing this point in a parenthetical aside, Phelps notes, "Relativism is not construed as pernicious; 'pluralism' conveys more accurately the idea that reality is too complex to be encompassed by any single truth or perspective on it" (32).

Phelps' work consistently aims to (re-)integrate reading and writing to construe each as inseparable from the other. She implies that the "dominant" Process approach to composition separated them unnecessarily and for reasons related to its terminology and/or its root metaphor(s). But, in arguing for this reintegration, she does not discard *process* but instead simultaneously redefines it—as "the cooperative enterprise whereby writers and reader construct their meanings together"—and places it within an alternate network of terms ("Dialectics" 14). In so doing, she "changes" (or, at least, hopes to change) "the root metaphor of composition from that of creation to one of symbolic interaction" (14). Again—and at the risk of redundancy—this symbolic interaction is contextualist and thus, in some senses, transactionalist. In defining her terms by proliferating terms, Phelps states,

> Context (also system, field, whole, ecology, relation) refers to the total set of relationships from which particular entities and qualities derive. . . . A contextualist theory is one in which all parts are not only interdependent but mutually defining and transactive. . . . This premise holds for the system in general, and specifically for the relationships between subject and object, observer and observed. Neither is fixed; the line between the two is neither sharp nor stable, because each is derived from and defined by the constantly new relationships in which it participates. (*Composition* 32–33)

In this light, writers (those who might otherwise be called "human individuals") are considered to be "multidimensional systems not clearly distinguishable from their social and physical environment" (34).

Of course, Phelps' arguments here will sound familiar to contemporary compositionists and writing studies scholars, given the current, collective fascination with writing ecologies and/or the ambience of rhetoric. And, as I have indicated but not yet commented upon, the term *ecology* pops up quite often in Phelps' discussions of symbolic interaction and contextualism. In fact, though Marilyn Cooper is often credited with introducing an ecological approach into composition studies with her April 1986 "The Ecology of Composition," Phelps did so three months earlier, in the January 1986 issue of *Rhetoric Review*. In "The Domain of Composition," she presents a "very abbreviated sketch of a view of written discourse as interaction." In this interactive conception, she writes, "Written discourse as symbolic action can only be understood ecologically, in terms of its rich interaction among acts, meanings, and reality, rather than by a reduction of its texture to ideal elements and rules." This ecological conception, she argues, would entail "an interpenetration of writing, the mental world of writer and readers, and the life-world in which they live" (185). Inasmuch as I want to conceive of ecological composition as a postprocess approach to rhetorical invention, Phelps' work here might seem to be postprocess or proto-postprocess. Indeed, in *Composition as a Human Science*, she explicitly critiques Process for "its inadequacy to articulate a comprehensively ecological framework for composition" (41). I will not characterize her scholarship as postprocess, though, given her apparent, prolonged resistance to such labels. Even so, I cannot help but note how it accords with postprocess approaches in other ways.

In Chapter 5, I will demonstrate that Kent's proto-postprocess theorization often occurred outside the conventional (i.e., first-year) bounds of composition, that *Paralogic Rhetoric* was understood at the time of its publication to imply a movement toward writing in the disciplines (i.e., teaching writing within its relevant activity systems), and that the after-life of postprocess theory has entailed a further movement away from composition and toward writing studies. Consider, then, how Phelps explains the ramifications of her contextualist approach in *Composition as a Human Science*:

> If we apply contextualist criteria, there is no principled way to restrict the responsibility for such teaching to a particular age or setting. . . . Thus we have grounds for enlarging the teaching responsibilities of composition to encompass the origins of literacy in cultural experience and its continuing growth and application to practical contexts, such as work or public life, within the individual's personal history. (71)

For Phelps, contextualism implies (at least) three major shifts: in the age of the learners (a shift to lifelong learning); in terms of who can teach (a shift in favor of those involved in the activity system); and in the setting for education (a shift toward teaching within the activity system itself). In a later elaboration, she states, "The newly vigorous contextualist or ecological orientation to literacy recognizes that the learner lives in a cultural and specifically linguistic world, and thus highlights the interpersonal dimensions of natural literacy learning" and it "emphasizes . . . participating in literacy events" (114). One learns to write by writing in the culturally and linguistically inflected settings in which one finds oneself, alongside others who also appear there.

CODA: ON MAPPING THE EDGES OF POSTPROCESS

In writing a history such as this, one faces unavoidable questions concerning categories. Over and over again, I have been forced to ask, *how far do the edges of postprocess extend?* The answers to this question are always ultimately arbitrary, but also revealing.

There's an old cliché that says, "If it walks like a duck and it quacks like a duck, well, then, it must be a duck." By this logic, similarities are obvious, and one shouldn't over-think them. But, from my perspective here, a lot hinges on *likeness*, which can always be construed (and, more to the point, *constructed*) broadly or narrowly.

The better you know a thing, the more you care about its fine-grained distinctions. For much of my life, my brother and I were roughly the same height and weight, we had the same hair color, similar eye colors, the same skin tone, and at least some shared facial features. Yet, whenever people would tell my mom that we looked alike, she'd become either insulted or perplexed. She could see that I have her eyes and chin, but my brother has my dad's nose and smile, and so on down the line. Those distinctions *mattered* to her, but they couldn't and didn't to most people who encountered us. And, to some degree, that hurt her.

Now, I am not trying to equate these relatively academic musings with a mother's love for her children. Even so, I imagine, I am writing this book to those willing to make such fine-grained distinctions, some of whom may even have emotional stakes in my depictions.

In quite a few respects, as I hope this chapter has shown, what came to be called postprocess was itself an instance of a broader series of shifts in composition and writing studies research throughout the 1980s and 1990s. Even so, I want to refuse the impulse to subsume Nystrand's and Phelps' research into the history of postprocess simply as interesting or odd examples of it—one considered to be "not theoretical enough" and the other surprisingly considered to be "too theoretical." To do so would be to privilege that which one can name—because a name has been pre-given—at the expense of that which is not yet named. One could just as easily say that Kent's proto-postprocess work is an instance of whatever Nystrand was doing at the time or whatever Phelps was doing at the time. Likewise, of course, one could create some new category—one can *always* create a new category—and subsume Nystrand and Phelps and postprocess into it. Such a gesture would present certain merits. I take Nietzsche to be correct in identifying concept-formation (that is, categorization) as the fundamental move toward knowledge-making. But, I also follow him in lamenting whatever is lost, stripped away, cast aside in order to produce a semblance of likeness. The gain always implies a loss, and so one is forced to ask: is the gain worth it, and to whom?

In this light, when asked the question, *how far do the edges of postprocess extend?* I have attempted to answer: just far enough, and no farther.

CHAPTER 4.

OH, CANADA: THE BIRTH OF POSTPROCESS NORTH OF THE BORDER

Postprocess tenets have been considerably more influential within the scholarly discourse(s) of composition and writing studies than has been acknowledged to date. In some cases, they have even functioned as "unformulated conventions," widely shared though generally un-acknowledged conceptual premises. To justify these claims, I have dis-entangled the tenets from the category that has been used to join them together, *postprocess*, then identified their prevalence in scholarly discourses that are not commonly considered to be postprocess. I will apply that procedure in Chapter 5, as I trace the origins of contemporary "post-composition" approaches to writing instruction, particularly writing studies and/or writing about writing pedagogies, through postprocess. I'll also employ a similar operation in Chapter 6, as I demonstrate that the dominant contemporary theories of invention are postprocess approaches. In both of those cases, I hope to show that postprocess represents the un-named or un-acknowledged "umbrella" category that might join together those otherwise disparate intellectual formations. While scholars certainly benefit from distinguishing ecological approaches to composition from posthumanist ones, I believe that there's also something to be gained by acknowledging the underlying externalist (and thus postprocess) inventional scheme that each pre-supposes, then by separating them off from internalist (and thus Process) inventional schemes. But, this is not the only way to demonstrate the heretofore unacknowledged impacts of postprocess principles.

Unlike Process, which can trace its lineage through two quasi-manifestos, Barriss Mills' 1953 "Writing as Process" and Donald Murray's 1972 "Teach Writing as a Process Not Product," those who coined the terms *post-process* and *postprocess* didn't do so to characterize their own theories of writing and/ or approaches to writing instruction. Nor, with the exception of Judith Langer's relatively inconsequential 1984 usage, did they attempt to inaugurate a new era of research or approach to instruction. Instead, the terms *post-process* and *postprocess* were applied retroactively to pre-existing works. Thus, postprocess principles must have been circulating through (at least some branches of) the discipline before *anything* had been deemed *post-/postprocess*. In the last chapter,

I demonstrated that interpretive conceptions of writing circulated widely before *writing is interpretive* found its place in postprocess' "three-part mantra." To do so, I focused on the works of Martin Nystrand and Louise Wetherbee Phelps, both of whom rightly positioned their own works as representative examples of larger scholarly endeavors, but neither of whom has been commonly acknowledged as a postprocess pioneer.

In this chapter, I will trace an alternate genealogy of postprocess writing theory and pedagogy. When Anthony Paré identified a post-process pedagogical approach in his 1994 "Toward a Post-Process Pedagogy; or, What's Theory Got to Do with It?," he offered a name to a series of pedagogical methods, grounded in a rigorous conceptual framework, already being applied by a coterie of scholars—Russell Hunt, James Reither, and Douglas Vipond—at Saint Thomas University in Fredericton, New Brunswick, Canada. In many respects, what Paré calls a *post-process pedagogy* could just as easily have been called a Saint Thomas pedagogy or a Hunt-Reither-Vipond pedagogy; those scholars are *that* central to Paré's formulation.

Before proceeding onward, I would voice an important caution. Throughout this book, I am distinguishing between post-process, as introduced by John Trimbur and defined as the "leftwing trajectory of the social turn," and postprocess, as introduced by Irene Ward and defined as an externalist and paralogic conception of writing (Trimbur, "Taking" 109). I want to affirm, then, that Paré's notion of post-process much more closely resembles what I am calling *postprocess* than what I am calling *post-process*. Indeed, although I am examining Hunt, Reither, and Vipond in their own, separate chapter, they would fit just as well in any of my three other genealogies of postprocess. Like the scholars I examined in the previous chapter, they aimed to (re-)integrate transactive theories of reading into theories of writing. As should become clear, they belong equally well within genealogies of writing studies and writing about writing that I will present in the next one. And, notably, scholars associated with those fields, including Michael Carter, Elizabeth Wardle, and Douglas Downs, have acknowledged their conceptual debts to Reither, in particular. My sense is that if Hunt's and Vipond's contributions were more commonly cited and discussed, those scholars would receive similar credit as intellectual forebears. Finally, I will analyze Reither's "Writing and Knowing" myself as a precursor to externalist inventional schemes in Chapter 6.

Admittedly, according to one set of metrics—that is, textual citations—this Canadian version of post-/postprocess has been relatively inconsequential. Although Trimbur and Paré independently coined *post-process* within months of each other, Trimbur's article has been cited more than 225 times, whereas (at the time of my writing) Paré's has been cited fewer than ten. Only two texts that

I consider in this book, Richard Fulkerson's "Of Pre- and Post-Process" (2001) and Paul Kei Matsuda's "Process and Post-Process: A Discursive History" (2003), even cite Paré. And, when they address his work, they do so in cursory fashion. Fulkerson writes, "I believe John Trimbur and Anthony Paré get the credit/blame for introducing the term 'post-process' into our scholarly discourse in separate articles in 1994," and then two sentences later remarks, "I'll return to Trimbur" (97). He never returns to Paré. When Matsuda mentions Paré, he places him in a footnote to a discussion of Trimbur's article, not in his article's main text. But, of course, textual citations are neither the only nor the best way to account for disciplinary knowledge construction. To understand fully the impact that Hunt, Reither, and Vipond had on their academic discourse and inquiry community, I believe one must also examine their non-textual contributions.

In presenting Hunt, Reither, and Vipond as postprocess theorists, I want to affirm their substantial contributions to the field in terms of their pedagogy, their conference organizing, their presentations and interactions at conferences and institutes, and their editorial work. For instance, the core principles described in Reither's "Writing and Knowing" were instantiated in the form of a particular pedagogy (collaborative investigation, often including inkshedding) and implemented at a uniquely structured academic conference, Inkshed. The pedagogical method of inkshedding also provides a conceptual basis for at least one textbook, *Conversations about Writing: Eavesdropping, Inkshedding, and Joining In* by M. Elizabeth Sargent and Cornelia C. Paraskevas. In addition, as late as 1989 (and perhaps later), Reither was offering a free-and-open-to-the-public writing seminar entitled "Writing and Knowing" at McGill University (*Inkshed* 8.2). And, as recently as 2017, the Inkshed/CASLL Press was the only Canadian scholarly press devoted specifically to the discipline of composition studies (MacDonald, "Farewell" 1–2). Writing in 1989, Richard Coe would therefore affirm Reither's monumental importance to constructing a community of writing instructors in Canada:

> Those of us in Canadian universities and colleges whose speciality is composition/rhetoric realized, just under a decade ago, that our connections ran mostly through the United States, that we came together most frequently as an informal Canadian caucus at composition conferences in the United States, that we communicated with each other about our research through U.S. publications, and so forth. In response to this realization, we—read "Jim Reither, with help from his friends, for he supplied the impetus"—created a Canadian newsletter, started an "occasional" working conference (which

> has, in fact, now met annually since 1984), and helped reorient and transform English Quarterly into a respected academic journal. This tripod—newsletter, journal and conference—now supports the primary cross-Canada community for those who study and teach writing in the universities, colleges and corporations. ("Write a Letter" 20)

Without Reither and his colleagues Hunt and Vipond, the subsequent history of writing instruction in Canada would have looked very different.

In examining Hunt, Reither, and Vipond, then, I will focus on three areas in which they offered impressive intellectual contributions: first their scholarly writing, which was often produced collaboratively; second, the innovative pedagogical schemes they developed and implemented, especially two inter-connected elements they called collaborative investigation and inkshedding; and, third, the newsletter-that-became-a-conference-and-also-an-academic-press that Reither and Hunt founded and edited, Inkshed. Though, as we'll soon see, these elements are not so easily separated, I'd still like to pursue them in this order. After passing through these examinations, I'll turn to Anthony Paré's 1994 "Toward a Post-Process Pedagogy." Contextualizing Paré's argument in light of the Inkshed community—especially the works of Hunt, Reither, and Vipond—shows a version of post-process (surprisingly similar to what I am calling postprocess) to have a separate, Canadian genealogy.

THREE MEN ON AN ISLAND—AND THE OLDER-THAN-WE'VE-ACKNOWLEDGED ABOLITIONISM

From a postprocess perspective, all writing is invariably and inexorably collaborative, given that (externalized) minds cannot produce thought "on their own." Reither and Vipond present an early formulation of this idea in their 1989 article "Writing as Collaboration." By their reasoning, writing is "impossible—inconceivable—without collaboration" and it is collaborative "from beginning to end" (856). From that perspective, there wouldn't be much sense in trying to distinguish the amount of collaboration required to produce one text versus another. But, applying a more traditional definition of collaboration, which might uphold the possibility of solo-authored texts, one would distinguish levels of collaborative-ness. Under such a conventional viewpoint, the writing processes employed by Hunt, Reither, and Vipond (and their other co-authors and peer reviewers) would appear very, even unusually, collaborative.

Reither and Hunt would publish and present together several times, as would Hunt and Vipond (and/or Vipond and Hunt). They often worked in close quarters, and the physical particularities of their text-production were very easy to idealize. As Hunt told me, "We often, while drafting, sat at one computer and swapped the keyboard back and forth" (personal correspondence). "Writing as Collaboration," a text attributed to Reither and Vipond, includes a case study of the publication of Hunt and Vipond's 1986 "Evaluations in Literary Reading," a text that Reither and two other colleagues at Saint Thomas, Alan Mason of the anthropology department and Thom Parkhill of the religious studies department, had variously read and responded to (857). And, as an interesting historical footnote: at the close of "Writing as Collaboration," Reither and Vipond extend their gratitude to "the trusted assessors—the enablers—who helped workshop this paper": Hunt, Paré, and Karen Burke LeFevre, the author of *Invention as a Social Act* (866). And this is not to mention the other notable members of their scholarly collective: Richard Coe and Andrea Lunsford and Lester Faigley—all prominent figures in the discourse of social and/or collaborative writing. Coe, now commonly cited as an intellectual forebear of ecological composition, served on the editorial board of *Inkshed* from 1983 (issue 2.1) through at least the late 1990s. Lunsford, who taught at the University of British Columbia from 1977–1986, published brief notes in the newsletter as early as 1983. Along with Lisa Ede and C. Jan Swearingen, she published an article entitled "Collaborative Writing: Perspectives by Incongruity" in a 1990 special issue on collaborative writing (*Inkshed* 9.2). She also served on the Inkshed Conference organizing committee at various points. Faigley, with whom Reither had studied during his year as a visiting scholar at the University of Texas-Austin from 1981–1982, also served on the newsletter editorial board from 1991 until 1998 (Phelps, "Four Scholars" 88).

As Reed Way Dasenbrock has argued, Thomas Kent's postprocess theories pointed toward two primary ends—first, reintegrating theories of reading with theories of writing, and second, teaching writing in the disciplines ("Review" 103). Hunt, Reither, and Vipond likewise pursued these goals, though approaching them from separate angles and arriving at slightly different conclusions. While affirming the necessity of hermeneutic guessing and the invariably interpretive nature of writing, Kent tended to focus on highly granular or localized concerns: how interpretation occurs at the level of individual utterances. The three scholars from Saint Thomas University also applied reader-response literary theories to their models of writing and/or writing instruction, and they likely would have assented to Kent's insights. But, their own examinations also emphasized another way that reading and writing inter-connect: one's reading (and research) practices provide one with the facts, figures, anecdotes, and insights—in short, the contents—of subsequent writing acts. In "Writing and Knowing," for instance, Reither states, "Academic writing, reading, and inquiry are inseparably linked; and all three are learned not by doing any one alone, but by doing them all at the same time. To 'teach writing' is thus necessarily to ground writing in reading and inquiry" (625).

In affirming the inter-connection of reading and writing, of course, Reither's theories would also heavily overlap with Judith Langer's and Louise Wetherbee Phelps'. Like them, he sought a means for dispensing with the (false) Product/ Process dichotomy on which much Process theorizing had attempted to ground itself, and aimed to conceptualize writing processes so as to account for the role of prior products. In "Writing and Knowing," which is notably sub-titled "Toward Redefining the Writing Process," Reither writes, "Academic writing, reading, and inquiry are collaborative, social acts, social processes, which not only result in, but also—and this is crucial—result from, social products: writing processes and written products are both elements of the same social process" (625). And, in that article's final sentence, he affirms, "It is time to redefine the writing process so that substantive social knowing is given due prominence in both our thinking and our teaching" (626). Thus, for Reither, as for Langer and Phelps, a suitably robust conception of the (social) writing process would need to account for the role of other people's texts and authors' interactions with those texts in the act of writing.

Hunt, Reither, and Vipond were jointly suited to integrate reading and writing into a model of language development, particularly in terms of writing ability. Hunt's primary training was in eighteenth century literature and literary theory, Reither was trained as a Shakespearean, and Vipond was an expert in cognitive psychology and psycholinguistics. As Vipond explained to me, "My interest early in my career was 'text comprehension.' Russ's interest was 'reading,' so we were really coming at the same thing from different angles" (personal correspondence). Those three also sought to incorporate others into their efforts at reading-writing integration: the newsletter that became *Inkshed* was first called *Writing and Reading/ Theory and Practice*, and, as *Inkshed*, it would later carry the subtitle "A Canadian newsletter devoted to writing and reading theory and practice."

To begin this exploration, I want to dwell on Hunt's work. At least on the southern side of the U.S.-Canada border, Hunt may not be considered a "major" disciplinary figure in composition and writing studies. Though he was prolific, his articles were generally published in Canadian journals (e.g., *English Quarterly* and *Inkshed*) or other non-U.S. outlets (e.g., *TEXT*), in journals focused more on literary studies (e.g., *Poetics* and *Reader*), or in edited collections. As a result, his work did not achieve the level of influence that, in my estimation, it merited and continues to merit. Even so, I would affirm, it is remarkable: excellent and well ahead of its time.

Hunt begins his 1983 article "Literature is Reading is Writing" with a simple observation: "Recent research into language and language learning processes has helped us realize that we don't actually understand enough about how reading and writing relate to one another" (5). Throughout the 1980s, then, he and Vipond would examine the social dimensions of reading in several articles: "Point-Driven Understanding: Pragmatic and Cognitive Dimensions of Literary Reading" (1984), "Crash-Testing a Transactional Model of Literary Reading" (1985); "Evaluations in Literary Reading" (1986); and, with Lynwood C. Wheeler, "Social Reading and Literary Engagement" (1987). Their insights on reading eventually become relevant to writing instruction, but they were not solely or immediately so.

That first text, "Literature is Reading is Writing," is interesting in its own regard, though. There Hunt notes the connection between reading and writing posited by current-traditionalism (as explained by Richard Young): "a one-directional, causal" one, in which "reading good texts causes—or is at least a major factor contributing to—good writing." Hunt notes various problems with this model, including the most basic: "there is simply no evidence that it works" (5). Then he proposes an alternative relationship, drawn from a more conceptually robust notion of reading, now considered to be "as active a process as writing," a task "not governed by the text" but instead "what Kenneth Goodman calls a 'psycholinguistic guessing game' that is actively played by readers" (6).

Hunt argues for a conception of meaning—whether textual or gestural or otherwise—as "a joint, mutual product, the result of cooperation and sharing—a transaction—between two people" (6). This view of reading undercuts the current-traditional assumption that reading good texts invariably leads to good writing. "There isn't much we can say about the consequences of reading," Hunt argues, "because reading varies so much from one case to the next" (6–7). Therefore, he concludes, "We cannot simply use texts to teach writing. We have to teach reading as well"—but a particular form, what Roland Barthes would call "writerly" reading. In this approach to reading, the reader actively generates questions and hypotheses and engages with the text in something very much like a dialogue; the reader's "attention is predominantly constructive . . . not looking at things, but at relations between things" and attempting to discern the text's "'Point': the pragmatic, interpersonal, social purposes and intents of the text's author" (7).

In the sort of reading that focuses on the author's "point," Hunt and Vipond elsewhere argue, "Meaning is not seen as something to be located in the text, but instead as something to be negotiated between readers and texts within situational constraints" ("Contextualizing the Text" 10). They draw this focus on the situationally contingent nature of meaning from Louise Rosenblatt who conceives of reading as *transactional*, rather than *interactional* ("Shunting Information" 131). In a *transaction*, Rosenblatt notes, "the elements or parts [of a phenomenon] are seen as aspects or phases of a total situation," whereas, in contrast, *interaction* implies "the impact of separate already-defined entities acting on one another" ("Viewpoints" 98, 97). Thus, in her theory of reading, Rosenblatt distinguishes between the *text*, that is, "a set or series of signs interpretable as verbal symbols," and what she calls the *poem*, a catchall term for any literary work that comes into being in a transaction mutually dependent on a reader and a pre-existent text ("Poem as Event" 127). A transactional theory of reading is interested in poems, not texts. And, within this framework, the poem is considered to be "an event in time. It is not an object or an ideal entity. It is an occurrence, a coming-together, a compenetration, of a reader and a text" (126).

Hunt and Vipond would follow Rosenblatt in pursuing a transactional conception of reading but offer their own revisions to her model. Rosenblatt had distinguished between two primary sorts of reading—*efferent* reading, in which the reader focuses on what will be taken away from the text, and *aesthetic* reading, which is oriented more toward an experience of the text (*The Reader, The Text* 24). Hunt and Vipond would rename these two types (calling them *information-driven* and *story-driven*) and add a third: *point-driven*. To read in a point-driven way, they argue, is to collaborate, to attempt to "'make contact,' with a narrator or writer." In light of Rosenblatt's terminological distinctions, then, one can better understand Hunt and Vipond's claim that the *point* in point-driven reading "is not something that is 'in' the story at all; rather, the terms refer to an activity—a pragmatic, inherently social activity" ("Shunting Information" 134).

Much like other postprocess thinkers, understanding reading and writing as interpretive (or transactive) events led Hunt to question the utility of conventional academic writing tasks—and even the utility of conventional writing classes. Hunt begins his 1993 "Texts, Textoids, and Utterances," by remarking on his own efforts to "put meaning at the center of all the written language used in connection with my classes." *Meaning* is understood here in a specific way: not "as something that's in text or language" but instead "meaning as a social event" (113). Here Hunt forwards a dynamic, situationally contingent and socially determined notion of textual meaning, exploring how it impacts reading and writing instruction. During the 1988–1989 academic year, he had taken a sabbatical leave in Australia and Germany and "re-discovered" the works of Bakhtin and other genre theorists. As a result, he came to understand the utterance, "any instance of language in use, bounded by a change of speakers," as the "basic unit of analysis for understanding language" ("Traffic in Genres" 214). After considering Bakhtin's insights, Hunt was also forced to "abandon the idea that genres were external, fixed forms," learned by mastering abstract rules. Instead, he came to see that genres are learned through "authentic dialogue," that is, instances of language use in which all parties attempt to infer each other's intentions and respond to them (216). But, after arriving at these abstract conclusions, Hunt could not help but recognize a flaw in commonplace writing pedagogies: the authentic dialogues necessary for language development were unlikely to arise in classroom settings. The typical academic essay, Hunt argues, is "neither created by the student nor understood by the teacher as an utterance; rather, it [is] bracketed, set aside, considered, evaluated. If it is a dialogue, it is one conducted *around* the actual text, one which brackets the text out as a sort of hypothetical instance" (216–17).

Writing in the March 1989 issue of *Inkshed*, Hunt theorizes about genre in response to the work of Anne Freadman, an Australian scholar of comparative literature. In so doing, he sets up a contrast between a Process approach to writing instruction and what he would call a "genre approach," one that closely resembles the pedagogies of postprocess scholars. In her article "Anyone for Tennis?," Freadman compares genre to a game "consisting, minimally, of two texts in a dialogical relation" (97). She demonstrates that the game has rules, but that the "rules" merely delimit the possible moves that one can make; they neither define the game nor provide meaningful instructions about strategy (95–96). Tennis, of course, requires two players, and no one can make a tennis "shot" without that shot being directed at another player within the context of a game. Without those two elements (another player, a game), one can only ever hit a tennis ball, one cannot make a *shot*. Likewise, to complete the analogy, a genre *is* a genre because of dialogic response and turn-taking.

Drawing from this analysis, Hunt concludes, "For me, the most powerful use of the tennis analogy is [Freadman's] assertion that you can only pretend to play in the classroom, and that won't work" ("Process vs. Genre" 16). And, this conclusion entails practical consequences: instructors must "offer our students a situation in which their writing counts for something that matters to them, in which it's read for what it says rather than to be evaluated, in which writing and reading have authentic social consequences." They must, in other words, construct an educational setting "in which their shots are part of an authentic game" (17). Now, to be sure, these ideas sound quite similar to those espoused by Joseph Petraglia, David A. Russell, and the other contributors to *Reconceiving Writing, Rethinking Writing Instruction* (1995). But, it's important to remember that Hunt was making this case five years earlier. In closing my discussion of Hunt as a "solo" author, though, I'd like to turn to another text, one that not only shared the post-composition tendencies of Petraglia's edited collection—but one that anticipated them by *more than a decade*.

At CCCC 1984 (New York City, March 29–31), Hunt delivered a presentation entitled "Language Development in Young Children and in the Composition Classroom: The Role of Pragmatics." That presentation outlines many principles that would circulate throughout Hunt's subsequent work and distills them for oral delivery. It also anticipates and/or prefigures many of the basic principles of genre- and/or activity-theory-oriented versions of postprocess to an astonishing extent. Hunt begins that presentation by directly stating his opposition to cognitivism, and more particularly its "particularly damaging" and "sterile conception of [language] learning" as "something that occurs in the individual learner, in isolation, as a sort of accumulation of individual capital" (1). In contrast, for Hunt, language learning is "in its very nature so profoundly social, intersubjective and transactive" (2–3). Drawing variously from the works of Lev Vygotsky, A. R. Luria, Charles Sanders Peirce, and M. A. K. Halliday, Hunt offers a pragmatic approach to writing instruction that "examines the relationship between language and the social world" (3). In this conception, language acts as "a vehicle for relationships," and Hunt affirms that it is best acquired "in use, when we are attending not to language itself but to something else" (9, 11). As he does elsewhere, Hunt then argues that "language learning is strongly dependent on a rich and genuine pragmatic context" but also frames quote/unquote "school writing" as being profoundly "denuded of pragmatic motives" (12–13). At best, when instructors gesture toward pragmatic ends for writing, they invite students to pretend or simulate authentic situations (13). These insights have major ramifications; Hunt writes,

> What I find particularly difficult about the rethinking I propose is that it casts doubt on virtually every strategy that I have used as a teacher of writing. It casts them all into crisis— traditional essay writing, freewriting and related exercises, journals and diaries, sentence combining and fluency drills and exercises. None is supported by the kind of pragmatic network in which successful language learning occurs. . . . [Some students]—among my students, they are the vast majority—sometimes learn specific skills in areas like rhetor- ical strategies, organization, sentence structure, and so forth, but regularly—this is, I think, the writing teacher's universal lament—the skills don't transfer into other areas and they don't last. They don't transfer and they don't last because they haven't been learned the way we learn language for use and for keeps—in the service of our relations with others. (13–14)

In other words, this social (that is, dialogic and/or pragmatic) conception of language learning not only demonstrates the inherent flaws in many of the most foundational elements of Process-era writing instruction; it also explains why the lessons of writing instruction do not transfer to other contexts.

As an antidote to current-traditional pedagogy and as a means of extending Process in profitable directions, Hunt advocates creating situations "in which writing is the medium of a dialogue, in service of a collaborative attempt to learn and as a way of exploring ideas and establishing relationships," placing emphasis "clearly and unequivocally on the exchange of ideas, information, and values rather than on the texts as object and as evidence of skill levels." However, he doubts whether such an effort could succeed, given the accreted, institutionalized norms and values of composition pedagogy. And, once more, the entailed conclusion is severe. In plain terms, Hunt offers a radical conclusion, "This means inevitably, I think, that we must be prepared to consider the abolition of writing courses as such" (14).

In both versions of his chapter on the "new abolitionism," Robert Connors repeats the same claim: "In the research for this essay, I could not find anything written between 1975 and 1990 in the field of composition that called for general abolition of the [first-year composition] course" ("Abolitionist Debate" 57; "New Abolitionism" 19). Thus, unearthing Hunt's presentation at CCCC—which should fall squarely within the field of composition—complicates this history. He represents an early—perhaps even *the earliest*—exemplar of what Maureen Daly Goggin and Susan Kay Miller would more accurately call "reconceptualists," rather than abolitionists. As those two scholars note, reconceptualists did not so much call "for the abandonment of writing instruction" but rather "for the dismantling of the current system in order to build new, more effective ones" ("What Is New?" 94).

In my personal correspondence with Hunt, I asked him how he felt about the "New Abolitionism." Agreeing with my characterization of him as a conceptual precursor, he stated,

> We—I think particularly I—were certainly conscious abo-
> litionists, before Sharon [Crowley] announced it. I've just
> been going back through Inkshed newsletters and noticing
> that I called for abolition (knowing it was never going to
> happen, in large part because of the social and economic and
> academic institution that had grown up around the comp
> class). We thought of abolition, I think, because we found it
> possible to imagine a writing environment that didn't include
> comp classes: we lived and taught in one. . . . So, yes we were
> abolitionist— but I never had the sense that we'd been erased
> [from the histories told by Connors and others]. We really
> weren't noticed—as you've said in your chapter. And I cer-
> tainly never had any sense that abolition was in the cards, or
> that anybody was likely to take my recommendation seriously.
> (personal correspondence)

In light of his call for abolition, I would note an important terminological choice: in his CCCC presentation, Hunt addresses writing courses, not composition courses. In his estimation, not even WAC courses, as they are generally implemented, can solve the issues he has identified:

> Their aim, like that of traditional "comp course" assignments, is regularly to produce text for evaluative purposes. Sometimes their aim is exclusively to evaluate the student's grasp of the subject matter; occasionally, the more "responsible" teachers in other subjects will evaluate papers for "writing" as well. But in neither case is there a genuine purpose or audience for the writing, nor is there likely to have been reading out of which, and in response to which, the student's utterance genuinely arises—or writing to which it will in turn give rise. ("Language Development" 15)

This is not to say that writing ability cannot be learned, though. Indeed, the central thesis of Hunt's work is that it *can* be learned—but that it must be learned in social contexts in which it is acquired in use. One solution, he argues, would be to create a course "whose avowed and genuine aim is the learning of something other than language—some course with its own, autonomous 'subject matter'—and [then to] introduce written language in a genuinely functional way into that communal learning situation." This "pragmatic web" might then "form a scaffolding for language development, and for the establishment and flourishing of that pragmatic imagination which allows fluent and accomplished writers to produce text which seems pragmatically whole even in the absence of such a web" (16). In other words, Hunt advocates something more like (what has come to be called) Writing in the Disciplines, but which he has elsewhere called Writing *under* the Curriculum: "constructing situations for student writers which offer them immersion in the social situations which occasion and use writing . . . and subordinate explicit instruction to the situations where the apprentice writer can best profit from it" ("Afterword" 380).

Hunt describes a course that might achieve these ends, using his own introductory literature and eighteenth-century lit classes as examples and focusing on five educational components:

1. Assignments in which students *report* to the other students;

2. Assignments in which students summarize articles and other works for members of the class who have not read those works themselves;

3. Situations in which spontaneous exploratory writing is circulated, anonymously or not, and responded to, anonymously or not;

4. Situations in which students engage in genuine, written dialogue and/or multilogue concerning the ideas included in their work—whether with their instructor or with other students;

5. Situations in which the instructor does not merely attempt to explain rhetorical approaches but "actually models them by participating in the writing community— by performing the same tasks, for the same purposes— both anonymously and not. ("Language Development" 17)

At the close of his presentation, Hunt affirms that the particular assignments are less important than the underlying disposition toward language learning they represent. At last, he states, "A pragmatic perspective has the power to change our thinking and our teaching at least as dramatically as did the cognitive perspective . . . and I think it's time to start exploring it in earnest" (18).

COLLABORATIVE INVESTIGATION: A PEDAGOGY THAT CAME TO BE CALLED *POST-PROCESS*

Originally located in coastal Chatham, New Brunswick, Canada, Saint Thomas University moved inland to Fredericton, 175 kilometers (110 miles) to the southwest, in 1964 (Spray and Rhinelander 515). At the time, its English department had only three members, one of whom would leave soon thereafter, and no departmental chairperson (522). Reither was added to the faculty for the 1967–1968 academic year, and Hunt followed one year later (590). When Vipond joined the Psychology department in 1977, the university's largest academic units had six members each, and so, as he explains, "It was inevitable that we rubbed shoulders with people from other departments." For what it's worth, the likelihood of Reither and Hunt meeting Vipond was even higher: English and Psychology shared the same floor of Edmund Casey Hall (Vipond, personal correspondence).

Those attending Saint Thomas were primarily first-generation college students from rural New Brunswick, and the literacy panic sweeping the United States at the time was felt at Saint Thomas, as well (Hunt, personal correspondence). Thus, in 1978, Saint Thomas initiated a first-year writing requirement, with courses taught by faculty from across the disciplines (Spray and Rhinelander

649). With Reither directing the Writing Programme, classes implemented a Process approach, "built around sentence combining and other 'state of the art' ideas," and employing Flower's textbook *Problem-Solving Strategies for Writing* (Hunt, personal correspondence; Vipond, *Writing and Psychology* ix). Vipond volunteered to teach his first (and what would become his only) course in that Programme during its third year (Vipond, *Writing and Psychology* ix). But he left it changed all the same, carrying the Process approach to teaching back into his Psychology courses. In 1985 the Programme disbanded altogether (Spray and Rhinelander 649–50). As Hunt explains, "It only lasted a few years, in large part because departments didn't share our view that literacy was not the English department's sole responsibility; still, while it lasted we introduced almost a quarter of the faculty . . . to the idea that faculty should all take responsibility for literacy" (personal correspondence). Around that time, Reither, Hunt, Thom Parkhill of Religious Studies, and Vipond began implementing collaborative investigation and inkshedding as central elements of their courses (Vipond, *Writing and Psychology* x).

In many of their works, Hunt, Reither, and Vipond end by explaining the practical implications of their theories. In doing so, of course, they follow the genre conventions of scholarly articles in composition studies. However, it seems clear to me that they are not so much applying their theories to practice, as though the two were or could be separate. Instead, their work demonstrates a dialectical connection between theory and practice. To the extent that they make theoretical claims, these seem to derive from practice, and they are consistently revised in response to iterative, practical applications. In a retrospective, definitional presentation from the 1999 Inkshed Conference, Hunt explains the origins of the eponymous practice:

> "Inkshedding" began as a practice in the early eighties, when Jim Reither and I began trying to make "freewriting" (which we had learned about from writers like Peter Elbow) into something dialogically transactional . . . to give writing a social role in the classroom, and thus to create a situation in which the writing was read by real readers, to understand and respond to what was said rather than to evaluate and "help" with the writing. We did this in our classes by asking students to free write in response to a shared experience . . . and then passing the freewritten texts around and asking readers to mark passages in which the writing said something "striking," something that seemed to them interesting or new or outrageous. ("What Is Inkshedding?" 3)

Just a few paragraphs later, however, Hunt also adds, "The ways in which inkshedding functions—and the ways it has been instantiated—have grown and changed, of course, since then." And, after noting that inkshedding could serve as "a reasonable synecdoche for [his] basic stance as a teacher," Hunt admits that it "turned out to have a number of implications, many of which we hadn't anticipated at all." In texts produced while inkshedding, for instance, students demonstrate a more profound "anticipation of audience" ("What Is Inkshedding?" 3). Furthermore, inkshedding would not only "broaden the bandwidth" of classroom conversations and reduce the degree to which the first utterances would dictate all others, it could also increase the likelihood that each utterance could be "heard" in a meaningful way (4). That is, given that inkshedders' texts receive "*immediate* reading and response," the practice immerses writers in an "authentic social transaction" (6, 5).

Hunt, Reither, and Vipond had two primary language instruction methods: inkshedding and collaborative investigation. In my estimation, the former has quite clearly had better branding (a cooler name, an eponymous newsletter and conference) than the latter. Even so, I would still position it as somewhat derivative of collaborative investigation and less educationally central. Indeed, Reither does not address inkshedding directly in "Writing and Knowing" or (with Vipond) in "Writing as Collaboration." In one instance, Hunt frames it as being one of two "fundamental and related strategies" employed within collaborative investigation—the other of which "doesn't have a name" ("Speech Genres" 249). In another case, he calls it "the central strategy" in collaborative investigation ("Traffic in Genres" 217). But, he always frames it as being a component of the larger educational method, collaborative investigation.

The (now defunct) professional organization that sprung from *Inkshed* came to be called The Canadian Society for the Study of Language and Learning (CASLL), a name that indicates a key supposition of its founders. As Coe notes, "Learning to write and learning other things [are] part of the same process and should be thought about together" (qtd. in Williams "Voicing" 58). Or, as Vipond would argue, indirectly referencing Reither's 1985 text, "To understand writing as social process we have to understand more about how knowledge is created and used; 'writing and knowing' are inextricably linked. By this account, we need to be as concerned with knowing as with writing" ("Review: *Frames*" 4). This idea is likely correct in the abstract, but ecological (e.g., institutional and/or bureaucratic) factors may have helped to call forth its realization. In Andrea Williams' words, "Such an epistemic approach to writing fits the Canadian institutional contexts where writing instruction is likely to be situated in the disciplines rather than in first-year writing courses" ("Voicing" 58). I would like to consider, therefore, how Hunt, Reither, and Vipond attempted to cultivate dialogic classroom spaces where subject-matter-learning and learning-to-write could occur simultaneously.

Hunt defines collaborative investigation directly and concisely: "In general, it entails creating a situation in which the class organize themselves into a team to investigate cooperatively some specific topic, using writing as the fundamental tool for that organizing, that investigating, and that cooperation" ("Texts, Textoids" 123–24). However, a more extensive explanation appears in Reither and Vipond's "Writing as Collaboration," in which they argue that "both writing and knowing" are "impossible—inconceivable—without collaboration." In presenting a version of collaborative inquiry, they attempt to expand then-conventional understandings of collaboration beyond "short-range activities such as coauthoring and peer editing" to include "a long-range collaborative activity we call 'knowledge making'" (856). At its most basic theoretical level, this collaborative knowledge making implies that "all of us who write must ground our language in the knowing of those who have preceded us. We make our meanings not alone, but in relation to others' meanings, which we come to know through reading, talk, and writing" (862). In practical terms, collaborative knowledge making entails placing each student into a research team, a "community-within-a-community," that must "investigate a more or less original scholarly question or field" (862–63). Each team must then work "collectively to develop, through reading and writing, its own knowledge claims, and cooperatively to find ways to fit its knowledge claims into the knowledge of the larger community" (862). In the midst of all this, the teacher does not simply orchestrate student actions—as those become increasingly complex but also increasingly student-driven. The instructor also acts "as an expert co-researcher, modeling the process" by contributing to it (863).

In a separate text, "Time for the Revolution," Reither argues that the promise of student-centered, Process pedagogy was never truly realized; what was a "revolution" in theory never amounted to one in practice. While instructors shifted their focus from "finished product to invention (and perhaps even to revision)," they still continued to assign context-free, a-rhetorical tasks" (11). Instructors simply substituted one set of rules (about products) for another about processes. But, even these new rules were "false and misleading about actual writing processes," and so the potentially revolutionary Process approach was "trivialized, bastardized, into a non-process—and, to boot, into theoretical and practical nonsense" (11–12). Even though, he argues, "the notion of writing as social process is an even richer idea than writing as (cognitive) process," it could still suffer the same fate (12). It could be ruined in practice "by taking a new set of rules (this time about disciplinary forms, formats, and conventions) and trying to lay on a few 'social' activities" (12–13).

Thus, if instructors were ever to maximize the potential of social theories, they would need to dispense with "the same old current-traditional designs for writing (and other) courses" (13). They would need to re-design their courses to be social from the ground up. Rather than attempting to instruct students about abstract or detached principles of/for writing—even social principles—instructors need to establish conditions in which students learn language skills (including writing and reading) in the process of learning how to learn (i.e., skills in "inquiry"), all while learning about the subject matter of the course in question (Reither and Vipond 863). Summarizing how all of this operates at the end of "Writing as Collaboration," Reither and Vipond present a wholly integrated model:

> In short, [students] learn to write by reading. Or, more
> accurately and importantly, since there is no such thing as
> knowing how to write (there is only knowing how to write in
> certain genres for certain audiences of certain subjects in cer-
> tain situations), they learn how to learn how to write. Perhaps
> most important of all, students learn that writing and know-
> ing are collaborative acts—vital activities people do with other
> people to give their lives meaning. (866)

This final sentiment sounds very much like a postprocess position—especially in its assertion that "there is no such thing as knowing how to write," of course. Even so, I think it's important to acknowledge a central premise of "Time for a Revolution"—that what now sounds like postprocess to some of us (or *to me*, at least) may once have appeared as a logical extension of Process itself. Reither writes, "The idea that writing is process remains revolutionary, requiring revolutionary ways of thinking about and teaching writing. Those revolutionary ways must become the subject of our thinking, our teaching, and our ongoing conversation. No issue in the study and teaching of writing is more important than this" ("Time" 13).

INKSHED: A DIFFERENT KIND OF NEWSLETTER, A DIFFERENT KIND OF CONFERENCE

In the first issue of what would come to be called *Inkshed* (then entitled *Writing & Reading/Theory & Practice*, or *W&R/T&P* for short) Reither explains his impetus for writing. He and Hunt—along with other Canadian scholars—had attended several recent conferences in the United States, getting "caught up in the energy of the 'revolution' going on there in the fields of writing and reading/theory and pedagogy." At the same time, they had become increasingly frustrated by the logistics and financial costs of engaging in those conversations. Therefore, at the 1982 Wyoming Conference, seven Canadian scholars—Chris Bullock, Anne Greenwood, Russ Hunt, David Reiter, Jim Reither, Susan Stevenson, and Kay Stewart (who would become the second editor of *Inkshed*)—decided to launch a newsletter. The first issue (October 1982) was sent to more than eighty Canadian instructors, though the subscribers list would quickly climb into the hundreds (*W&R* 1.1., page 2; *Inkshed* 2.5, page 1). In that first issue, quoting from Chris Bullock, Reither states, "This newsletter will be 'interested in approaching writing and reading and literacy as serious subjects of interest in their own right, not just as 'problems' or fodder for testing or as objects of administrative technique'" (*W&R* 1.1, page 2). That is, as Louise Wetherbee Phelps notes, Reither "makes crystal clear . . . [that] the study of written language . . . is to be undertaken for its own sake, not as instrumental to pedagogy" ("Four Scholars" 99). *Inkshed* would, in other words, reject what Lynn Worsham and Sidney Dobrin later called the "pedagogical imperative"; it would allow theoretical explorations of writing without demanding that each result in direct classroom application(s).

Even in its earliest incarnation, two other, enduring elements of the *Inkshed* ethos appear: a light-hearted, comical tone and a commitment to dialogic and/or social authoring. Reither, apparently, had not been happy with his initial newsletter title, and so he closes the first issue with an advertisement: "LET'S-HAVE-AN-END-TO-UNWIELDY-TITLES-CONTEST, " noting that he would send a set of "six—no, make it eight—coasters (advertising an assortment of genuine German beers and stolen from genuine Gasthausen all over West Germany) and a brand new disposable BIC razor" to whomever might propose the best title for the subsequent issues. In that first-issue, Hunt (who was then on a sabbatical at Indiana University) appears in the publication information as the newsletter's "far-flung correspondent." In subsequent issues, he would be listed as the editor in charge of fashion (issue 2.6), obituaries (3.3), consumer affairs (3.4), and entertainment (3.5), as well as the punctuation consultant (4.4), research director (5.3), and silent partner (4.5). But, though Hunt would seldom comment on the topics for which he was institutionally credited, he *would* frequently contribute, as would many other scholars, including the newsletters various "provincial correspondents" (who came to be called "consulting editors").

On the third ever page of *W&R / T&P*, Reither notes, "In the long run, this newsletter may well self-destruct: what we need is a journal" (issue 1.1, page 3). More than thirty years later, the newsletter's publication-run would end; however, it never self-destructed in the fashion Reither imagined. It never became a journal. And, quite crucially, its status as a newsletter—and avowedly *not a journal*—indicated something fundamental about Reither's ethos as an editor and its social or dialogic function within the field of Canadian writing instruction. Writing in *Inkshed* 5.6 (1986), Reither states,

> My idea of *Inkshed* has been, from the first issue (though I didn't have the language back then), that this newsletter ought to be a "parlor" in which people carry on their conversations about writing and reading theory and practice. It is *not* a journal, privileging text over discourse, monologue over dialogue. It never should be. It's a place where people talk with other people, collaborating with one another in the search for meaning in their fields and their worlds. It's a place for exploration, not domination. ("Editorial Inkshedding" Dec. 1986 1)

Reither's commitment to collaboration is evident across nearly every issue he edited. In issue 3.2 (1984), he frames his role as being a "compiler" and not an "editor." In this light, he states, "Inkshed's primary functions are those of the bulletin board and the podium. . . . *Inkshed* is not something I do. It's something you do" (5). In the editor's introduction to issue 4.1 (1985), this time entitled "Epistemic Newslettering; or, *Inkshed* as a Mode of Learning," Reither reminds readers of the newsletter's goal. It was not designed "only to *serve* the community of academics in Canada" interested in its topics but "also to help develop and promote such a community" (1). In this light, then, he presents an "exhortation," encouraging readers to fulfill their "obligations to participate as full members of this community we're trying to build." *Inkshed*'s status as a newsletter and not a journal encouraged participation in several ways: allowing authors to "publish more exploratory, less 'finished' pieces of writing than a journal ordinarily can," as well as "those observations, findings, or ideas that seem genuinely important but not really substantial enough to work up into full-length articles." It also lowered the barriers that might keep readers from becoming contributors or even just engaging in scholarly conversation, thereby allowing them to "determine not only the kind of forum it will be, but also the kind of community *we* will be" (2). Reither therefore reasons, "The pages of *Inkshed* ought to be a stage on which the activities of participating in, constructing, and developing a scholarly (or 'interpretive') community are acted out" (3). Similarly, in one of the newsletter's final issues, Horne summarizes the newsletter's purpose and function: "Its reason for being was to create a community in which to discuss, or facilitate dialogic interaction—the same purpose, it seems, as the inkshedding writing activity" ("Inkshed: History" 8).

Just as *Inkshed* was to be a very different sort of academic publication, the yearly gathering that it spawned was to be "a different sort of conference" (*Inkshed* 3.2, page 2). In their first advertisement for Inkshed I, a "working conference" to be hosted by their own institution, Saint Thomas University, Hunt and Reither "welcome proposals that promise to involve participants in active and constructive ways." That is, they intone, "Sessions should do more than present the products of inquiry, they should also engage the participants in the processes of inquiry" (*Inkshed* 2.6, page 9). In *Inkshed* 3.2, while offering up a tentative schedule, the organizers explain the logistics of the event. The conference would not include concurrent sessions so that "as far as possible, all participants will share the same experience." Furthermore, after six of the seven sessions, attendees would engage in inkshedding together, after which "a series of *ad hoc* editorial committees (of registrants) will select from and edit, conference staff will print and publish, and one session will be based upon, the texts produced." In this way, then, the texts produced during inkshedding would "form part of the continuing verbal exchange at the conference, supplementing and deepening the oral discussions." By structuring the conference to include "exploratory writing," its organizers were "putting our money where our mouths have been"—that is, implementing the concepts that the *Inkshed* newsletter had endorsed (*Inkshed* 3.2, page 2). In subsequent years, Miriam Horne notes, "conferences were held in isolated settings away from distracting factors such as shopping or sightseeing"; as a result, "inkshedders had nothing to do but participate in the conference." And, given the conferences' remote locales, "the dialogic engagement was also facilitated by the fact that meals were taken together, everyone was lodged in the same building, and a bar was usually present" (Horne, *Writing* 44).

PARÉ'S POST-PROCESS PROCLAMATION

Though the document in which Trimbur first uses *post-process* is a review of books by C. H. Knoblauch and Lil Brannon, Kurt Spellmeyer, and Patricia Bizzell, he uses the term to refer to a more general tendency in the field. In the most relevant passage, he refers to those books as "statements that both reflect and (especially in Bizzell's case) enact what has come to be called the 'social turn' of the 1980s, a post-process, post-cognitivist theory and pedagogy . . . ." (109). Thus, when it appears in Trimbur's text, the adjective post-process appears in an appositive position, syntactically equivalent to post-cognitivist but presumably not meaning the same thing, and modifying and/or explaining the social turn of the 1980s. That is, for Trimbur, the social turn was post-process. And, clearly, Trimbur uses the term social turn as a means of echoing others; the social turn is the name that the phenomenon in question has "come to be called." But, even if Trimbur originally used the term *post-process* to refer to the whole social turn, he clearly signaled internal divisions within that movement, noting, for instance, its "leftwing trajectory." In the years following Trimbur's initial pronouncement, subsequent scholars primarily employed *post-process* to reference scholars, theories, and pedagogies associated with that left-wing trajectory.

Similarly, Hunt, Reither, and Vipond could not help but recognize a wide array of "social" theories of writing and writing instruction. In a 1993 article, Hunt repeats a criticism that had once rightly been leveled at *Process*, bemoaning the over-use of *social* to mean any and everything: "And so at conferences we begin to make jokes about how often the word 'social' can be allowed to appear in the program. We struggle to keep the term from becoming so general, so widely used, that it no longer means anything" ("Texts, Textoids" 113–14). Whatever the individual political commitments of the scholars from Saint Thomas may have been, though, their critiques of other social approaches were far less ideological than those associated with Trimbur's post-process. Instead, they oriented their efforts toward increasing the classroom-level effectiveness and impact of social theories and pedagogies. In a 1988 *Inkshed* article, Vipond writes, "We've heard a lot lately about writing as 'social process,' but it's easy to shrug off the term as simply the latest buzzword. Thanks to the efforts of scholars such as Jim Reither, however (*College English*, October 1985), it's becoming clear that to understand writing as social process we have to understand more about how knowledge is created and used; 'writing and knowing' are inextricably linked" ("Review of 'Frames'" 4). And, indeed, Reither and Vipond begin "Writing as Collaboration" by declaring non-social visions of writing passé: "The case for writing's social dimensions no longer requires arguing." Even so, they suggest, social theories had not produced "a corresponding transformation in the ways writing is conceived and dealt with in our classrooms," and so they endeavored to bring that change about (855).

Hunt and Vipond worked together over the course of a decade to formulate a social conception of reading, and, in Hunt's writings especially, the question of how meaning emerges is the central question of a social approach to writing instruction. For Hunt, meaning is not "something that's *in* texts or language." Instead, he argues, "It seems to me far more powerful and useful to think of meaning as a social event" (113). Meaning is socially derived, but one must therefore also re-think the social in light of this novel conception of meaning. In Hunt's estimation, "These implications are easy to lose sight of; but I think once we've lost them we're really not talking about treating language as social any more" (114). Though Hunt isn't as concise as one might like in defining *meaning*, he does provide a useful illustration of his viewpoint:

> If you listen to any naturally occurring oral conversation for
> more than two or three minutes, in fact, you discover that

> the meanings of the overwhelming majority of oral utterances
> are in fact determined not by their semantic properties and
> syntactic structures, but much more powerfully by a sort of
> unspoken, continuously renegotiated social contract between
> the participants in the conversation. ("Texts Textoids" 115)

Though we need not return to a full exploration of these ideas here, suffice it to say that Hunt sees collaborative investigation and inkshedding as the means of exercising and enacting this social perspective in academic contexts.

Reither also distinguishes between what he had set out to do and what was generally practiced in the social turn. In "Time for the Revolution," he writes, "Now there's another good idea making the rounds. The notion of writing as social process is an even richer idea than writing as (cognitive) process. Thinking of writing as a social process tells us a whole lot more about what writing is, where it comes from, what its uses are, how and why we learn it." However, in a way we might now expect, Reither adds, "But even as this idea enlivens and enriches our conversation, we strip it of its essentials and its power as we bring it into our classrooms," primarily by treating it as something that can simply be layered on top of "the same old current-traditional designs for writing (and other) courses" (12). Though he doesn't directly say it, Reither indicates that this sort of layering had been, to date, the primary method of the social turn. Just as the potentially radical Process approach had been "trivialized, bastardized, into a non-process—and, to boot, into theoretical and practical nonsense," so too was the social turn being trivialized and bastardized into something non-social. But, as we now know, Reither did believe in an alternative. A suitably (that is, rigorously) social approach to writing instruction would need to embed student writing within meaningful, authentic learning contexts—it would need to involve something like collaborative inquiry in its robust sense.

In "Toward a Post-Process Pedagogy," Paré cites some authors generally associated with the social turn, most notably David Bartholomae, Berlin, and Faigley. Although he never uses the term *social turn* himself, he admits that "fragments of a social theory of writing" are broadly shared. And, he presents the central claim of Trimbur's post-process—that all language use represents a struggle over depictions of reality—as one of the "four key fragments of a social view of writing" (4). (For what it's worth, the other three refer to the epistemic, formative, and intertextual dimensions of language use.) But, whereas Trimbur and other post-process scholars would credit social power structures (of race, class, and gender) for the dominance and/or prevalence of hegemonic ideologies, Paré takes the comparatively apolitical view that the best arguments win (5).

When the adjective *post-process* appears in Paré's article (including in the title), it's always applied to a *pedagogy* (4, 6). And, importantly, Paré's thinking seems to be very much in-line with Reither's and Hunt's and Vipond's. A pedagogy that would "mak[e] school writing a social act," he argues, could not simply draw from "one or another of the beliefs" he had previously described. It would instead need to "draw on all of them" (6). Paré also theorizes six primary implications of a social theory of writing for a "post-process writing pedagogy." To justify the first of these, that students should "write as part of ongoing activities," he cites Hunt; then Reither; then Vipond; then an article co-authored by Reither and Vipond—all within the space of a page. Drawing from Hunt, he notes that academic writing tends to be "disengage[d] . . . from the context of use and human purpose," which leads students to write "textoids," rather than actual, meaningful texts. Drawing from Reither, he argues that non-academic writing often succeeds where academic writing fails because, in non-academic contexts, "writing is a secondary activity . . . always in the service of the discourse community's work." The "work" of schooling is "inquiry, research, speculation, reflection, debate, analysis" and so forth, and, to be clear, "writing can be used to get that work done." To explain how to use writing to "get something done," Paré cites his own efforts working with engineering students. But, his very next example refers to "Douglas Vipond's psychology class at St. Thomas University in Fredericton," which had "prepared a booklet on psychology for Susan MacDonald's grade nine class at Dalhousie High school," after an extensive process of research and correspondence. Then, Paré immediately notes that Reither has described "a number of projects that engage students in collective inquiries," referencing his work with Vipond, as well (6). Between this first reference to Hunt and this last reference to Reither and Vipond, no other scholar (besides Paré himself) is cited.

When Paré presents his second implication, that students should "write with new technologies," he refers once more to Hunt, who "has made ambitious use of locally networked computers to turn his literature courses into collective inquiries," in which "virtually all classroom 'activity' occurs on the computer" (7). Paré does not defend his third principle ("Explore conflict and difference in writing") by way of Hunt, Reither, or Vipond. But, he does return to them to justify his fourth: "Write as one of many voices." To help students write as "contributors" to their "disciplinary conversations," rather than merely as "commentators," Paré advocates inkshedding. To assist students in "writing in many different roles"—his fifth post-process pedagogical implication—Paré endorses collaborative investigation (though he does not call it by this name). He writes,

> To help develop expertise in the classroom, a teacher might
> begin by breaking complex topics into sub-topics and dividing

> reading or research responsibilities among the students. Or,
> better yet, have the students explore the topic and devise their
> own investigations of sub-topics. Each student becomes an
> expert . . . and reports back to the whole group. (8)

But, even here, the influence of Hunt, Reither, and Vipond is not done. In justifying his sixth and final implication—"write collaboratively"—Paré turns to Reither once more (8). I do not believe I am over-stating my case, then, when I say that Hunt, Reither, and Vipond *are* the genealogy of post-process north of the U.S.-Canada border.

At the start of this chapter, I argued that Paré's post-process more closely resembles paralogic, externalist postprocess than the left-wing trajectory of the social turn. To conclude, I would like to consider, then, how Paré's notion of post-process moves beyond Process and how it aligns with what I am calling *postprocess*. In one of the few histories of post-/postprocess to even reference Paré's work, Paul Kei Matsuda writes,

> Like Trimbur, [Paré] used the term [*post-process*] in referring to
> the view of "writing as a social act" in contrast to the cognitive
> view of writing that emerged "when psychology was the dom-
> inant influence on composition studies." Despite the title of
> his article, however, Paré used the term "social process" (p. 4)
> several times in his article, suggesting the ambivalent position
> that the social view of writing occupied in relation to process
> theories and pedagogy. (73)

Matsuda is, of course, largely correct. For Paré, a post-process approach is decidedly not an expressivist or cognitivist one, and he uses the phrase "writing as a social act" to indicate as much. It's also true that "social" views of writing hold an ambivalent position within the histories of Process and post-/postprocess. Though I don't necessarily disagree with Matsuda, I would still add a few points here.

First, when Paré refers to writing as a "social process," he is making a declarative statement about how writing emerges. It is a process, to the extent that it emerges or unfolds in time, and to the extent readers co-construct meaning with writers. But, it is social to the extent that it is dispersed or distributed. Though Paré discusses post-process pedagogical methods and employs the phrase "writing is a social process," he carefully avoids equating post-process pedagogical methods with "social" Process approaches to writing instruction. Indeed, in his second paragraph, he quite clearly affirms that "we have moved beyond process"—that is, a Process approach to writing instruction.

Second, even while admitting that writing is a "social process," Paré seems to distance himself from that formulation. I think, like Reither, he is less interested in launching a full-scale critique of Process or even of the social turn and more interested in intensifying or rigorously extending them—even to the point that they become something else. In the first column of his text's first page, Paré affirms that cognitivists formerly "thought of writing as something that happened largely in the writer's head," but, now, "we have come to view writing as a social process." By the bottom of that column, though, he switches to an importantly different phrase: "I would like to explore the deceptively simple idea that writing is *a social act*," a phrase that he repeats twice more in the next column (4; emphasis added). On the next page he refers to "our understanding of writing as a social activity" (5). And he refers to his post-process pedagogy as a way of "making school writing a social act" (6). When the phrase "social process" appears again, it is not something that writing *is* but something that writing is *subsumed within*: "The thinking that writers do is part of a larger, social process and the texts they create are strands in a web of activity" (6); "by locating writing within the social processes that could and should constitute school work, we can re-unite the idea and the action of composition" (9); and "naturally, we must help students with invention, style, and arrangement . . . but those concerns will only have an impact on and make sense to our students in the broader context of a social process of writing" (9).

It's worth affirming, then, that (social) "action" rather than (social) "process" seems to be the key term for Paré or that, at minimum, any conception of writing as social process is bound up with it also being a social act. In this way, Paré's terminological preference places his theorization alongside (if not within) the genealogy of postprocess I have been developing throughout this book. Notably, Paré does not quote from Cooper and Holzman or from Kent. But, *Writing as Social Action* is, of course, the title of Cooper and Holzman's 1989 book. Cooper and Holzman admit drawing their terminology from Vygotsky ("and his American students"), and they directly oppose the "Cartesian idea of the self" and the "Romantic paradigm of the isolated writer thinking individualized thoughts." Noting that the "social aspects of writing have increasingly received attention within our profession, particularly in the last several years," the authors state their desire to be "very clear about what we mean when we say that writing is a *social activity*," importantly "emphasiz[ing] both parts of this term" (ix). And, at the same historical moment in which Paré was writing (1994), Kent was also arguing against *process* as a central term and for *activity*, in its place: "As strong externalists, we would stop talking about writing and reading as processes and start talking about these activities as determinate social acts. This shift from an internalist conception of communicative interaction . . . to an externalist conception that I have outlined here would challenge us to drop our current process-oriented vocabulary" (*Paralogic Rhetoric* 169).

In short, for Paré, as for Hunt, and Reither, and Vipond, a post-process mode of writing instruction looks very much like what I have called a postprocess approach. It entails constructing situations in which texts *do things*, in which students write and read and respond to one another, and in which their texts are written and read and responded to, as though they were meaningful utterances. That language is a social phenomenon is taken for granted. It is, to borrow a phrase from Joseph Petraglia, "the right answer to a really boring question." There are better *what-is-writing?* questions to ask, and better answers to give.

CHAPTER 5.

POSTCOMPOSITION: BEFORE AND AFTER POSTPROCESS

From the opening pages of his first monograph, *Constructing Knowledges*, Sidney Dobrin has examined the relationship between theory and practice in composition studies. In so doing, he has amply documented a pervasive view of theory among composition scholars: it is only valuable to the extent that it can "immediately affect classroom practice." Theory-skeptical scholars commonly enforce what he (following Lynn Worsham) has called the "pedagogical imperative," and thus disciplinary theorists are often forced to conclude their manuscripts with hasty and under-developed remarks concerning classroom applications (*Constructing* 64, 86–87). In contrast, Dobrin affirms that theories concerning writing can be both correct and valuable, even if (at first, and perhaps indefinitely) they hold no bearing on instructional conduct. Many organizations benefit from employing workers in Research and Development (R&D), even if the concepts they produce never pass from theoretical prototypes to production models, and so too can composition studies as a whole profit from the efforts of its dedicated theorists.

As I understand Dobrin and Worsham, resisting the pedagogical imperative amounts to theorizing freely without worrying about applications. Quite crucially, Dobrin does not argue that a theory—postprocess, for instance—should *never* be applied as a pedagogy or transformed into one; instead, he repeatedly insists that it should not have to be applied "immediately" in the form of pedagogy to be considered valuable (*Constructing* 63–64, 87, 147). By my estimation, Dobrin is not as anti-pedagogy as he is often imagined to be. Rather, in his contribution to the *Post-Process Theory* collection (1999), he himself considers some consequences that (paralogic hermeneutic) postprocess perspectives might entail for commonplace pedagogical practices. However, near his chapter's beginning, he cautions, "*At the outset,*" that is, at such an early stage in their development, "paralogic hermeneutic theories seem to be not readily translatable into manageable pedagogies" themselves ("Paralogic Hermeneutic Theories" 133; emphasis added). And, even more tellingly, in his final paragraph he writes, "As I mentioned earlier, I am not going to suggest ways in which pedagogies can or should be developed in order to accomplish the goals of these theories. I am not sure if such translations to practice are possible *yet*" (147; emphasis added).

Even when Dobrin offers his strongest admonition in this regard—"stop talking about teaching"—he presents it in the form of a "new mantra for writing studies," rather than as a commandment (*Postcomposition* 190). "Stop talking about teaching" is a statement one would repeat to oneself, so as to avoid the internalized dictates of the pedagogical imperative, which at every turn affirms the opposite: *explain how this relates to teaching*. As Dobrin argues, that mantra might help scholars "to step beyond the limits of thinking about writing in terms of classroom application and observation, calling instead for research that begins to tear down the very boundaries of the field in order to develop more useful, accurate theories of writing" (*Postcomposition* 190).

Notably, when Dobrin first launched his critique of the pedagogical imperative, he did so in a chapter in which he aimed "to show how one particular line of theoretical inquiry—postprocess theory—has been intruded upon by composition's pedagogical imperative in ways that have not produced workable pedagogies and have, in fact, denied major facets both of postprocess theories and theoretical pursuit in general" (63). Although Dobrin demonstrates the negative impacts of the pedagogical imperative on all theorizing about writing, it would remain conceptually tethered to postprocess in much subsequent research. As later scholars critiqued and/or extended his logic, however, some became confused on what resisting the pedagogical imperative would entail. The suggestion that scholars should not *have to* turn postprocess into a pedagogy was transformed to mean that scholars *should not* turn postprocess into a pedagogy. Thus, oddly, the critique of the pedagogical imperative transformed into an anti-pedagogical imperative. And, as Hannah J. Rule has pointed out, that anti-pedagogical imperative has produced negative consequences for postprocess, in particular: "it has led to cautiousness—even a moratorium—on rethinking pedagogical and process assumptions through certain postprocess and other postmodern claims" (*Situating* 15).

Dobrin illustrates two primary problems with the pedagogical imperative: it damages the field of composition as a whole, inasmuch as it constrains theoretical knowledge-making, and it damages the theories themselves. With reference to the first, he reasons, "Issues about discourse, language, and writing that exist beyond the classroom and that do not directly impact classroom practice must also be studied if we are to understand their operations. Theory does not necessarily have to inform pedagogy. The anti-intellectual positions that find theory useless unless it leads directly to classroom application deny a responsibility to the field" (*Constructing* 28). In addition, the knee-jerk tendency engendered by the pedagogical imperative—*theorize, then apply theory in practice as soon as possible*—"often . . . denies particular theories their revolutionary potential, discredits certain theories before they have been thoroughly explored, and, in effect, neutralizes the innovations individual theories offer the field in favor of already inscribed assumptions and practices" (64–65). Sometimes, the pedagogical ramifications or logical extensions of a given theory are not obvious or evident at first glance, and when hasty implementations fail, those setbacks can depress or even cancel future attempts.

Implicit with Dobrin's critique of the pedagogical imperative is a belief he commonly and extensively defends: "Composition studies' primary object of study is not writing or even the teaching of writing, as the field often claims; the field's primary object of study is the (student) subject" (*Postcomposition* 4). By his accounting, "such a focus greatly limits . . . what can be known about writing," and "it has fostered an anti-theoretical climate within the field," ultimately producing "intellectual stagnation" (4, 7). That is, most writers do not write for academic purposes, and academic writing (however broadly defined) only represents a miniscule subset of all writing produced worldwide within a given timespan. In addition, the distribution and circulation of academic texts follow much more predictable patterns than do those of non-academic ones. Many of the most interesting developments in the recent history of writing—especially those brought about by digitization—have relatively little to do with (narrowly defined) academic writing or academic writers. But, if knowledge-making in the field is constrained by what Paul Lynch calls the "Monday Morning Question"—"This theory (or idea, or philosophy) you're proposing is great and everything, but what am I supposed to do with it when the students show up on Monday morning?"—then theorists are implicitly prohibited from exploring those developments and their ramifications (*After Pedagogy* xi).

Therefore, in texts dating from the turn of the millennium onward, Dobrin has often conspicuously placed his own theorizing outside the bounds of composition studies proper, sometimes coining new disciplinary designations to do so. At one point or another, he has situated his own work within discourse studies, a term introduced by Stephen Yarbrough in *After Rhetoric*; ecocomposition; postcomposition; and/or writing studies (*Ecocomposition* 2; *Natural Discourse* 14, 83). For instance, he identifies the "the primary agenda" of his 2011 book *Postcomposition* as justifying "a move beyond the academic work of composition studies in favor of the revolutionary potential of the intellectual work of writing studies, specifically the work of writing theory, an endeavor likely best removed from the academic work of pedagogy and administration," that is, composition (24).

As a longtime exponent of postprocess and editor of one of the two primary edited collections on the subject, *Beyond Postprocess*, Dobrin understands his call towards disciplinary reform to be directly connected to postprocess theory, in particular. "At its core," he reasons, "postprocess serves as an institutional critique and an attempt to show that writing theory can sever itself from the sacrosanct subject as the central imperative of writing studies" (*Postcomposition* 129).

By this account, postprocess provides the tools—even the weaponry—necessary to sever the tie between writing research and writing pedagogy. Therefore, *Postcomposition* operates "with the intent of violence"; the book "does not work toward resolution; it is intentionally a moment of resistance, of violence" (2, 188). That violence works toward a concrete goal: a postcomposition discipline, writing studies.

Dobrin's career evidences a notable, long-standing preoccupation with the question "What is writing?" In his 1997 review of texts by Chris Davies, Joseph Harris, and James C. Raymond, he writes, "Perhaps the question 'what do we do?' is not the question we should be asking; rather, we should ask 'what is writing?'" ("Review" 698). However, by Dobrin's account, the discipline of composition has been so transfixed with the student writer (i.e., "the sacrosanct subject") and writing instruction (following the pedagogical imperative) that it has not attended to writing itself. In contrast, Dobrin affirms "the agency of writing itself, be it identifiable agency of specific texts, the recurring agency of writing in multiple, networked formations, or the intellectual agency of a concept, idea, or theory," all of which he contrasts with "the agency of the subject or even of the writing-subject" (78). When he employs the term writing itself, he generally connects it to a few key principles: ecologies (50, 56), circulation (58, 78), writing as system (140), viscosity (184), and, in a somewhat surprising (re-)turn, the posthuman agent, whom he conceives of as "indistinguishable from writing itself" (188).

Responding to *Postcomposition*, Bruce Horner strongly critiques Dobrin's logic, doubting that the violence he calls for is necessary. In Horner's words, "We might respond to calls to transform composition into writing studies as welcome and unremarkable, on the one hand, and yet also impertinent, asking for work to begin that in fact has long been underway ("Rewriting Composition" 471). In other words, Dobrin has failed to account for—and even to acknowledge—versions of writing studies that have emerged from alternate theoretical frameworks. Rather, per Horner once again, "Dobrin's references to writing studies ignore large swaths of scholarship that can already lay claim to such a name." As a result, in his work, "writing studies appears to be only just emerging *ex nihilo* in the work of a handful of theorists: something new and at odds with all that has come before" ("Rewriting" 459). That is, Dobrin pretends that "hefty reams of scholarship" on the subject do not exist and "effectively clears the field of theorizing by deeming (at least some) extant theorizing something else" (459, 460).

For Horner, "far from representing a new identity for composition," writing studies has "always been part of composition" (471). He has not been alone in making this claim. In "Where Did Composition Studies Come From?" (1993) Martin Nystrand, Stuart Greene, and Jeffrey Wiemelt provide documentary evidence that would support Horner's claim. They figure the "emergence of a composition research community" in the 1970s as coinciding with "the emergence of scholarly thinking and empirical research about writing qua writing"—that is, *writing itself* (271, 272). In other words, for Nystrand, Greene, and Wiemelt, the modern incarnation of composition studies has never existed apart from writing studies. Of course, their history focuses on texts published in empirical and teaching-focused journals—the kind of scholarship that is anathema to Dobrin. But, the erasure of those texts from Dobrin's history is precisely Horner's point. Whereas Dobrin believes that composition has yet to transcend pedagogical concerns, Nystrand, Greene, and Wiemelt argue that it only "emerged as a discipline as its focus began to transcend traditional problems of effective pedagogy" and became instead a discipline featuring "coherent research programs . . . marrying empirical methods to theoretical conceptions" (272, 271). In other words, Dobrin sees writing studies emerging after the death of composition (as it is presently conceived: an administrative and pedagogical enterprise); in contrast, Nystrand, Greene, and Wiemelt suggest that composition itself was born from writing studies.

Ultimately, I am sympathetic toward some elements of Horner's critique. It's true that Dobrin could do more to acknowledge the writing studies research that distantly pre-dates his reformist calls. He might also do more to recognize the theoretical work occurring in that domain, even if it hardly resembles the continental-philosophy-inflected theorizing he prefers. However, a charitable reading might acknowledge that his vision for writing studies looks fairly different from the (sub)discipline that Nystrand, Greene, and Wiemelt describe: one heavily indebted to linguistics and the social sciences. Thus, Dobrin's proposition isn't as redundant as Horner presumes. In *Postcomposition*, Dobrin does acknowledge prior conceptions of writing studies, citing works by Charles Bazerman, John Trimbur, and Susan Miller. While he finds things to praise in those conceptions, he believes that Bazerman's is too pedagogically oriented, Trimbur's too vague in its methodological aims, Miller's too concerned with writ*ers* rather than writ*ing* (25–27). As Dobrin notes, "Ultimately, *Postcomposition* proposes a form of writing studies"—not the only one, but one of several—"one that moves beyond composition studies' subject-distracted view of writing and theorizes about writing" (27).

In this chapter, I want to lay aside Dobrin's scholarship, exemplary though it may be. Instead, I want to demonstrate that postprocess, through the gradual course of implementation in pedagogical form, has already arrived at something also called *writing studies*. Indeed, it seems quite similar to the thing Dobrin has proposed—and it may even be the very same thing. Near the start of their introduction to *Beyond Postprocess*, an edited collection published in the same year as

Postcomposition (2011), Dobrin, J. A. Rice, and Michael Vastola ask a seemingly non-rhetorical, historical question that they never quite answer: has postprocess "ushered in an era of *postpedagogy*? . . . a point within composition studies where new ways of thinking about writing fundamentally refuse any codifiable notion of the relationship between the writing subject and the texts it produces, as well as the 'practical' scholarship expected to proceed from that relationship" (3). I want to posit an answer: Yes.

As I will demonstrate, the form of writing studies that has already arisen via postprocess is postpedagogical in the sense that Dobrin, Rice and Vastola had hoped that it might be. As they note, postpedagogy is "not opposed to composition studies pedagogical imperative, but more interested in questions and theories of writing not trapped by disciplinary expectations of the pedagogical" (14). Stated differently: postpedagogy does not eschew teaching altogether; instead, it re-imagines what teaching might look like, if it were guided by the assumption that what we used to call *teaching* is impossible, given that writing isn't what we used to think it was during the Process era. It also moves the scene of theorizing "outside the classroom or other pedagogic scenes—even nonclassroom-based projects like service learning or community-based writing—in favor of inquiries that are not limited by processes of pedagogy" (17).

To illustrate the genealogy of this form of writing studies, I trace several concurrent and often parallel developments in the history of postprocess: theorizing writing as a form of communicative interaction; defining genres according to their functions, not their formal elements; attempting to teach genres within their relevant activity systems; renouncing the prior goals of generalized or generic composition courses; paying closer attention to *transfer*; and espousing Writing across the Curriculum and/or Writing in the Disciplines and/or Writing about Writing as an antidote to the ills of composition studies. Many, though not all, of these trends exist within an easily identifiable origin point for postprocess, Kent's *Paralogic Rhetoric*. And, indeed, early readers of that text understood it to be calling for a profound rethinking of institutionalized writing instruction, one in which "students would write public discourse intended to get things done in the world rather than discourse thought of as practice" (Ward, "Review" 186; c.f., Dasenbrock, "Review" 104). Kent did not precisely anticipate Dobrin's version of a postcomposition writing studies, but he did call for an end to composition instruction as it was then conceptualized.

In what follows, I don't want to argue that postprocess *created* or *caused* writing studies, or writing in the disciplines, or genre/activity theory, or research on transfer. I want to suggest, instead, that it has always been inextricably bound-up with and connected to these pedagogical methods and scholarly trends—some of which may have propelled *it*. I also want to demonstrate a further historical claim. If composition is narrowly defined as an academic discipline focused on student writers and institutionalized (first-year) writing instruction—a definition Dobrin seems to espouse (*Postcomposition* 3)—then postprocess emerged outside the bounds of composition at its very outset.

In some sense, postprocess was always already postcomposition, even if it has infrequently been recognized as such. One of the central arguments of this book is that postprocess *has* produced real but heretofore unrecognized effects on the field of writing instruction. To make that case, this chapter analyzes proto-postprocess texts published in non-composition venues, distantly removed from the conversation concerning (quote/unquote) "high postprocess theory" in mainstream composition journals. Some of those texts were authored by Kent. But, several others were authored by his colleagues at Iowa State University or by their graduate students. Like Kent's proto-postprocess texts, many of his colleagues' works were also published before the (unhyphenated) term *postprocess* came into existence (in 1994) or very shortly thereafter. Unsurprisingly, then, those texts have seldom been considered to be *postprocess,* even though they bear certain postprocess markers. Thus, the impact of postprocess on non-first-year-composition forms of writing instruction has not been sufficiently appreciated.

The role of Iowa State scholars in the development of postprocess is not necessarily a secret, of course. Four of the fifteen contributors to the 1999 *Post-Process Theory* collection—Nancy Roundy Blyler, Helen Rothschild Ewald, Kent, and David R. Russell—worked there. But, I want to widen the scope of my analysis beyond just that one collection, especially by considering texts published prior to it. While I'll focus on works by Russell and Blyler, and briefly discuss Ewald here, I also want to draw attention to postprocess postcomposition texts written and/or co-written by Charlotte Thralls, Rebecca E. Burnett, and several Iowa State graduate students, highlighting Clay Spinuzzi, Rue Yuan, and Elizabeth Wardle, in particular. After two contextualizing digressions, I'll close this chapter by discussing institutional reform proposals and efforts that bear postprocess markers and that march under the banner of writing studies.

Since I'll focus so closely on texts written by Iowa State scholars, let me explain what I hope to accomplish in doing so—as well as what I am decidedly not attempting to demonstrate. In my Introduction, I affirmed the importance of oscillating between levels of historical scale, from the local to the global and back again. By examining the works of professional communication scholars at Iowa State, I demonstrate that paralogic hermeneutic ideas made noticeable theoretical and practical impacts on one midwestern university campus. In addition, I want to show that postprocess concepts took an unusual migratory pattern. As Blyler has noted, guiding concepts (e.g., the Process approach) often enter "mainstream" composition scholarship before trickling down to professional and technical writing ("Process-Based Pedagogy"). However, paralogic externalist ideas filtered into professional writing scholarship before composition scholars at other universities ever discussed them. In saying all of this, though, I am not arguing that postprocess theories revolutionized professional communication scholarship and transformed that field once and for all. They did not. Nor do I even intend to show that they revolutionized the scholarly and pedagogical methods of an entire English department. They did not.

Iowa State was not a postprocess oasis. Many of its faculty members were engrossed in professional writing and/or writing in the disciplines research, and the vast majority of them never published works addressing postprocess in any way. Understandably, they had separate interests and investigated different issues. Furthermore, emergent postprocess theories and pedagogies did not immediately extinguish interest in dominant Process approaches. During the mid-1980s, while Kent wrote his proto-postprocess texts, his colleagues Glenn J. Broadhead and Richard C. Freed were demonstrating that professional communication scholars still had "little idea how current theories of composition"—by which they mean Process theories—"apply to writing in the business world" (3). Likewise, Blyler was—entirely rightly—demonstrating that Process models had not yet impacted professional writing scholarship and arguing that they ought to do so ("Process-Based Pedagogy"). Similarly, in 1989 Charles Kostelnick explored "affinities" and connections between the respective Process movements in writing and design ("Process Paradigms"). In other words: even while Kent was making his turn toward postprocess, many of his peers were fully engrained in Process, aiming to extend it into new domains.

When Iowa State scholars endorsed postprocess ideas and/or adjacent concerns in the 1980s and early 1990s, they did not call them *postprocess* because that term did not yet exist. In line with Kent's practice at the time, the term they used most commonly was *paralogic hermeneutics,* though David Russell would use the simpler term *externalist.* But, another important caveat presents itself: their texts demonstrate substantial disagreements in their approaches and perspectives. In articles published between 1987 and 1992, for example, Kent ("Schema Theory"), Blyler ("Reading Theory and Persuasive Business Communications" and "Shared Meaning and Public Relations Writing"), and their colleague David D. Roberts ("Readers' Comprehension Responses in Informative Discourse") would all oppose the traditional distinction between reading and writing and endorse a negotiated concept of meaning—a cornerstone of postprocess. However, whereas Kent would theorize widespread implications for writing instruction, Blyler and Roberts would "limit" the scope of their findings to particular examples. Blyler concludes "Reading Theory and Persuasive

Business Communications" with a simple affirmation: "In this article, reading theory has been used to derive guidelines for the tacit arguments present in persuasive business communications" although she admits not having analyzed "every type of persuasive business communication nor exhausted the possibility for additional reading-based guidelines" (395). Similarly, in line with the norms of social-scientific research, Roberts admits the "limited scope and qualitative focus of [his] study" before suggesting how his results "might suggest studies" that could extend them (146).

I would note one final point here: Kent's colleagues tended to frame paralogic, externalist (i.e., *postprocess*) approaches as conceptual advances over expressivist, cognitivist, and rhetorical ones, that is, as being preferable to most—but not all—Process approaches. At the same time, some of them placed postprocess concepts on equal footing with social constructionist ideas (see: Blyler, "Theory and Curriculum" 225–37; Burnett and Kastman, "Teaching Composition"274–78). In the terms I have been employing, then, some Iowa State scholars framed both post-process and postprocess as conceptually superior to Process, but did not see either as inherently preferable to the other.

THEORIZING BEYOND NARROW BOUNDS: THE ORIGINS OF POSTPROCESS IN PROFESSIONAL COMMUNICATION SCHOLARSHIP

The most famous passage in *Paralogic Rhetoric* may be Kent's (commonly misunderstood) claim that "writing and reading—conceived broadly as processes or bodies of knowledge—cannot be taught, for nothing exists to teach" (161). His fundamental point, which the very next sentence explains, is that "certain background skills" (e.g., grammatical constructions, the use of topic sentences, and so forth) "can be taught," but that even mastery of those skills cannot guarantee successful communication (161). Expanding on this claim elsewhere, Kent distinguishes between composition, which he believes can be taught, and writing, which he believes cannot. To ground this argument, he employs the term *composition* "primarily and narrowly to mean the study of the composing process" and *writing* to indicate "a kind of communicative interaction" ("Paralogic Rhetoric: An Overview" 149). Of course, even when he refers to "the composing process," Kent means something more than just stages and strategies. From his perspective, composition remains teachable because "we certainly may teach systematically and rigorously subjects dealing with how texts operate, how texts shape understanding, and how texts function within different social contexts," that is, "issues such as semantics, style, cohesion, genre, and so forth" ("Principled Pedagogy" 432; "Paralogic Rhetoric: An Overview" 149). If composition were reoriented to teach about how texts work (that is, how readers read—but also, what texts can *do*), rather than how to write (in the Theory-Hope-ful sense of *do this and you will succeed*), then the discipline could be conceptually tenable. As Kent concludes, "Our current and future students will always need to know how texts operate, how texts shape understanding, and how texts function within different social contexts" ("Principled Pedagogy" 433). Translated into contemporary terms: students will always need writing studies courses, even if they cannot "learn to write" in generalized first-year writing courses.

Within his own constrained usage of the terms, Kent claims that writing cannot be taught, but he indicates that it can (indeed must) be learned, over and over again. In focusing on the unteachability of paralogic, hermeneutic writing, however, critics often occlude Kent's practical assertions about how such learning might come to pass. In *Paralogic Rhetoric*'s final chapter, Kent forwards a more robustly and profoundly collaborative vision of instruction that might take place beyond the conventional bounds of composition studies (164). In this version of (what has conventionally been called) writing instruction, students and teachers would work closely together—even on a one-to-one basis—to construct texts that would respond to and act within "specific communicative situations," thereby taking part in "communicative interaction with others within and outside the university" (169).

In outlining the conditions in which the ability to write can be learned, Kent imagines a context very different from the traditional, generic, first-year composition classroom. The final section of *Paralogic Rhetoric* urges eliminating "traditional writing and literature courses" and notes that, in an appropriate institutional shift, "faculty in disciplines outside English departments would need to be retrained in order to take responsibility for the written discourse generated in their courses" (169). Or, as Dasenbrock explicated the book at the time: "Kent's theories move in two directions simultaneously: first, toward a greater integration of reading and writing, and second, towards writing-across-the curriculum [or, really, what we would now call Writing in the Disciplines], since engineers learn to write like engineers by writing as engineers" ("Forum" 103-04). But, Kent's arguments in this direction predate *Paralogic Rhetoric*. And, just as crucially, he refined many of his positions beyond the bounds of "mainstream" composition scholarship.

Now, if I were to mention that Kent edited and then co-edited *JAC* for several years in the mid-to-late 1990s, I assume that many readers of this book would register that fact either as (A) already known or (B) not particularly surprising. However, he also edited the *Journal of Business and Technical Communication* (formerly the *Iowa State Journal of Business and Technical Communication*) from 1990–1994 (*"Remapping"* 12). I imagine that fact is considerably less familiar, at least to readers of *this book*. I mention Kent's editorship here because it's quite relevant to an argument I'd like to extend: postprocess didn't all-of-a-sudden *start* to press writing instruction beyond composition in the 2010s. Rather, it sprung from other branches of writing instruction (i.e., what was once called "advanced composition") in the first place—more than thirty years ago. Before postprocess theories were applied to composition pedagogy, and even before they were introduced into the scholarly discourse of composition studies, they offered a conceptual interrogation of writing (itself), more generally.

The Kent who published "Paragraph Production and the Given-New Contract" (1984) in *The Journal of Business Communication* is not a postprocess thinker *per se*. Nonetheless, he advances some proto-postprocess arguments. Contra later accusations of postprocess impracticality, he also demonstrates direct concern with the pedagogical implications of his insights. Kent asks in his second paragraph, for instance, "How do we transform important current research into practical teaching tools?" And, in his article's final sentence, he asserts "If current rhetorical theory is going to come alive for *all* our students and not just those in our graduate programs, our work, it seems to me, should be directed as much toward practice as theory" (45, 65). In this instance, he concerns himself principally with the "given-new contract," which he notes, is an "extension of [H. P.] Grice's 'Cooperative Principle,' the dictum that speakers and listeners must cooperate with one another in the quantity, quality, relation, and manner of their communications" (46). Crucially, the given-new contract closely resembles Davidson's emphases on hermeneutic guessing, triangulation, and the principle of charity, which formed the foundation of Kent's paralogic rhetoric. Kent explains the Given-New contract as follows:

> [It] is a conventionalized agreement between communicators. Communicators must agree that while communicating they will share a "mental world" where all parties know what is given information and what is new. When communicating through written discourse, the writer assumes the greater share of responsibility for fulfilling the contract, for he shoulders the burden for the alignment of his texts with the reader's linguistic and extra-linguistic context. (46)

Importantly, at this stage of his career, Kent presents himself as developing only "a tentative first step toward a more complete teaching methodology" (45). That statement, of course, raises the question: *was he already imagining paralogic hermeneutic postprocess here?* We are left to wonder. In any case, the Kent of "Paragraph Production" is surprisingly concerned with delineating the nuts-and-bolts of a lesson that would require "three to four meeting periods" (53). Even more importantly, he presents this approach within the pages of a business communication journal and explains its utility in business-communication terms.

In 1987 Kent published two articles in non-composition venues that would provide a bridge between his earlier thinking on the Given-New contract and his eventual move toward postprocess as such: "Schema Theory and Technical Communication," published in the *Journal of Technical Writing and Communication*, and "Genre Theory in the Area of Business Writing," published in *The Technical Writing Teacher*. In both cases, he emphasizes the role of the reader in constructing textual meaning and demonstrates that communicative transactions are not and cannot be rule-governed; he frames effective communication as the result of on-the-spot negotiations, rather than application of pre-existent formulas.

In "Schema Theory," Kent recites three commonplace dicta for technical writing: to move from "old" information to new; to move from the most "general" information to the most specific; and to employ recognizable formats. The first of these, of course, closely resembles the Given-New contract. In this text, Kent employs Schema Theory to explain why the aforementioned principles *work*. He defines a schema as "a mental representation that helps us to organize information"; for instance, when one thinks of an *office* one imagines desks, computers, etc. (244, 246). Kent then affirms that schemata "mediate between the individual and the external world" (244). However, he also affirms that schemata act as "a kind of dialectic, transactional process that facilitates and promotes meaning production." Writers need to know about schemata, Kent argues, because they guide readers' textual interpretations, providing a "common ground between writer and reader," though not one that could be established through any kind of rule-bound structure or format (248–49). In this light, schemata might be best regarded as "*contracts* or agreements between reader and writer," inasmuch as they emphasize "the *process* of information transfer" (249). Importantly— and here is where the proto-paralogic-hermeneutic gesture emerges—schemata are not static or rule-bound. Instead, "writers must continually seek out the common ground, the contracts, the cooperative agreements, the mental representations shared between writer and reader" (249). Ultimately, Kent suggests, these schema-theory insights might lead technical communication instructors "toward a more interactive, reader-centered approach to composition" (251).

"Schema Theory" begins with a discussion of the given-new contract (243) and ends with a substitution: by the conclusion, Kent prefers to discuss *genres* as opposed to *schemata*. He writes, for instance,

> We should understand that, to a large extent, we teach *genres* in our technical writing courses. . . . When we view these

genres as mental representations that help a reader organize
information or, in other words, as schemata, they become
strategies and processes that writers employ to help readers
process information. Genres are not rule-bound documents.
So, from this perspective genres become a process through
which writers meet the expectations held by their readers.
(249)

"Genre Theory in the Area of Business Writing" seems to pick-up at this point.

At the outset of that text, Kent briefly describes the "traditional" view of genres—"rigid taxonomies composed of synchronic conventions that may be codified into normative rules" (232). But, he soon notes, this conception leads to a serious difficulty for business writing pedagogy: infinite regression. If one attempts to create "production rules" that could apply to every document, one would inevitably need to revise those rules to account for each instance in which the new text deviated from generic norms. "The writer's work, then, would be perpetual," Kent argues: "He or she would be forced to memorize periodically a new series of checklists, or would be forced to consult a new catalogue containing updated checklists" (235–36). However, an alternate vision of genre as "hermeneutic structures that help writers and readers make sense of the world of discourse" might provide more useful insights for pedagogy (237). Though he doesn't employ Davidsonian terms here, Kent seems to indicate that prior theories—even those derived from previous, successful acts of communication—have little guidance to offer for subsequent interactions. One does not proceed in communication by knowing in advance how to proceed, rather one proceeds through interpreting while communicating.

In the latter half of his article, Kent explains three central implications of genre theory: "(1) no text is ever genre-less; (2) no text is ever reader-less; (3) no text is ever culture-less" (237). Readers interpret texts based off of their assumptions about the texts' genres and, similarly, writers craft texts to conform to genres. As a corollary, he argues, "So, in a pragmatic sense, writer and reader agree to cooperate by employing genres and by responding to them in ways that both writer and reader expect" (238). This cooperation is not governed by "*definitive* and *untemporized* rules," though, because genres are dynamic and negotiated. This constituent negotiation of genre dovetails with Kent's second insight—that no text is ever reader-less. Given that readers co-construct genres, instructors should "seek to move beyond production rules for the manufacture of texts."

Here, without directly acknowledging his purpose, Kent seems to take a forceful jab at Process approaches, which he conceives of as being too monologic and internalist and which act as though "only the writer's concerns are important." A better approach to writing instruction might instead provide "flexible guidelines that help a writer discover the expectations held by her reader" (239). His final assertion, that no text is ever culture-less, moves in an even more externalist direction. Kent argues that "genres change as our reading expectations change," which its itself a function of "cultural life, our ideology, politics, economic conditions, and so forth"; in this light a genre is "a repository of cultural history" (239). In presenting this argument, it seems to me, Kent applies semantic externalist principles to textual forms, rather than (just) individual words.

Drawing from these insights, Kent presents six elements of a hypothetical business writing textbook. The first and last are especially notable here. "First," he writes, "our book would contain no generic formulas, no rules, no checklists" (240). After rattling off four more points, he concludes, "Finally, our textbook would show students that writing, like thinking, cannot be reduced to formulas" (241). Whether Kent had intended to repeat himself isn't clear to me. But, either way, rejecting formulas is both the alpha and the omega of his business writing approach. In closing, he acknowledges that "our imaginary textbook would be a strange book by today's standards," but he also expresses some optimism that it might not always seem so strange. As genres tend to do, perhaps business writing textbooks might evolve. Indeed, he contends, "Business writing, I believe, is destined nonetheless to move away from the narrow view of writing as sets of rules, checklists, and formulas and instead, move toward a wider view of writing as a dialogic, dynamic, and social communicative process" (241). The pedagogical arguments that Kent presents here may not be quite as paralogic or externalist as positions he would later endorse, but they're surprisingly close, and they demonstrate his thought moving in that direction.

In the following years, Kent's work would turn more directly turn paralogic hermeneutics, and he'd publish those insights primarily in "mainstream" rhetoric and composition journals: *College Composition and Communication*, *College English*, *JAC*, and *Rhetoric Review*. He'd return to professional writing scholarship in 1993, though, with "Formalism, Social Construction, and Interpretive Authority," published in *Professional Communication: The Social Perspective*. For what it's worth, that text is discernibly postprocess, and it echoes many claims from *Paralogic Rhetoric*, which was published that same year. For example, Kent affirms the need to "shift from talking about writing as either a process or a conventional act to talking about writing as a hermeneutic interaction," and urges instructors to "drop our current process-oriented vocabulary and begin talking about language-in-use" (90). And, in a somewhat surprising (though intellectually consistent) move, he also urges the end of institutionalized professional-communication instruction, just as he had for composition. He states, "Collaboration might replace teacher-centered instruction. . . . The professional writing teacher would become an adviser or, better yet, a consultant," and further, "for our institutions, traditional professional writing courses would be eliminated" (90). He even suggests that "this paralogic-hermeneutic instructional method also would create complex problems for the discipline of professional writing" as a whole. In particular, it would force instructors to concede that "writing instruction is a misnomer" because no body of knowledge exists to be taught and, furthermore, "good writing—as a transcendental category—does not exist" because good writing is nothing more than good hermeneutic guessing (91).

In terms of the account I am telling, *Professional Communication: The Social Perspective* presents one other interesting item. That text was edited by Nancy Roundy Blyler and Charlotte Thralls, longstanding writing partners and professional communication scholars at Iowa State. The two co-founded what was then called the *Iowa State Journal of Business and Technical Communication* (now *JBTC*) and co-edited it for several years before Kent took over the role in 1990. In their own chapter, "The Social Perspective and Professional Communication: Diversity and Directions in Research," Blyler and Thralls indicate that the "social perspective" in writing research should not be considered "a monolithic paradigm"; rather, "significant differences exist among socially oriented theorists and researchers." They therefore differentiate between three primary social forms of writing instruction—the "social constructionist," the "ideologic," and the "paralogic hermeneutic"—and show how each addresses four primary concepts: "community, knowledge and consensus, discourse conventions, and collaboration (5–6). Thus, a year before either of the terms was popularized, Blyler and Thralls were distinguishing between what I have called *post-process* and *postprocess* and demonstrating how each differs from social constructionism. To anyone seeking a thorough delineation between those schools of thought, I would strongly recommend that text, or Blyler and Thralls' follow-up to it, "The Social Perspective and Pedagogy in Technical Communication," which also considers a fourth social perspective, the "social cognitive."

IOWA STATE IN THE EARLY YEARS OF PARALOGIC HERMENEUTICS, PART I: DAVID R. RUSSELL

I'd like to turn now to texts authored by Kent's colleagues at Iowa State University. First up: David R. Russell. Postprocess is best defined as an externalist, paralogic conception of communicative interaction and attendant transformations in writing instruction. Though Russell is most commonly acknowledged as a historian of and leader in the WAC/WID movement, he was certainly aware of major postprocess tenets, and his work applies them, even when avoiding the term *postprocess*. Dobrin's postcomposition question—*what* is *writing?*—emerges in Russell's work, as well. Although both focus on what writing *does* after inscription (that is, as it circulates), they arrive at different conclusions. Of course, some conflict is attributable to their theoretical attachments: Dobrin to complexity theory and French post-structuralism; Russell to Russian psychology, genre theory, and activity theory. In any case, I want to turn to two of Russell's most-easily-categorized-as-postprocess works here: "Vygotsky, Dewey, and Externalism" (1993) and "Activity Theory and Its Implications for Writing Instruction" (1995). In the former, Russell attacks "general-composition courses"; in the latter, he critiques "general writing skills instruction," another name for the same thing. In both instances, his relies on a definition of writing that opposes many Process-era disciplinary conventions. If anything, I find these works to be *more* postprocess than his chapter in *Post-Process Theory*—at least insofar as they authorize readings of Russell's work that might advocate (more disciplinarily radical) postcomposition and externalist positions. In contrast, his *Post-Process Theory* chapter seems to me to be invested in maintaining the discipline's institutional or administrative status quo. There he writes, "The task is not to toss out 'the process approach,' by demarcating a 'post-process' era" and he continues, "the task rather is to extend the activity system of the discipline of composition studies" (91). After discussing those theoretical texts, I'll turn to Russell's large-scale history of the WAC/WID movement, a narrative in which he was himself implicated.

In "Vygotsky, Dewey, and Externalism," Russell notes that "general-composition courses take as their starting point the philosophical premise that the student—his or her intelligence, aptitude, behavior, skill, and so on—can be abstracted from disciplinary content," and thus they have been "oriented toward the *how* of writing, not the *what* (174). In contrast, as Russell carefully delineates, Vygotsky and Dewey opposed such a *what-versus-how* severing. They conceived of the "content of the disciplines . . . not [as] a static repository of universal truth and method . . . but an organized set of social practices and activities" (177). In discarding the "Cartesian epistemological split between Subject and Object, scheme and content," they also discarded the "individual/social dichotomy," demonstrating that the social "give[s] rise to consciousness and cannot be understood without it" (178). Thus, any notion of human development would need to include the social as a fundamental, constituent element. One could not plausibly conceive of development as a simply interior, abstracted process. To develop (in any activity or sphere of action) would mean to develop socially, together with others. In this conception, even "mind is social, historical"—that is, in the terms I have been using, externalist (182).

Notably, these premises would lead Russell toward a very postprocess set of conclusions. He writes,

> Because almost all thought and action are socially mediated, rather than biologically or transcendentally determined, it is never possible to reduce thought/action to a closed logical system, to predict with certainty the thoughts or actions of a person or group. This means that speech and writing (and their acquisition) are paralogical, to use Thomas Kent's term. (182)

By Russell's account, an externalist conception of mind directly refutes the underlying premises of expressivism. As he reasons, "Learning to write doesn't happen *naturally* through some inner process . . . if only we free students from the oppression of external authority" (184). According to this rationale, "realizing one's human potential" does not require removal from external constraints or restraints, but instead it "comes *through* society, history, culture—and therefore through disciplines—not in spite of them or by transcending them" (185). And, here is the key: in this externalist conception "growth in writing" entails "mov[ing] toward acquiring the genres, the habits of discourse, the voices of social groups involved in organized activities *while* students more and more fully participate in (either directly or vicariously) the activities of those groups and eventually contribute to and transform them—not *before* they participate in them" (186).

In this final turn, we see the distinction between Russell's externalist conception of writing in (the activity systems of) the disciplines, as compared to the Process-era conception of discourse communities. Insofar as the earlier approaches were internalist, they did not (and perhaps could not) refuse the distinctions between form and content, between what the mind is and what the mind knows (i.e., knowledge), or between language and/or communication *as such* and the uses of language and/or communication within particular, situated contexts. They often attempted to teach students the discourse conventions of specific disciplines without immersing or engaging students in the behaviors of those disciplines; thus, students were asked to employ genres—which Russell would conceive as forms of social action—without any sense for the actions they might be employed to conduct or complete. In contrast, Russell calls writing "a matter of learning to participate in some historically-situated human activity," and he argues that "it cannot be learned apart from the problems, the habits, the activities—the subject matter—of some group that found the need to write in that way to solve a problem or carry on its activities" (194). Writing, in this sense, is inseparable from what it does. Functionless writing—the decontextualized academic essay, for instance—is not *real* writing. For Russell, to be sure, these insights point toward one final conclusion: the need to "drop the abstraction (and perhaps the institution) of general composition courses in higher education" (195). If those courses do not teach writing as it exists in nearly every other instance—as a doing, and an action—then *they* have no useful function.

Russell extends these insights in "Activity Theory and Its Implications for Writing Instruction," which appears in Joseph Petraglia's edited collection *Reconceiving Writing, Rethinking Writing Instruction* (1995)—a group of essays directly confronting the *what is writing?* question. There, while demonstrating that "writing is an immensely protean tool that activity systems are always and everywhere changing to meet their needs," he draws an argument from the postprocess script: people do not "'learn to write,' period." Instead, he argues, people acquire genres through their use in activity systems; in this sense, "learning to write means learning to write in the ways (genres) those in an activity system write" (56–57).

To illustrate this point, Russell employs a memorable and effective comparison between playing ball-games and writing. This analogy clearly undercuts the idea that skills unproblematically generalize across activity systems. Facility in one form of ball-playing (say, driving a golf ball) does not map onto all other forms of ball-using (e.g., putting a golf ball, let alone bowling, or serving a tennis ball, or playing arcade pinball). Even though baseball games begin with the seemingly generic command to "Play Ball!," and football and basketball players often describe themselves as *ballers,* no one seriously believes that skill in one sporting arena implies an ability to *play ball* generally. Indeed, many team sports evidence a division of labor with different players specializing in different ball-related tasks (e.g., throwing, versus catching, versus kicking, versus punting a football). In the sporting context, in other words, the impossibility of generating or developing a generalized ball-aptitude is widely accepted. However, the polite fiction of generalized writing skills is the foundation on which traditional composition courses have been built—an unsteady one, indeed.

Writing, Russell demonstrates, has generally been assumed to be a generalized tool, and compositionists have assumed that one who acquires dexterity with that tool might then apply their skill more or less un-problematically whenever and wherever they pleased. As a result, compositionists have attempted to construct courses in "general writing skills instruction" (GWSI). However, just like ball-skills, writing abilities are so context-(i.e., activity system)-dependent that gaining facility with one form says nothing about one's ability to use another. But, while the most generalized conception of writing is the most problematic, other (somewhat less) generic forms still present problems.

Russell also distances his approach from Process-era, social-epistemic conceptions of "academic" or "universal educated discourse" (UED). When compositionists saw themselves as cultivating academic discourse, they certainly demonstrated greater conceptual complexity than those who believed simply in a generalized but vague notion of "good writing" (usually tied to essayistic or literary style). However, they still did not follow their own arguments far enough. In arguing that academic discourse differs from non-academic discourse, why not further differentiate disciplines from one another? From an activity theory perspective, Russell argues, "There is no distinctive genre, set of genres, linguistic register, or set of conventions that is academic discourse or public discourse per se, because 'academia' and the 'public' are not activity systems in any useful sense for writing instruction" (60). Furthermore, although illusory, those categories (i.e., "academia" and the "public") produce real—and really detrimental—effects: they "create and preserve the false notion that there can exist 'good writing' independent of an activity system that judges the success of a text by its results within that activity system" (60).

For reasons that will become evident later, let me note one final point about Russell's chapter. After presenting a prolonged argument about the merits of WAC/WID for improving students' writing in a way that general writing skills instruction cannot, Russell offers a curricular proposal. "Groups of scholars and researchers in a range of disciplines . . . specifically study the role of writing in human activities," he notes; "It is thus now possible and, I believe, desirable to teach a general introductory course *about* writing." In such a course, he argues, students wouldn't necessarily strive to improve their skills as writers—the goal of composition instruction since its American foundation(s). Instead, such a course would teach students "what has been learned about writing in those activity systems that make the role of writing in society the object of their study" (73). For Russell, a move away from traditional conceptions of composition, oriented toward general writing skills instruction and seeking to cultivate universal educated discourse, might imply a move toward Writing Studies or what, through the work of his former Ph.D. advisee Elizabeth Wardle, has come to be called Writing about Writing.

In addition to his theoretical texts, which illuminate the conceptual underpinnings of the WAC/WID movement, Russell also recounted the long history of teaching writing beyond the confines of first-year composition courses—and even outside of English departments—in *Writing in the Academic Disciplines, 1870–1990*. What we now think of as Writing across the Curriculum (WAC) was not the first such movement, he demonstrates, only the first to go by that name. It also differed from prior ones in its pedagogical approach: "Instead of examining writing as a single set of generalizable skills and its teaching a set of generalizable principles and techniques, new lines of investigation have examined writing as a constituent of communities, differentiated by the structure of knowledge and the activities of each community" (299). WAC in the early 1990s could be seen as an extension and/or application of the Process-era notions of social constructionism and discourse communities.

However, as Russell notes in an update for the book's second edition, something began to change during the 1990s. Scholars in the (sub-)field began to differentiate between WAC, which they characterized as an exercise in *writing to learn* (or "writing *about* the subjects disciplines study"), and Writing in the Disciplines (WID), which they characterized as *learning to write* (or "learning to write *in* the ways disciplines do"). Jonathan Hall parses the distinction clearly, WAC "believes that it is teaching transferable writing skills, and aims for a general academic analytical language, while WID suggests that there is no such thing as a single scholarly language, only the various specific languages indigenous to particular disciplinary communities" ("Toward" 7).

But, the increased prevalence of WAC and WID were not the only notable reforms to 1990s writing curricula. As Russell demonstrates, "The relations between the writing-across-the-curriculum movement and first-year composition (FYC) programs got much more complicated in the 1990s." In particular, the successes of WAC "lent a certain credence to recent abolitionist calls" to do away with first-year composition courses altogether (313–14). This was not the first period in which abolitionist calls circulated throughout the field, to be sure. However, prior calls for abolition always arose from outside of composition, among those who doubted that writing could be taught at all. In contrast, in the words of Robert Connors, the 1990s "new abolitionists" were a group "trained as compositionists from an early point in their careers" who arrived at "exactly the opposite conclusion: that writing can be taught, and that experts are needed to teach it, but that the required freshman course is not the most effective forum for attaining the ends we seek" ("New Abolitionism" 23). WAC/WID didn't merely undermine FYC by being successful. The tangible or quantifiable results mattered, of course. But, just as importantly, the principles underlying WID themselves call out for the end of conventionalized composition instruction *as such*. The premises entail the conclusion. Russell hints at this point in *Writing in the Academic Disciplines*, reasoning, "But if one sees writing (and rhetoric) as deeply embedded in the differentiated practices of disciplines, not as a single elementary skill, one must reconceive in profound ways the process of learning to write" (15). And of course, Russell himself subscribed to these perspectives, as did the subjects of my last chapter, Russell Hunt, James Reither, and Douglass Vipond.

From here I'd like to go (at least) two directions at once. But, given the linear nature of print, of course I can't. I'd like to jump to the work of Joseph Petraglia, who edited and contributed to the *Reconceiving Writing* collection. I'd also like to connect Russell's articles to the work being done by his peers at Iowa State. Since I can't do both, though, a quick reminder: Russell worked at Iowa State; so did Helen Rothschild Ewald, and Nancy Roundy Blyler, and Charlotte Thralls, and Kent. Many of those scholars were/are, like Russell, more commonly associated with WAC/WID and/or Professional Communication and/or Technical Communication. (The boundaries get blurry in a hurry.) Even so, they were also quite knowledgeable about postprocess in the paralogic, externalist sense, and they brought those insights into their own branches of scholarship and teaching.

A BRIEF DIGRESSION: JOSEPH PETRAGLIA'S REJECTION OF A "REALLY BORING QUESTION"

Let us depart briefly from Ames, Iowa to discuss Petraglia, a somewhat strange figure in the history of post-/postprocess, inasmuch as he (A) earned his Ph.D. from Carnegie Mellon, scholarly home of Flower and Hayes; (B) unapologetically called himself "committed to a cognitivist framework for understanding writing" ("Writing" 79); and (C) employed the key terms *post-process* and *postprocess* in a seemingly haphazard fashion (c.f., "Is There Life," especially 49–50). Unsurprisingly, then, other commenters have disagreed about how to categorize his work. Foster calls him someone who "self-identif[ies] as post-process but who do[es] not necessarily partake of Kent's theory," a position I find demonstrably false, inasmuch as Foster never adequately demonstrates that he (or any author in *Reconceiving Writing*, for that matter) self-identifies as post-/postprocess (*Networked Process* 13). That is, she never presents a sentence in which he says, "As a postprocess scholar . . ." or even implicitly indicates an affiliative stance. Elsewhere, John Whicker slots Petraglia beneath the heading of "authors who don't reject process" ("Narratives" 506), a position I also find demonstrably false.

If anything, I would categorize the Petraglia of his published record as someone who *does* reject Process but doesn't self-identify as post-/postprocess—largely because his primary conceptual interests are not those of Kent but much closer to those of, say, Russell or Aviva Freedman, or even more so Michael Cole and Lauren Resnick. The works he seems to like the most don't originate in or speak directly to the context of first-year composition in the United States. As a result, he has a more expansive sense of what writing is and what writing instruction can be.

For Whicker, Petraglia's key admission is that *post-process* "signifies a rejection of the generally formulaic framework for writing that process suggested" but does not dispense with "the fundamental observation that an individual produces text by means of a writing process." Instead, Petraglia considers the insight-as-"mantra" that "writing is a process" to be the "right answer to a really boring question" (53).

Per the current analysis, I want to pause and ask what I hope will not be a tedious meta-question. Rather, I think it's legitimately worth asking: if "writing is a process" is the answer to a really boring question, *what is the question?*

One might, for good reason, suggest "What is *writing?*"

I do not want to rule out that possibility. I accept its correctness as more-or-less self-evident. But, I think that Petraglia is trying to lead toward something more interesting (i.e., less "boring") here. As Sianne Ngai demonstrates in *Our Aesthetic Categories*, interestingness is a function of the circulation of information (defined in Gregory Bateson's sense of *differences that make a difference*). It's a measure of novelty within sameness, or of deviation from generic norms. I think Petraglia is suggesting that compositionists have continually raised the question—*what is writing?*—in a way that has supposed its own particular and singular, unchanging answer: *writing is a process.* But, there are, to be sure, end-lessly other things that writing is besides a process. It's a visual and/or physical and/or virtual marking, a tool, a mode of self-expression, something that circulates, and so forth, and so on. One could employ those exact same three words— *what is writing?*—to ask very different kinds of questions and thereby arrive at very different answers. This is one of the other things that writing is: iterable. When Dobrin insists that we have not yet begun to ask the question of what writing is, I think this is what he means, more or less: we have not yet begun to ask other versions of the same question. By continually answering the same way, by turning *writing is a process* into a mantra, we have not let the question iterate, proliferate, take on new life as it circulates, mean other things, enter into new spaces, change *us.*

Petraglia's own chapter of *Reconceiving Writing* is deeply concerned with the distinction between ill-structured and well-structured problem-solving. For him, how a question is posed matters. Thus, for Petraglia (or so it seems to me, at least), genuinely interesting versions of the *what is writing?* question could be asked. And, he seems (to me) to be quite invested in asking them.

How, then, might he answer a more interesting version of the same old question? Among other things: whatever else it may be, writing is *not* the thing that general writing skills instruction has assumed that it is or could be: "a master-able body of skills that can be formed and practiced irrespective of the formal context of the writing classroom" ("Writing" 80). When he initially outlines GWSI instruction, Petraglia employs a notable set of scare-quotes, displaying his skepticism: "General writing skills instruction sets for itself the objective of teaching students 'to write,' to give them skills that transcend any particular content and context" ("Introduction" xii). To explain what writing is, at minimum, one would have to say that it isn't *that*. However, my purpose here isn't chiefly to outline GWSI but to argue for Petraglia's postcomposition, postprocess-ness.

For Petraglia, I would argue, disavowing the GWSI view of writing instruction *does* seem to be a movement away from Process, if Process is understood to be co-terminous with a historically specific, widely shared, disciplinary approach to teaching *composition* (though not necessarily "basic writing, technical writing, writing-intensive content courses, or creative writing") (xi–xii). While noting that his sketch of GWSI is "highly abbreviated," he still affirms that it is "no strawman." Rather, he argues, "It is a curriculum that an overwhelming majority of writing instructors is paid to teach, that practically every composition textbook is written to support, and the instruction for which English departments are given resources to deliver" (xii). The fiction of general writing skills produces all sorts of real effects and, thus, GWSI is also *real*. Dispensing with the fiction, though difficult and disciplinarily traumatic, would therefore produce all sorts of real effects, too.

For Petraglia, even when it aspires to create "authentic" writing experiences in which students engage less-well-structured problems, composition is still too "school-bounded" ("Writing" 88). In this context, students may learn how to "do school," but the things that they end up doing—"*appearing* to address an audience, *looking like* you have a purpose, and *pretending* to be knowledgeable"— are too different from real-world, ill-structured writing tasks to avoid what he calls pseudo-transactionality, "the illusion of rhetorical transaction" ("Writing" 89, 92; "Spinning" 19). Although Petraglia is chiefly concerned with opposing GWSI, not Process *per se*, he still makes a handful of characteristic postprocess gestures, both in *Reconceiving Writing* and in his contribution to *Post-Process Theory*. I want to focus on three of them.

First, Petraglia affirms a turn toward the environment or ecology. At the close of "Writing as an Unnatural Act," for example, he states, "If one agrees with the contention that writing, in its fullest sense, cannot really be taught, we might then turn our attention to how we could at least provide the environments in which it naturally occurs" (94). This statement, it seems to me, anticipates his later diagnosis of the postprocess mindset: "In conclusion, we have become much more interested in the ecology in which writing takes place than in the mere fact that writing is the outcome of a variety of steps and stages" ("Is There Life" 62).

Furthermore, in defining the scare-quoted "'natural habitat' of the academic writer," Petraglia presents three key propositions. The second of those—"the natural writing assignment derives much of its rhetorical nature from reading" is most pertinent for our present purposes, as it reflects his second characteristically postprocess gesture: blurring the lines between reading and writing. Petraglia justifies this move in *Reconceiving Writing* (95–96) and in his contribution to *Post-Process Theory*. In the latter case, he advocates for "a reconceptualization of what it means to 'teach writing,' and argues that "this reconceptualization requires that the discipline let go of its current pedagogical shape . . . and instead deploy its efforts to inculcate *receptive* skills," rather than pursue a "generic writing *techne*." For Petraglia, this receptivity might resemble the "rhetorical sensitivity" models theorized by Roderick Hart and Don Burks, which "direct a student toward the selection of those aspects of his or her self that could, and perhaps should, be rhetorically transformed when confronted with particular social conditions and situations" ("Is There Life" 62).

Finally, Petraglia concludes both chapters with very similar arguments about the end of composition. In *Reconceiving Writing* he argues that "general writing skills instruction—perhaps the very notion of the composition classroom—is an idea whose time has gone" ("Writing" 97). But, this fact shouldn't lead to despair for instructors nor to "disaster for the rhetoric and writing field" (98). Different, important work remains to be done, but—as Petraglia's final verbal omission indicates—it will be work for *rhetoric* and *writing*; it won't be work for *composition*. In *Post-Process Theory* he remains dubious about "the ability and willingness of writing professionals to evolve not only post-process, but post-composition." Even so, he acknowledges that another field, writing studies, might already "be growing up alongside and within composition" and that it might "one day be in a position to challenge the status of composition as the main site of professional identity" (63).

Iowa State in the Early Years of Paralogic Hermeneutics, Part II: A Group Effort

Before taking our recent (de-)tour into Petraglia's work, I mentioned that Russell's texts could lead toward a different hyper-textual jump: to a discussion of the scholars working at Iowa State University during the 1980s and 1990s. Among enthusiasts of (theoretical, narrowly construed) postprocess, Kent and Russell are likely the most well-known of this group. However, to demonstrate that postprocess postcomposition had a broad(er than generally recognized) impact, I want to look at that Iowa State coterie, including the works that some of their doctoral students produced while in Ames. I'll also focus on one prominent alumna of their graduate program: Elizabeth Wardle.

I mentioned earlier that four Iowa State faculty members published chapters in *Post-Process Theory*: Blyler, Ewald, Kent, and Russell. Other than Kent, Ewald most directly engaged with postprocess tenets, especially externalism, by way of Bakhtin. Her "Waiting for Answerability," for instance, provides an exemplary

treatment of Bakhtin's work at the hands of social constructionists and externalists. By her account, Bakhtin himself was not an externalist, but some of his ideas
moved in that direction, and he provided conceptual equipment for those who
would move the field from social constructionism to externalism (340, 336).
However, inasmuch as I want to focus on the existence of postprocess theory
beyond the bounds of (first-year) composition, I must depart from Ewald here.
Although she published professional communication scholarship consistently
throughout the 1980s, occasionally in the 1990s, and again in the 2000s, those
texts do not typically engage postprocess concepts. Ewald did coordinate Iowa
State's doctoral program in Rhetoric and Professional Communication in the
1990s ("Waiting" 331), and a published syllabus from her graduate-level *Theory
and Research in Professional Communication* course includes several postprocess
texts (Ewald, "Iowa State" 49–50). So, I assume that she still impacted some
professional communication scholars' viewpoints on the subject.

Let us turn, then, to Blyler. In the early 1990s, she (solo-)authored one article that I would characterize as proto-postprocess, "Reading Theory and Persuasive Business Communications," and two that would introduce paralogic
hermeneutic principles into professional communication scholarship: "Shared
Meaning and Public Relations Writing" and "Theory and Curriculum: Reexamining the Curricular Separation of Business and Technical Communication."
Those articles don't necessarily *endorse* postprocess, and I don't mean to over-
state the importance (which is minimal) of paralogic hermeneutics to her overall arguments. Even so, in both articles, Blyler presents paralogic hermeneutics
as a rejection of positivism, "the belief that the mind, as a windowpane, mirrors reality and that discourse simply records what the mind has apprehended"
("Theory" 226). In "Shared Meaning" she "investigate[s] the rhetorical means by
which meaning is shared" between readers and writers (304) and explains how
paralogic hermeneutics explores "the interaction of communicants as they share
theories or interpretations of discourse" (303). In "Theory and Curriculum,"
she categorizes paralogic hermeneutics as a "social view of discourse," alongside
social construction. She presents its difference clearly, though:

> Paralogic hermeneutics addresses the issue of socially medi-
> ated meaning by positing that meaning is negotiated directly
> by communicants as they interact, rather than being deter-
> mined in advance of an interaction by any factor, including
> the community membership and internalizing communal
> views that social construction appears to require. (230)

In an uncodifiable and open-ended process, communicants guess at each
other's meanings and re-adjust their interpretations accordingly, she notes, but

"these guesses and expectations . . . only 'more or less' coincide" and any "agreement reached about meaning is always imperfect (230–31). This final point is notable because, that same year, Blyler would also publish "Teaching Persuasion as Consensus in Business Communication," a text that would implicitly disavow many of paralogic hermeneutics' key claims about the impossibility of perfect interpretive alignment.

The faculty at Iowa State were at the forefront of postprocess in its initial stages, and their graduate students would eventually carry forth the banner, both in articles written during their ISU years and as they went forth into their professorial careers. Lee-Ann Kastman Breuch's 2002 "Post-Process 'Pedagogy'" may be the most-well known text in this regard, though I will not discuss it here because it was published in a "mainstream" composition journal. For similar reasons, I'll lay aside Iowa State graduate student Lee Libby's "Passing Theory in Practice" (1997), an early application of paralogic hermeneutics to hypertext theory. Instead, I'd like to discuss two professional-communication-related texts: Clay Spinuzzi's 1996 "Pseudo-Transactionality, Activity Theory, and Professional Writing Instruction" and Rue Yuan's 1997 "Yin/Yang Principle and the Relevance of Externalism and Paralogic Rhetoric to Intercultural Communication." Those articles lay-out their primary foci in their titles, but a few additional comments may be merited.

Spinuzzi connects Petraglia's insights on pseudo-transactionality, Vygotskian activity systems, externalist hermeneutic guessing, and professional writing. He concludes that students need not learn professional writing exclusively within professional activity networks (or "ANs") but that, at the same time, "teaching students generalized communication strategies without reference to localized ANs will not help much either"; instead, "students should join other ANs and use the professional writing classroom as a forum for discussing them and as an opportunity to examine their practices" (304).

Yuan's article draws from the postprocess contention that no shared language is necessary for communication to take place: communication depends on aligning passing theories, not on sharing prior theories. Yuan demonstrates that Process-approaches, especially those endorsing discourse community models, "assume that culture is generalizable" and thus engage in negative and/or harmful stereotyping by "ignor[ing] or suppress[ing] the heterogeneous elements of a society" (300, 301). In contrast, a paralogic externalist approach would lead "intercultural communicators [to] treat each person and each interaction as different and, in so doing, [help] them avoid cultural stereotyping" (316).

I'd also like to argue that Iowa State alumna Elizabeth Wardle, whose work is most commonly associated with the writing about writing approach to first-year composition, and who is commonly figured as an advocate for writing studies, has carried forth the postprocess torch. But, before we can go forward in that direction, we may need to go sideways and backwards: to earlier works in writing studies.

THE END OF COMPOSITION: AN IN-DENIAL POSTPROCESS TEXT . . . ?

I began this chapter by addressing Dobrin's *Postcomposition,* particularly its call to move the field of composition toward (a form of) writing studies, which might finally ask the question of *what writing is,* and which would not (feel the need to) tether all theories of writing to the pedagogical scene of collegiate writing instruction. However, I also presented Bruce Horner's critique of *Postcomposition*: that it dismisses or ignores quite a lot of scholarship in a branch of composition also called writing studies that has already done the sort of work it requests. Here, I'd like to turn to a text that Dobrin does quote, David Smit's *The End of Composition Studies.*

At the outset of his book, Smit identifies "the teaching of writing" as composition's "primary reason for being," or, within the punning parlance of his title, its *end (End* 2, 1). Framing composition as a teaching subject is, of course, the exact sort of gesture that would irritate Dobrin—a point Smit understood. In his only citation of Dobrin, Smit rightly characterizes him as "argu[ing] that the field ought to devote itself to theory in the abstract, and that the relevance of theory to practice should not be a major concern of the profession" (*End* 7). I don't think Smit is correct on this point; as I read him, Dobrin does not advocate for a wholly theoretical discipline but one that might clear a large, dedicated space for theorizing. Even so, Dobrin does consistently express displeasure with the application of theory as pedagogy. Thus, when he assesses Smit's efforts to move the discipline beyond composition as "applaudable" but still far too concerned with pedagogy, the gesture is hardly surprising (*Postcomposition* 10).

In Dobrin's estimation, *The End of Composition* "in fact, argues that writing as phenomena cannot be studied independent of the local contexts in which it is taught and learned (10)." Or, stated differently: for Smit, according to Dobrin, the only way to study writing is to study writing instruction. This is not a precise description of Smit's work, though. While he is certainly more concerned with teaching and learning (i.e., pedagogy) than Dobrin, Smit says nothing of the sort on the page Dobrin cites. The closest he comes is arguing that "writing may not be a global and unified phenomenon," that "writing ability may be very context-dependent," and that "writing teachers"—who, for Smit, are importantly *not compositionists*—need to "participate in" and "know about the workings of" the discourse communities into which they would enculturate students (166). If

I understand Smit correctly, he does not claim that writing can only be studied where it is taught and learned, as Dobrin claims of him. Instead, he argues that writing can only be learned within particular activity systems, and thus it should only be taught by those who themselves write within those particular activity systems. This is an importantly different claim.

Notably, in the same text where he denounces Dobrin, Horner spends quite some time comparing *The End of Composition Studies* to *Postcomposition*, ultimately to conclude that both suffer from a lack of imagination. Smit's work, to be sure, is easier to attack on these grounds. He opens his book with a startlingly pessimistic claim: "For all practical purposes, the major concepts, paradigms, and models we have to work with" in analyzing what writing is, whether it can be learned, and how one would need to teach it "are already known and widely accepted, that there is little hope we can reconceptualize writing in startling new ways." Smit even asserts, "Indeed, it strikes me that viable alternatives to current concepts, paradigms, and models are inconceivable" (*End* 2). But, despite their differences—Smit refusing to believe in the possibility of *the new*, Dobrin consistently fetishizing it—the two share a fundamental similarity. In Horner's estimation, the two texts "declar[e] the field to be at an end," instead of "pursuing ways of thinking that field differently" (Horner, "Rewriting" 464). Ultimately, Smit proposes "little that is different from WID curricula already on the books, inflected with dominant free market ideology." For what it's worth, Bethany Davila launches a similar critique of *The End*, arguing that Smit "situates himself within the writing across the curriculum (WAC) camp" and therefore the book "reads as a continuation of Joseph Petraglia's *Reconceiving Writing, Rethinking Writing Instruction*, a pivotal book on composition studies and WAC." Smit wants to position himself outside of this tradition, but I don't think he succeeds.

Although Smit has few nice things to say about postprocess, his vision of a renewed composition sounds *extremely similar* to the postprocess postcomposition I have been documenting in this chapter, all the same. He claims to present an argument outside or beyond it, but his premises accord very closely with its central claims. Indeed, the phrase *post-process* only occurs once in *The End*. On page 8, Smit writes,

> Whether or not "process" teaching was ever very widespread, books and journals are starting to appear touting such phrases as "post-process" and "after theory" with no indication of what the discipline should teach other than "process" or what it should study "after theory." Theorists as different as Thomas Kent, Aviva Freedman, and Joseph Petraglia offer substantial arguments from language philosophy, empirical

studies and classroom observation that writing cannot be
taught. What then should writing teachers *do* in the classroom? The answers vary.

Smit's tone seems to imply that this lack of a unified disciplinary direction,
this variation is a problem. Indeed, when he argues that composition has reached
its conceptual (dead?) end, he notes that all subsequent accounts will be quote/
unquote "postmodern," that is, "historicized, contextualized, and contingent,"
and thus "limited" (2). He laments, as well, the trouble that compositionists will
therefore face in "reaching any kind of consensus about the teaching of writing,"
noting that, "in that direction I see our only hope for significantly improving the
teaching of writing in this country" (12).

These gestures strike me as odd, or at least inconsistent with his earlier scholarship. Smit had once criticized another scholar, Daniel Royer, for believing that
"important philosophy should be 'systematic' and 'coherent' and 'speculative.'"
In contrast, he had noted, "I think such a philosophy is impossible" ("Reply to
Royer" 380). That is, in his earlier works, Smit seemed to endorse a postmodern,
non-systematic, incoherent vision for writing instruction, one that might attend
to individual students and localized practices.

But, in his swift dismissal and subsequent omission of post-/postprocess from
The End of Composition Studies, I don't believe that Smit meant to criticize Kent
or Freedman or Petraglia, really. Instead, his criticism seems more an exercise
in ground-clearing, of making his own argument seem different enough to be
worth saying at all. On the very next page, he effectively endorses their ideas—
that language is heteroglossic, that "meaning is a matter of interpretation," and
that "the way we understand one another through language is primarily interpretive, a matter of hermeneutics"—even citing Kent to do so (9). He then
claims that "composition studies as a field has only tentatively begun to take the
implications of these tenets seriously." That is, "the field continues to talk about
writing, to think about writing, and to teach writing, as if it were a global or
universal ability" and therefore "the field continues to foster writing in generic
'writing' courses" (10). His own work, I would argue, attempts to counter-act
those tendencies in more-or-less postprocess ways. So far as I can tell, then,
there's no reason for Smit to swipe at postprocess except to avoid having to work
through it, rather than alongside it. So, he swipes at it, then he ignores it.

In fairness to Smit, his primary contention is an important one: compositionists know what does and does not work in writing instruction, but that
knowledge has not brought forth changes to pedagogical conduct. In this light,
learning more about writing or even writing instruction may not provide "the
solution to the crisis in composition studies." And, indeed, that solution might

instead need to arrive by way of "political action," a point to which I suspect Horner might begrudgingly assent. Or, if not that, then, "perhaps more fancifully, a spiritual reawakening" (12). It's on his next statement that I want to pause, though. He writes,

> To improve writing instruction we will have to radically restructure the way writing is offered in the undergraduate curriculum. If writing is indeed greatly constrained by context, if we learn to write certain genres by immersing ourselves in the discourse of a community and by using writing to participate in that community, then it makes sense that writing as a subject at the post-secondary level should be taught in those academic units most closely associated with the knowledge and genres students need or want to learn. As a result, I believe that writing instruction should be not be [sic] the primary responsibility of English departments and writing programs; rather, writing instruction should be the responsibility of all the various disciplines of the university. In other words, we must put an "end" to the hegemony of writing instruction by composition studies as a field. (12)

Here, in essence, Smit argues for writing in the disciplines. He even follows it up by opposing (what I will later call) the Realpolitik objection to postprocess: that it may be good in theory, but its practical implications will lead to writing instructors losing their jobs. Contesting that conclusion, Smit states, "Of course, this does not mean that professionals in composition studies will find their work coming to an end" (12).

To be fair, Smit's proposal does add something new to the mix: that composition instructors be trained directly and explicitly in the discourse of some non-composition academic field, as well. But, otherwise, it's all very familiar: the version of Writing in the Disciplines that comports with a postprocess perspective or attitude. Since no generalized form of writing exists, students would not be enrolled in generic writing courses or encounter generic writing teachers (159, 162). In this model, students would enter into particular discourse communities and study with tutors or mentors who engage in the activities of those discourse communities (141, 155). To actualize such reforms, students would need more than just the typical sorts of required writing courses; they'd need to be taught writing in the various academic and professional disciplines by professionals in those fields. Of course, by the end of the book, Smit concedes that his "program may not be as revolutionary as it sounds; that it may indeed be fundamentally evolutionary because over the past twenty years, individual institutions have been gradually implementing programs that go in the direction that I recommend" (183). He also admits, "Obviously, the most effective way to accomplish this sort of cooperation has already been modeled by writing-across-the-curriculum and writing-across-the-disciplines programs" (193). But, one wonders here: why start out so controversial only to fall back onto something so broadly accepted?

I cannot answer that question.

Instead, I want to latch onto one final point.

The previous section of this chapter concerned graduate students at Iowa State who had taken postprocess beyond its commonly acknowledged (narrow, First-Year Composition) bounds. I ended by asserting a desire to discuss the work of Elizabeth Wardle. But, I needed to contextualize her work. We are now prepared to turn to it.

ELIZABETH WARDLE, WRITING ABOUT WRITING, AND POSTPROCESS WRITING STUDIES

Wardle's work dove-tails with Smit's in two ways: by considering what Smit calls "disciplinary knowledge" and contemplating how writing skills transfer from one context to the next. Six pages into a chapter called "What Does It Mean to Be a Writing Teacher," Smit announces his purpose clearly, writing, "The large issue I am raising here is whether there is something we might call *disciplinary knowledge*, which all writing teachers ought to share by the very fact that they are writing teachers" (*The End* 65–66). After suggesting that several theorists have attempted to "professionalize" the field by offering a view of writing as a "global and unified phenomenon," Smit notes that "obviously, the entire point of [his] analysis" is to prove the contrary. For Smit, there is no such thing as disciplinary knowledge because nothing systematic or fully generalizable can be known about writing. From this point, he presents his stipulations for what a writing teacher should look like (166) and then summarizes those points: "The model here is of teacher-practitioners, who know how to write particular kinds of discourse themselves, and are self-consciously reflective about their own writing and how that writing participates in the workings of the larger discourse community, and are capable of sharing their knowledge and insights with others" (167). For Smit, because all knowledge-that-counts-as-knowledge about writing is contextual and contingent (i.e., in his terms "post-modern"), nothing is sufficiently known about writing that could make *it* the subject of such a course. Thus, compositionists ought to become educated in the discourse conventions of some other, knowledge-producing fields, so that they might then teach students to write within them. Wardle, it seems to me, accepts many of the fundamental arguments that Smit presents but arrives at a very different policy proposal.

As I'll primarily discuss Wardle's work from the late 2000s, it's worth mentioning her resistance at that time to being called a post-process scholar. Although, judging from the textual record, I hope (and believe) that she might agree with my categorizing her work as postprocess, though in a rather constrained way. In a July 26, 2007 response to one of Alexander Reid's blog entries, Wardle states,

> Maybe I am resisting a label but comfortable with the tenets, though, frankly, I haven't ever found any clear tenets of post-process theory. If it's that any description of processes, however complex, don't (as you say) "describe the material events by which texts are produced," well, I would agree. But I don't think the process researchers would *disagree.* If it's more along the lines of Kent, that writing is not teachable, I don't completely buy it. But I guess if I take everything I do believe we have learned from genre theory, activity theory, and the whole social turn, we have to seriously question what it is that *can* be taught. I don't believe that nothing can be taught, however. ("Comment on 'What Should'")

In a subsequent blog entry, Reid would present an extended response to Wardle. There and elsewhere (e.g., *The Two Virtuals* 5, 23), he defines *post-process* in line with Trimbur's definition, as "an attempt to capture the various ways that rhet/comp scholars have moved beyond, built upon, and/or rejected the dominant writing process school of thought" and "a recognition of the social and cultural dimensions of writing" (Reid, [Post-] Post-Process Composition"). To that entry, Wardle presents a request for Reid to "help [her] out a little more" by answering a question: "does post-process necessarily entail cultural studies or an emphasis on liberatory pedagogy . . . ?" And, in light of this question, she reasons,

> If we are talking about post-process as recognition of the social and cultural dimensions of writing, then activity theorists, genre theorists, etc. would be post process, and so would I. But if one must adopt a cultural studies approach in the writing classroom or a Freirean liberatory pedagogy in the classroom, then genre theorists and activity theorists are not (necessarily) post-process, and neither am I. ("Comment on '(Post) Post-Process Composition,'" 26 July)

In this instance, I cannot help but note that Wardle distinguishes between two forms of post-process—the first of which roughly resembles what I have been calling *postprocess* and the second of which sounds quite a lot like (in my terms) *post-process*. While she accepts the first label for herself, she rejects the second. Eventually, in a subsequent reply, Wardle offers a self-identificatory concession: "It would be far more meaningful for people to classify us (and others) in a more specific way—as genre theorists, as activity theorists, even as Joseph Petraglia groupies. But just saying we are 'post process' could mean things that we do espouse as well as things that we definitely do *not* espouse" ("Comment on '(Post)-Post-Process Composition," 27 July). Given the semantic confusion(s) of postprocess and post-process, I certainly understand her reluctance to be considered a post-/postprocess scholar. More precise categorizations of her work exist, including ones that might not distort understandings of what she does and does not believe. Even so, given that Wardle willingly self-identifies as a genre theorist, I would remind the reader of an important fact: before the term postprocess existed, Kent himself was a genre theorist, as well. His first book was entitled *Interpretation and Genre*, Chapter Six of *Paralogic Rhetoric* is entitled "Paralogic Genres," and, as this chapter has demonstrated, his earliest texts on (professional communication) writing instruction apply genre theory to it. In a very real way, there is no postprocess theory without genre theory. And, as an additional side-note, Anis Bawarshi has analyzed postprocess across the grain of genre theory on a few occasions ("Beyond Dichotomy"; "Writing Post-Process").

To understand how Wardle's work stands within the tradition I am constructing here, let us turn now to her published scholarship. To initiate their 2007 "Teaching about Writing, Righting Misconceptions," Wardle and her co-author Douglas Downs recite a series of claims that feel ripped-from-the-pages of Smit's *The End of Composition*—until they don't. They note that first-year composition is typically asked to prepare students to write a form of generalized academic writing that simply does not exist and to provide those students with writing skills that would transfer unproblematically from one site to the next. But, of course, the question of transfer is considerably more complicated. Furthermore, the field—which they call "writing studies"—has "largely ignored the implications" of "more than twenty years of research and theory" and has "continued to assure its publics (faculty, administrators, parents, industry) that FYC can do what nonspecialists have always assumed it can," that is, create or produce "good writers" in one or two semesters of generalized writing instruction (553, 552). Downs and Wardle frame the negative impact of these "unsupportable assurances" in a different light than Smit does, though. If we continue to recite these proclamations and teach these courses, all the while knowing that they cannot work, then "we silently support the misconceptions that writing is not a real subject, that writing courses do not require expert instructors, and that rhetoric and composition are not genuine research areas or legitimate intellectual pursuits." They therefore argue for a reimagining of composition, one that would teach "*about writing* . . . as if writing studies is a discipline with content knowledge to which students should be introduced," instead of simply aiming to teach students "'how to write in college'" (553).

This is, of course, a solution to a problem that has haunted postprocess from its earliest stages. If the logical extension of postprocess is that writing should be taught with small-scale (i.e., as close to one-to-one as possible) mentorship relationships by knowledgeable practitioners who produce the genres in question and circulate them within the relevant activity systems, then what do you do with the fact that most composition instructors seem to have an obsolete knowledge base?

You could, as Kent suggests, try to create more writing intensive courses within the disciplines (*Paralogic Rhetoric* 169–70).

Or, you could, as Smit suggests, attempt to train compositionists in some other knowledge base (214, 220–23).

Or you could, as many universities have done, establish cross-disciplinary collaborations or "learning communities," in which first-year composition courses are "linked" to courses in other academic disciplines. However, as Wardle elsewhere demonstrates, students in such learning communities often import the subject matter of other disciplines into their composition essays without meaningfully engaging the genres or activity systems of the disciplines in question. Thus, she expresses doubt that such composition courses can prepare students to write *in* those disciplines any better than generic or non-themed courses could ("Cross-Disciplinary Links" 10, 13).

As a final alternative, as Downs and Wardle suggest, you could recognize that a field of scholars has been at work learning things about writing—what it is, what it does or can do, how people learn to do it to the degree that they *can*, and so forth—for quite a long time. You might, therefore, ask those scholars to teach their students what they themselves know about writing and help to cultivate those students' writing skills within a writing studies discourse community. You might, in other words, take the postprocess directive to replace first-year composition courses with writing in the disciplines ones to its logical extension—and teach first-year composition *as though it were itself a writing in the disciplines course.* As Wardle notes elsewhere, many composition assignments "mimic genres that mediate activities in other activity systems," but their "purposes and audiences are vague or even contradictory" within the FYC context ("Mutt Genres" 774). By asking students to write about writing studies knowledge within a writing studies course, instructors could avoid these "mutt genres." Instead, a more theoretically defensible approach would ask students to create "boundary objects," which might "actively function as bridges to the varied disciplinary genres students will encounter" (782).

Teaching students to write by teaching them about writing would not, however, entail a one-size-fits-all model for writing about writing; as Downs and Wardle admit in a 2013 retrospective: "Not even Downs and Wardle have a Downs and Wardle approach" ("Reflecting Back"). If one wanted to avoid Downs' and Wardle's "empirical" method of writing about writing, one could follow Deb Dew in exercising a "largely rhetorical" approach, or Barbara Bird's "rhetorical and philosophical way," or Shannon Carter's "ethnographic focus on literacy" or Betsy Sargent's "somewhat epistemological approach" (Wardle, "Continuing the Dialogue" 176). To the extent that writing about writing implies anything stable, it would be "the underlying set of principles: engage students with the research and ideas of the field, using any means necessary and productive, in order to shift students' conceptions of writing, building declarative and procedural knowledge of writing with an eye toward transfer" ("Reflecting Back").

And here we arrive at the other way in which Wardle's thinking and theorizing dovetails with Smit's: the question of transfer. To my mind, the scholarly fascination with transfer seems decidedly postprocess to the extent that it refuses definitions of universal or stable "writing ability" and dismisses the existence of a unified genre called "academic writing" as an illusion. At the same time, I must admit, the reasons that transfer scholars provide for these refutations generally have little to do with paralogy or externalism. In addition, the underlying assumptions of "transfer" discourse add some complexity—worth puzzling over and working through—to Kent's (in)famous argument that each act of writing is so radically singular that nothing learned in one instance can guarantee communicative success in any other and thus, at most, one can become a "better guesser." Transfer holds open the possibility that some stable core (or cores) of knowledge or ability *can* prove useful from instance to instance, even if there are (still) no guarantees.

For present purposes, I want to turn to Wardle's 2007 "Understanding 'Transfer' from FYC," which begins with a nod to Smit. There she acknowledges that *The End of Composition Studies* "summarizes what we know as a field about the transfer of writing-related skills from first-year composition to other courses and contexts." At the time, she admits, that collective knowledge base amounted to "very little." By 2007 only "a few theoretical discussions of writing transfer and FYC, writing centers, and advanced writing courses" had been published, and none of the three case studies that had investigated transfer was "initially or primarily interested in transfer." The vast majority of transfer-related research in existence concerned the transfer of writing abilities from academic to professional contexts (65).

A large portion of "Understanding 'Transfer'" documents Wardle's efforts to study generalization—her preferred conception of transfer—by applying a writing about writing approach at the University of Dayton in 2004 (70–81). Drawing from that research, Wardle affirms "the importance of context and activity to generalization." In particular, she argues, "Students needed context-specific support from their teachers and peers to successfully complete new writing tasks." As she would herself acknowledge, the context-dependence of pedagogical intervention might seem to make FYC unnecessary. Even so, Wardle identifies "*meta-awareness about writing, language, and rhetorical strategies*" as perhaps "the most important ability our courses can cultivate" (81–82). And so, in a departure from both Kent and Smit, she presents FYC as a workable site for such intervention; it can, she argues, "help students think about writing in the university, the varied conventions of different disciplines, and their own writing strategies" (82). Even with this optimism, though, she ends her article with a cautionary note: even a revised FYC would fail to have measurable impacts on student success beyond the first year, unless WAC and WID programs continue to grow and writing studies scholars continue to learn more about writing in other disciplines (82).

Wardle's theorizing about writing does not foreground externalism or paralogy, the two benchmarks of what I have been calling *postprocess* theories. Even so, it seems to merit *post*-prefixes in its relation to Process and to composition in another sense: insofar as it inverts the hierarchy of Process-era approaches to collegiate writing instruction. First-year composition has long been considered the foundation for improvement in student writing ability, the course upon which all others would need to build and from which other courses might extend their insights. Other courses could be added or subtracted from the curriculum, but FYC would always remain. Indeed, Wardle blames this odd institutional arrangement for the failures of writing instruction:

> FYC as preparation for writing in the academy has, after all, been our cornerstone enterprise, the course from which our discipline emerged. But therein lies the crux of the problem. In most cases, courses emerge from disciplines, not the other way around. . . . FYC began before the discipline and has long defied shaping by our disciplinary knowledge. ("Mutt Genres" 784)

According to conventionalized logic, advanced composition and WAC and WID courses might assist students throughout their collegiate careers, but they were never imagined to be *more important than* and certainly not *essential to the successful functioning of* first-year composition. In contrast, Wardle argues that first-year composition should only continue to exist to the extent that it becomes attentive and subservient to those other writing courses. Because any meaningful insights one might offer in FYC would need to be tailored toward their eventual extension elsewhere—that is, to student transfer—FYC has no place in a curriculum that lacks WAC and WID courses.

Furthermore, Wardle (and Downs, for that matter) is perfectly happy to reject the conventionalized goal of composition instruction, and she seems willing to eschew the term *composition*. In this sense, as well, she advocates for a postcomposition form of postprocess writing instruction. Sounding quite a lot like Kent, she urges instructors to "actively and vocally give up 'teaching to write' as a goal for FYC," for example, and she makes her reasoning clear: "There is no evidence that FYC has taught students to write for the university and none to suggest it will start to do so as soon as we discover the next best teaching method" ("Mutt Genres" 784). Although her revised curriculum might fill the institutional slot (in students' advisement forms) typically belonging to FYC, Wardle indicates that she prefer it be "called something like Writing about Writing" (784).

Likewise, although Downs and Wardle pitched their Writing about Writing course as an "FYC pedagogy" in their 2007 *College Composition and Communication* article, they also reliably employ the term *writing studies* to describe the larger scholarly field to which they belong, even attributing to it a forty-year history of investigating writing ("Teaching about Writing" 553, 555). In her generally affirmative and encouraging response to their work, Barbara Bird also makes the tactical choice to categorize their course as an example of FYC while identifying its "writing studies approach," which "goes beyond teaching writing processes and deeply engages students with the issues and concepts of writing" (169). She, of course, has not been alone in applying this writing-studies categorization. *Writing Studies* has become a much more common term within disciplinary conversations since Downs and Wardle "(Re)Envision[ed] 'First-Year Composition' as 'Introduction to Writing Studies'" in 2007.

As it relates to the place from which this chapter began, one final point is worth mentioning here. *Writing Studies*, as Wardle and Downs and Bird (and Russell, and Dobrin, and many, many others) employ the term typically denotes scholarly investigations into writing that need not apply directly to first-year composition. That is, it refers to scholarship that, whether implicitly or explicitly, rejects the pedagogical imperative. This is, of course, what Dobrin had hoped to call forth into being in his 2011 *Postcomposition*.

CODA: . . .BUT, IS IT POSTPROCESS OR (PARÉ'S) POST-PROCESS?

In a 2007 online interchange with Alexander Reid, Elizabeth Wardle distinguishes between two forms of post-process: one strongly reminiscent of what

I have been calling *post-process,* the other recognizable as a form of *postprocess.* Though she rejects an association with cultural-studies inflected and/or Freirean post-process pedagogies, she reluctantly admits that her work might be considered post-process, "if we are talking about post-process as recognition of the social and cultural dimensions of writing." As she notes, under such a conception, "activity theorists, genre theorists, etc. would be post process, and so would I." Those two conceptions are, of course, the dominant conceptions of post-/postprocess circulating in the scholarly discourse of U. S. composition and/or writing studies. However, as I demonstrated in Chapter 4, a third conception of post-process exists—a specifically Canadian one outlined by Anthony Paré in a 1994 article, which focuses primarily on the pedagogical methods of Russell Hunt, James Reither, and Douglas Vipond.

As I hope should now be clear, Kent and those three Canadian scholars shared an interactive or transactive vision of textual meaning. They all sought classroom methods that might foreground the role of the reader in constructing meaning. And they arrived at a similar conclusion regarding the viability of first-year writing courses: they ought to be abolished or *very* significantly reimagined. Kent, who taught professional and technical communication courses, could see the merits of WAC and WID courses, and he urged U.S. writing instructors to shift their pedagogical efforts beyond the bounds of first-year composition. The professors from Saint Thomas University did not need to be convinced to do so; their institution did not require—or even offer—generic composition courses.

Even so, the post-process pedagogy formulated by Hunt, Reither, and Vipond differs considerably from Kent's postprocess, paralogic hermeneutic approach. The former three sought to make writing the vehicle for conveying information among all course participants, students and faculty alike—and thus transforming the whole classroom into a discipline-specific-research activity system. In contrast, Kent's model would, in effect, have students ignore one another so as to engage very closely with the instructor in a one-to-one mentorship model.

But, as should now be clear, the post-process pedagogical methods proposed by Hunt, Reither, and Vipond *do* resemble those proposed by other scholars associated with Iowa State, namely David R. Russell and Elizabeth Wardle. In this chapter, I have argued that Russell's and Wardle's approaches might be considered both postprocess and postcomposition, and that they seem to resemble Sidney Dobrin's desire for a postpedagogical writing studies discipline. Here, I want to demonstrate that Wardle's work represents the point of convergence of U. S. postprocess postcomposition and Canadian post-process.

Now, in a limited and obvious sense, the works variously written by Hunt, Reither, and Vipond easily fit into a/the genealogy of postcomposition. Their ideas emerged outside the bounds of composition because composition, narrowly defined as generic, first-year academic writing instruction, did not exist in their Canadian context.

Instead, they oriented their insights about writing instruction toward instructing students in "subject matter" classes. Thus, compared to U. S.-based composition scholars, their attempts to theorize writing were not as constrained by pedagogical and administrative imperatives. Hunt, Reither, and Vipond were, in effect, teaching Writing in the Disciplines courses, or what Hunt preferred to call Writing under the Curriculum courses: "constructing situations for student writers which offer them immersion in the social situations which occasion and use writing . . . and subordinate explicit instruction to the situations where the apprentice writer can best profit from it" ("Afterword" 380).

By Reither's account, for writing courses to succeed, instructors "need to find ways to immerse writing students in academic knowledge/discourse communities so they can write from within those communities," and he notes that WAC, "when it's done well, seems to have a chance of doing that." Within the terms of his argument, doing WAC well entails what we might now call a WID approach: allowing students to "indwell an actual academic knowledge/discourse community, to learn, from the inside, its major questions, its governing assumptions, its language, its research methods, its evidential contexts, its forms, its discourse conventions, its major authors and its major texts—that is, its knowledge and its modes of knowing." Reither affirms that the name of this course wouldn't particularly matter and that "it need not be a writing course" ("Writing and Knowing" 624). Instead, the only real key is that the course involve collaborative investigation (625). So, yes, like Hunt's and Vipond's, as well, Reither's theorizing is not territorialized on or even around first-year composition and, in that relatively trivial sense it is postprocess but also postcomposition.

But, "Writing and Knowing," along with the other texts by Hunt, Reither, and Vipond that I've surveyed, also fits into my genealogy of postcomposition in other ways: citationally, as core texts within a public. Though, of course, alternate genealogies could exist—and I hope that others will eventually write them—I have elected to conclude this chapter's genealogy of postprocess postcomposition with the works of Elizabeth Wardle. The influence of Hunt, Reither, and Vipond and their Inkshed associates sometimes appears in Wardle's (and Downs') research in subtle ways. Although it includes no references to the triumvirate from Saint Thomas, Wardle's "Mutt Genres" article, cites a host of former inkshedders: Patrick Dias, Graham Smart, Andrea Lunsford, and even Paré. When discussing the "Challenges and Critiques" of their pedagogical approach, Downs and Wardle note that *"Few appropriate resources exist for first-year students"*—an issue they later attempted to solve with their own textbook, *Writing about Writing* ("Teaching" 574). However, in a footnote, they acknowledge that "the new book *Conversations about Writing* by Elizabeth Sargent and Cornelia Paraskevas" represents a "partial exception" (579). That text's subtitle is *Eavesdropping, Inskshedding, and Joining In*, and it includes an overview of inkshedding as an instructional method, written by Hunt.

At other times, though, the influence of the Inkshed collective is front-and-center. In their 2007 article introducing a writing about writing approach to first-year composition, Wardle and Downs define writing as "inseparable from content," citing Reither ("Teaching" 555). Then, when they begin to explain the "grounding principles and goals" of their Intro to Writing Studies course, they state, "The first of our shared beliefs corresponds with James Reither's assertion that writing cannot be taught independent of content. It follows that the more an instructor can say about a writing's content, the more she can say about the writing itself; this is another way of saying that writing instructors should be expert readers" (559). Now, this is not merely a reference to Reither, it is a rather direct re-statement of one of his key take-aways: "Academic writing, reading, and inquiry are inseparably linked; and all three are learned not by doing any one alone, but by doing them all at the same time. To 'teach writing' is thus necessarily to ground writing in reading and inquiry" ("Writing and Knowing" 625). Later, after explaining the readings they tend to assign, Downs and Wardle echo Reither once more: "If writing cannot be separated from content, then scholarly writing cannot be separated from reading"—or, Reither might add, from engaging in the (inquiry) activities of the discipline. Indeed, when Downs and Wardle describe the "tightly scaffolded" research assignments their students pursue, they sound quite similar to the collaborative investigation theorized by Hunt, Reither, and Vipond (562–64). Thus, it's somewhat unsurprising when they conclude, "In fact, throughout the course, as students exchange research tales, data, and questions, it is clear that the writing studies pedagogy answers Reither's and Kleine's calls for communities of inquiry" (564).

CHAPTER 6.

AROUND 1986: THE EXTERNALIZATION OF COGNITION AND THE EMERGENCE OF POSTPROCESS INVENTION

At the start of this book, I noted a straightforward historical fact: the scholarly discourse surrounding postprocess has fizzled and perhaps even ended. Yet, I also offered an equally verifiable, if somewhat more contentious claim: even if few scholars discuss postprocess *as such* these days, postprocess tenets and principles have gained widespread assent. They just haven't been called *postprocess*. As I hope to show, the externalist, paralogic view of writing forwarded by postprocess has proven especially influential within the scholarly discourse on rhetorical invention. In tracing out a genealogy of postprocess invention here, I also hope to continue an intellectual project admirably begun by Matthew Heard, Lee-Ann M. Kastman Breuch, Paul Lynch, and Alexander Reid: calling forth postprocess theory's pedagogical implications and applying them to particular acts of writing.

I have emphasized the inherent linguistic indeterminacy of *postprocess* elsewhere, even framing it as a positive feature of the underlying view of language, not a problem to be corrected. Here I would make a related point: one need not understand the meaning of the term in order to apply a postprocess approach. Indeed, as this historical account will illustrate, one need not even possess the term. Rather, many of the most robust contemporary approaches to invention exhibit postprocess tenets—and some of these theoretical systems present direct applications to composition instruction. In justifying this claim, however, I must assume an atypical argumentative stance, identifying two scholarly discourses as theories of postprocess invention, though neither is typically framed as a postprocess theory *or* as a theory of invention. I refer here to ecological and posthuman approaches to composing.

For the sake of clarity, let me note an important distinction regarding my use of the term *ecological*. The chapters in the 2001 collection *Ecocomposition: Theoretical and Pedagogical Approaches* can be categorized according to how they imagine the relationship between ecologies and composition studies. Some chapters present the ecological sciences, environmental activism, and sustainability as fitting subject matter for readings and assignments in "themed" composition courses. In other chapters, ecology becomes a metaphor or model for re-thinking the nature of the writing subject and the emergence of written texts. Marilyn Cooper strenuously advocates the latter conception in her Foreword, as do the collection's editors, Christian R. Weisser and Sidney Dobrin, in their single-authored chapters and co-authored Introduction. According to this understanding, *ecocomposition* might represent "the investigation of the total relations of discourse both to its organic and inorganic environment and to the study of all of the complex interrelationships between the human activity of writing and all of the conditions of the struggle for existence" (Dobrin, "Writing Takes Place" 12–13). For understandable and even charitable reasons, back in 2001 Dobrin and Weisser "resist[ed] . . . to some degree" their own "urge . . . to provide a concrete definition of *ecocomposition*," which might have constrained its meaning to their own preferred usage ("Breaking" 2). However, eventually the costs of conflating the two senses of *ecocomposition* became clear. Thus, at present, Dobrin's own personal website distinguishes between "distinct but overlapping subjects": "ecocriticism and ecocomposition, including questions of oceanic criticism" (i.e., the first definition) and "the ecological properties of writing" (i.e., the second). Here, likewise, I employ *ecological composition* to denote a theory of rhetoric and writing that contemplates the co-constitutive interaction(s) of subjects and their environs.

Throughout this book, I've argued that externalism (which implies paralogy) is the defining trait of postprocess theory and pedagogy. As I'll demonstrate here, the recent history of inventional theory evidences a steady broadening, which I will call an externalization, in its underlying concept of "mind." The vast majority of Process-era inventional schemes presupposed cognitive internalism, the idea that one's mind is separate from other minds and from the world in which those minds exist. In contrast, postprocess approaches—including ecological and posthuman versions—assume an externalist viewpoint: that no cognitive action can occur without the contribution of human and/or non-human others, including languages and various technological artifacts. By describing how externalized minds operate, ecological and posthuman theories help to account for the inventional act or event: how it happens, where it happens, among and with whom it becomes manifest. Each offers a broadened account of human (and, subsequently, non-human) cognition, thereby allowing for a different vision of the writer, the act of writing, and the written text.

To favor an internalist view of invention is often, by implication, to forward a vision of writing in which self-expression and clarity of presentation are paramount; one is a good writer for her ability to translate her own ideas into words and to employ approved grammatical standards. In contrast, complex or networked, postprocess forms of invention allow very different objects to qualify as writing (including things like databases and search engines, or even networks themselves) and advance very different definitions of quality, often favoring rhetorical outcomes over precise meanings (Johnson-Eilola, "Database" 220; Johnson-Eilola and Selber, "Plagiarism" 375). Furthermore, given the current media environment, in which texts blend together in constantly evolving media networks, "fragmentation" and "arrangement," that is, tearing apart and putting (back) together, are becoming increasingly viable forms of creativity. As Johndan Johnson-Eilola notes, quote/unquote "newness" seems less and less relevant with each passing day ("Database" 209–10). In networked spaces, creativity is increasingly becoming "the ability to gather, filter, rearrange, and construct new texts," to (re-)deploy texts within novel contexts, or, as he states elsewhere, "movement, connection, and selection rather than a mythical genius to pull inspiration from within" (*Datacloud* 134, 110).

Throughout this book I've argued that periodization matters—even to such a degree that historians cannot dispense with it, despite the challenges that it may and often does present. In breaking from the received wisdom about postprocess—that the term denotes an approach or mindset—here I suggest that it also refers to a period of compositional thought concerning invention. In *Postmodernism*, Fredric Jameson introduces the notion of the cultural dominant as a means for discussing widespread (though hardly universal) cultural tendencies. He argues that it is "only in the light of some conception of a dominant cultural logic or hegemonic norm that genuine difference could be measured and assessed" (6). In my estimation, since roughly 1986, postprocess has acted as a disciplinary cultural dominant for inventional thought, with its tenets (externalism, the impossibility of generalization, the unteachability of writing as such, etc.) providing the largely unspoken foundation(s) on which a host of divergent theories arise. Taking a cue from Raymond Williams, I assume that theoretical movements and the periods that they define inter-lock and/or overlap, such that, at any given moment, one might be emergent (e.g., postprocess), another dominant (e.g., Process), and still others residual (e.g., current-traditionalism). Following Sharon Crowley, I would date the emergence of Process to "around 1971" and, as I have already suggested, I place the emergence of postprocess—at least within inventional discourse—around 1986 ("Around 1971" 187). I prefer to remain silent concerning dates of dominance and decline as these may be impossible to identify accurately—via textual traces or otherwise. Of course, while dating the emergence of postprocess invention, I would also reaffirm a point made by Richard Young and Maureen Daly Goggin: "Different frames prompt different decisions about boundary markers" (31). In studying any other sub-field, one might arrive at a different periodization schema for postprocess. The other chapters in this text, I would argue, demonstrate as much; I have collected them all here not to unify them but so that they might collide or produce friction.

Although externalist principles were more-or-less absent from inventional scholarship prior to 1986, they're now everywhere—or pretty close to it. In addition to those that I'll focus on in later sections, they arise in the genre-based inventional schemes of Anis Bawarshi, which "extend the sphere of agency in the study and teaching of writing to include not only what writers do when they write, but what happens to writers that makes them do what they do (*Genre* 50; c.f., "Writing Post-Process"). They help guide the improv-oriented pedagogy of Hannah J. Rule (*Situating* 137, 143). They are present in Danielle Koupf's scrap-writing and critical-creative tinkering inventional schemes ("Scrap-Writing"; "Proliferating"). They are evident, as well, in Jacqueline Preston's assemblage-oriented approach, which asks students to conduct "traditional invention activities, such as mapping, brainstorming, and reflecting, but also [to produce] writing that on the surface is not readily identified as invention" ("Project(ing) Literacy" 44). They also inform the model of *distributed invention* that Kara Poe Alexander and Danielle M. Williams theorize as a sub-form of distributed cognition ("DMAC").

By focusing on inventional scholarship in this chapter, I offer one more postmodern *petit recit*—though one that dovetails, oddly enough, with one of the field's modernist grand narratives. In 1962, Elbert W. Harrington would write, "Most teachers know that rhetoric has always lost life and respect to the degree that invention has not had a significant and meaningful role" ("Modern Approach" 373). While I remain agnostic concerning the factual content of Harrington's claim, I would note its fairly widespread endorsement throughout the 1970s and 1980s by Richard E. Young and Alton L. Becker ("Toward a Modern Theory" 453), Janice Lauer ("Heuristics" 396), Lynn Worsham ("Question" 201), and George L. Pullman ("Rhetoric" 369), among others. In short, several (and perhaps many) scholars seem to have seen inventional research as a vital aspect of that newfound discipline, rhetoric and composition, during the years when Process reigned. Even so, as Kelly Pender states, "After the 1980s, compositionists weren't exactly lining up to the answer the question, What is invention?" (66). Pender has not been alone in puzzling over this historical curiosity.

In her 2002 book chapter, "Rhetorical Invention: The Diaspora," Janice M. Lauer points out a somewhat harrowing truth: the 1994 collection *Landmark Essays on Rhetorical Invention* had not included an essay written after 1986. Furthermore, in the years since then, scholarship devoted exclusively to invention had become "difficult to find." Lauer concludes, however, that inventional research had not disappeared but "migrated, entered, settled, and shaped many other areas of theory and practice in rhetoric and composition" (1–2). She also identifies more recent approaches as being "dispersed and localized, precluding any final characterization of a unified theory or common set of practices" (11). I do not intend to argue against Lauer here but instead to offer a parallel account.

While much inventional work did migrate into other areas around 1986, an entirely different strand began to emerge simultaneously—one with externalist instead of internalist presuppositions: a postprocess approach. Or, stated differently: as those researching invention increasingly came to reject internalist models of cognition for more social and ecological ones, a broad "crisis" began to emerge within that branch of Process theory—an event implicitly demonstrating how theoretically crucial internalism had always been. In addition, I would argue, the transition from Process to postprocess would necessarily entail the dispersal that Lauer notes, given that postprocess theories tend to focus on specific applications as opposed to generalized principles, and also a related disavowal—of invention as singular, settled, and resulting from direct human intention.

Because prior inventional theories held a foundational relation to internalism, this new, externalist scholarship was not initially recognized as relevant to invention *as such*. Indeed, it would take quite some time before externalist scholarship was—or perhaps even *could be*—seen as relevant to invention. To offer preliminary support for this claim, I'd like to turn to two articles published by Phillip K. Arrington in our focal year, 1986, as well as a chapter published by Janet M. Atwill in 2002.

Arrington's articles, "Tropes of the Writing Process" and "The Traditions of the Writing Process," both offer philosophically and historiographically sophisticated taxonomies of Process. For our purposes, though, his classificatory frameworks—and even the arguments he derives from them—are less crucial than what they implicitly indicate. In "Tropes" Arrington provides one ostensibly comprehensive taxonomy of Process approaches, defining each according to the master trope on which it relies (metaphor, metonymy, or synecdoche), all while demonstrating each model's implications for invention. In "Traditions" he offers another taxonomy, once again emphasizing inventional implications. And, this time he also illuminates the particular theory of mind underlying each one. Even in the all-too-common Process era tendency to divide "process" from "product," he argues, "Nothing less is at stake . . . than a theory of learning and, consequently, a theory of mind" ("Traditions" 2). Elsewhere, he writes, "Each tradition"—classical rhetoric, empiricism (i.e., cognitivism), and romanticism (i.e., vitalism)—"seeks to give us a model for the mind, for knowing, learning, and, finally, for language" (9). Yet, despite his preoccupations, Arrington does not mention an externalist approach to writing and/or writing instruction in either text.

Of course, one can encounter the limits of a model without yet knowing how to supersede it; many conceptual advances begin first with negative critiques before, eventually, someone advances positive claims toward whatever-comes-next. This phenomenon, I would argue, occurred in the transition toward postprocess invention. Charles Yarnoff's (1980) "Contemporary Theories of Invention in the Rhetorical Tradition" faults the internalism of several common inventional schemes but does not advance an externalist alternative. Notably, within my terminology, that text quite clearly advances a post-process approach to invention, concerned with the social (i.e., economic, political, racialized, gendered, etc.) elements of invention. Similarly, although he is chiefly concerned with discussing internalist inventional schemes, Thomas M. Rivers may himself endorse externalism in his (1982) "A Catalogue of Invention Components and Applications." In that text, Rivers affirms the value of ritual toward invention and indirectly suggests the importance of the writer's ecology (521, 525). He also seems to forward semantic-externalist concepts of invention (523–24).

In any case, here is the up-shot: in early 1986, even a very good scholar like Arrington, focused specifically on invention *and on theories of mind*, could claim to offer a comprehensive account of inventional schemes that did not include any externalist positions. This silence doesn't necessarily *prove* that none existed, of course. But, it does add some credence to two of my claims: first that such scholarship was only then—at that very time—beginning to emerge; second, that externalist scholarship was not initially seen as relevant to invention or offering a theory of invention.

In fairness to Arrington, I should note his objection to an earlier version of this account (i.e., to Lotier, "Around 1986"). He writes,

> Given the trope upon which theories of rhetorical invention
> have for centuries relied—of "hunting" and "finding"—it
> seems more historically accurate to suggest that *invenire* has
> always been an external process to some extent, as were
> the *topoi* rhetors relied on to invent arguments and appeals.
> Those codified *topoi* lay outside a rhetor's mind, as did opin-
> ions, the values and emotions of an audience, and much else,
> though the ability to discern, select, and combine what lay
> outside cannot even now, for all our technological wizardry,
> jettison a discerning human agent to perform these inventive
> acts. ("Most Copious Digression" 563)

I certainly agree that inventional thought has always been "external . . . to some extent." Even so, I would contend that the tropes of *hunting* and *finding* imagine the mind as a self-sufficient entity that can survey the external world without needing to rely upon it. A fully external account of invention would deny the distinction between hunter, hunted, and landscape by presuming that the hunter in question (i.e., the mind) exists only as a function of the other two. Similarly, working from an externalist perspective, I would frame the ability of Arrington's "discerning human agent" *to discern* as a function of language, symbols, and other external objects. To say as much isn't necessarily to "jettison" the human agent altogether but to re-think it nature (and its agency).

If Arrington's scholarship illuminates the (internalist) state of inventional thinking at the dawn of the postprocess period, Atwill's Introduction to *Perspectives on Rhetorical Invention* (2002), the same collection in which Lauer's "Diaspora" chapter appears, demonstrates just how long internalist suppositions would hold sway. By Atwill's accounting, "The very purpose of inventional strategies is to enable practice across rhetorical situations." She also distinguishes between two conceptions of postmodernism, one associated with Stanley Fish and the other with Pierre Bourdieu. Fish's model, she argues, "has been deployed *to challenge invention*," whereas Bourdieu's has *"significantly more to offer* to our understanding of invention" ("Introduction" xvi, emphasis added). Analyzing Atwill's work, John Muckelbauer clarifies the stakes of this distinction: "If invention is conceived as a tool in the process of generating persuasive claims and proofs for particular situations, it tends to be premised on a rather explicit model of consciousness-directed subjectivity [i.e., internalism]. Such an account is apparently irreconcilable" with Fish's version of postmodernism, in which "the subject cannot be bracketed off from contingency and context," that is, in which externalism is pre-supposed (*Future* 27). Ultimately, then, Muckelbauer concludes,

> What is noteworthy . . . is that Fish's approach doesn't appear to be of value [to Atwill] because it forces a humanist approach to question the basic premise of a transcendent subject and representational knowledge. . . . On the other hand, Bourdieu's approach is promising because it allows those basic premises to remain intact. (28)

That is, for Atwill, an internalist, "humanist" (rather than posthumanist) conception of subjectivity is so fundamentally intertwined with invention that challenges to humanist subjectivity are also challenges *to invention itself.*

In what follows, I will argue that externalist (i.e., postprocess) invention research began to emerge around 1986; however, I do not mean to imply that all inventional work became externalized, evidencing postprocess tenets at that time. Rather, this is the date of emergence for the earliest of such works. Indeed, none of the post-1986 works Lauer mentions in her own 2002 survey are ecological, posthuman, or explicitly postprocess in nature. Even so, the dispersed and localized nature of those theories, coupled with their resistance to theoretical generalization bears the marks of postprocess, and I cannot help but note the temporal coincidence of her schema with my own. Furthermore, the transition from Process to postprocess would necessarily entail the dispersal that Lauer notes, given that postprocess theories tend to focus on specific applications as opposed to generalized principles, and also a related disavowal—of invention as singular, settled, and resulting from direct human intention.

Finally, I would forward one more caveat: though my ensuing analysis focuses primarily on the intellectual history of an academic discourse, these theoretical transformations did not transpire in a vacuum, apart from more material, historical shifts. Within the United States and many similarly industrialized Western nations, the post-World War II era witnessed a number of massive transformations. On one hand: the industrial economy faded into the post-industrial, globalized and/or networked one(s). On another hand: the modern regimes of "culture" (that is, poetry, literature, philosophy, architecture, and art, etc.) gave way to the subsequent postmodern and the postpostmodern ones. On a third (prosthetic?) hand: in light of advances in information technologies and their corresponding assimilation into day-to-day practices, the human came to appear ever more obviously as the posthuman (or cyborg)—even if, as Andy Clark argues, humans are "natural born cyborgs" or, as N. Katherine Hayes demonstrates, "We have always been posthuman" (Clark, *Natural Born Cyborgs*; Hayles, *How We Became Posthuman* 291). Though they are importantly separate elements of the same spatial-temporal-technological-cultural-historical ecology, each of the three aforementioned conversions contributed to, supported, and extended the others in complex ways. And, of course, these transformations developed at uneven rates and they were unevenly distributed in physical space. As a result, even if one can easily articulate important distinctions between introspective forms of invention and externalist, ecological, or networked types, one cannot so easily attribute these changes to any single influence or set of influences. That is, insofar as the networked, externalist form of invention draws from and/or employs and/or produces objects designed for circulation and re-deployment rather than engaging in and supporting traditional forms of stable ownership, it is characteristically post-industrial; insofar as it arrives at or becomes instantiated within polyvocal assemblages, collages, and remixes, it is characteristically postmodern; insofar as it employs forms of systems-thinking and distributed cognition, it is characteristically posthuman.

The foregoing paragraph may sound abstract, so let us reduce the scale a bit: changes in compositional theory derive from more than just the intentional acts of composition theorists; they emerge in response to and with assistance from advances and adaptations in the ecology of writing, which is itself active in the productive process. Ecological and posthuman principles have become more central to composition's disciplinary consciousness because changes in the techno-linguistic-intellectual ecology of late-twentieth-century America have afforded novel possibilities for and practices of writing. In their application and use, the personal computer, the search engine, the wiki, and other information technologies have produced major shifts in the concept of invention, making the idea that writing had ever been individualizable seem ever more untenable.

IS THE "EXTENDED MIND" POSTPROCESS?
CAN IT BE(COME) POSTPROCESS?

Before proceeding onward, I want to justify the claim that ecological and post-human visions of writing accord with postprocess. That argument is more easily justified in relation to ecological models. Although postprocess most certainly did not *invent* ecological views of composing, the first three scholars to introduce such views into the discourse of composition studies all fit into the narratives I have told throughout this book. Richard Coe, author of "Eco-Logic for the Composition Classroom" (1975), was a prominent member of the Canadian Inkshed collective that Anthony Paré dubbed *post-process* and which, as I have shown, accords closely with postprocess in several important respects. Throughout the 1980s, Louise Wetherbee Phelps worked to unsettle Process from its status as the field's central metaphor and/or model, all while opposing Cartesian internalism. (For her references to ecologies, see "The Domain of Composition" and Chapter 1 of *Composition as a Human Science*). And, Marilyn Cooper, whom I will discuss more fully in a later section, saw "Thomas Kent's call for a 'postprocess' pedagogy . . . [as] a recognition . . . that composition studies still clings to a mechanistic rather than a systems view of writing" ("Foreword" xii–xiii). Likewise, in their early 2000s scholarship popularizing ecological views of writing, Weisser and Dobrin connected them directly to postprocess (Dobrin, "Writing Takes Place" 12; *Natural Discourse* 47). Scholars applying complex systems theory and/or chaos theory to writing instruction similarly demonstrate inter-connections between ecological and postprocess approaches (Kyburz, "Meaning" 510–11; Mays, "Writing" 560–63; Yood, "History").

To justify my more controversial contention—that posthumanist theories of writing can also be considered postprocess—I will turn to three texts. The first two appear in an indirect interchange in *Beyond Postprocess* (2011) between Thomas Rickert and Collin Gifford Brooke, on one side, and Byron Hawk, on the other. In short, Rickert and Brooke argue that postprocess has been insufficiently attentive to the issues raised by posthumanism and suggest that it cannot be reformulated in a posthuman direction. In contrast, Hawk presents a reimagined (or, in his terms "re-assembled") form of postprocess attentive to posthuman concerns. The third text, a 2012 dissertation written by Jennifer Rae Talbot, also supports the compatibility of postprocess and posthumanism, although Talbot frames their relationship differently than Hawk. By her account, postprocess has cleared the conceptual space within composition and/or writing studies into which posthuman theories could emerge.

If the *Beyond Postprocess* collection has a central preoccupation, it is the relationship between postprocess and technology. To be more specific: contributors Byron Hawk, Jeff Rice, Collin Brooke and Thomas Rickert, Cynthia Haynes, and Raúl Sánchez all fault postprocess for its inattention to technology and/or materiality more generally. Haynes, for instance, notes a historical curiosity: "postprocess pedagogy emerged outside the concurrent introduction of computing technology and interactive (distributed) writing activities that inflected the peak historical moment of process pedagogy" (147–48). That is, one group of scholars began investigating postprocess while another simultaneously began studying computerized/digital/new media writing, but the twain never converged. For Sánchez, both process and postprocess "were conditioned to look past or through the technologies by which writing takes place" (188). A question then arises: would a postprocess that addresses such concerns still be postprocess? In their chapter, Brooke and Rickert answer in the negative. In his, Hawk responds affirmatively.

Brooke and Rickert begin by reiterating a "commonplace": changes in technology produce changes in writing and rhetoric, and perhaps even in "the human being itself." To address such changes in light of digital media, they assert, scholars of writing will need to "reorient" their activities "beyond postprocess," given that "debates between process and postprocess have deflected attention from the material and technological changes that writing is undergoing." In this account, both Process and postprocess hold inexorably humanist underpinnings (163). Although the authors admit that "postprocess theory does open up space for getting beyond humanism," for them "it is hampered in advancing further by its humanist commitments to a linguistically mediated sociality that obscures more basic, even fundamental, relations to technology and materiality" (164).

If the discipline is ever going to address posthuman principles in a rigorous way, they suggest, it will need to move beyond postprocess. Postprocess theory's commitments are too rigid and thus limiting to its future capacity/ies or adaptability. In particular, its further progress is inhibited by its particular notion of hermeneutic interpretation (165–66); its sense that publics are human (166); and even its limited, semantic conception of externalism, which implicitly excludes vehicle externalism—that is, models of the extended mind (167–69). Thus, they state, "Put as directly as possible, in the current postprocess paradigm, there is no room to theorize, much less to begin the questioning that would intimate that the world and its objects are essential to the ability to think, speak, write, make, and act" (169). There is no way to arrive at an ecological or posthumanist or new materialist vision of writing through postprocess, they contend.

If I might interject here, I am skeptical about this line of reasoning. I acknowledge that Brooke and Rickert arrive at their dismissal of postprocess from a separate but parallel intellectual lineage, what has come to be called the Third Sophistic. Thus, they can tenably claim to identify postprocess' conceptual blind spots and limits—and even claim to think thoughts that postprocess has not yet thought. However, postprocess differs from Process-era social constructionism—i.e., it is not just another "social" pedagogy—inasmuch as Kent stridently opposes the idea that "different conceptual frameworks supply us with unique and incommensurate ways of looking at the world" (*Paralogic Rhetoric* 79). Thus, if there is room to theorize posthumanist questions within a non-postprocess scheme, they must also be thinkable within a postprocess one or translatable (in)to it.

Furthermore, I would argue, a theory/method/mindset—however one might define postprocess—can evolve, and many do. Indeed, many are re-shaped, strengthened and enhanced by direct critiques of them. Once postprocess was criticized for failing to evidence posthuman approaches, it faced the opportunity to reformulate itself. Whether or not it would have come to do so is a question that could only be answered in the future (anterior). I find no compelling reason to suggest that postprocess could not be re-articulated to account for the elements that it had to that point ignored. Indeed, even despite their strident criticisms, Brooke and Rickert are forced to acknowledge that "postprocess theory does open up space for getting beyond humanism" (164). Likewise, before discussing "two ideas that . . . quickly and radically move us into fresh territory," they are forced to concede that those very ideas "perhaps hav[e] a few ties to postprocess." The first of these is that "technology, environs, and human being can no longer be conveniently or neatly distinguished" (169). So, even in their own argument, the possibility of a reconfigured postprocess appears and reappears. Rather than focus on what postprocess seems to deny, then, one might dwell on/in what it enables or what it might become.

In his contribution to *Beyond Postprocess*, Hawk offers a rationale for just this sort of reimagining by, in his eponymous phrase, "Reassembling Postprocess" through ecological and posthuman premises. However, as I will use Hawk's work to ground my own re-articulation of postprocess, I feel compelled to acknowledge his sustained ambivalence toward postprocess. Just as 1980s-era cultural studies scholars accused "actually existing communism" of haunting (if not damning) their Marxist ideals, Hawk is ever careful to distinguish actually existing postprocess from "the promise of a postprocess paradigm" ("Reassembling" 81). In *A Counter-History of Composition*, he theorizes a "complex vitalist paradigm" for writing instruction that would offer "a focus on systems, dynamic change, complexity in both physics and the life sciences, an emphasis on situatedness, and an acceptance of the un-conscious or tacit elements of lived experience" (224). When he employs the term *post-process* (always hyphenated) in *Counter-History*, he doesn't differentiate Kent's approach from the one employed by Libby Allison, Lizbeth Bryant, Maureen Hourigan, and the various contributors to *Grading in the Post-Process Classroom*—a work that never really tries to step "beyond" Process. Hawk also argues that Kent's "dialectical approach to the social is still within Berlin's social-epistemic rhetoric"—not something outside of the Process paradigm (221–22). Furthermore, following Diane Davis, Hawk frames Kent's model of communicative interaction as insufficiently paralogic, not attentive enough to the otherness of the other, all of which makes him a "more traditional hermeneut" (222). Likewise, while affirming the efforts of Dobrin and Weisser to "push post-process further toward the concept of ecology," Hawk laments their reliance on expressivist and social-epistemic approaches, which keeps them from "pushing the concept of ecology to its limits" (222–23).

So far as I know, Hawk never heartily endorses postprocess, even as presented by its leading theorists. And yet, in his contribution to *Beyond Postprocess*, he presents a surprising admission. After summarizing a "complex, super-linear sense of process" that might theorize "situatedness [as] more complex than traditional communication triangle models," Hawk notes, "In [*Counter-History*] . . . I call this paradigm 'vitalist' for particular historical reasons, but as a paradigm or assemblage for our particular historical moment, postprocess works just as well" (81–82). There he affirms the possibility of a posthuman, vehicle-externalist postprocess. He credits postprocess with eschewing "universal and individual notions of the writing process," but notes that its vision of writing as a public, interpretive, and situated phenomenon is "still grounded in a humanist tradition." At the same time, though, he acknowledges that "postprocess theorists seem to desire" a way to "break out of traditional notions of the subject and process." So, he offers a posthuman reinscription of Kent's three pillars of postprocess: writing is public; writing is interpretive; and writing is situated. Hawk defines *public* in accordance with a new materialist or object-oriented ontology; *interpretation* as entailing Heideggerian "material embodiment" rather than simply hermeneutic guessing; and *situation* in line with a "Deleuzian ontology of assemblage" (75, 77). By rethinking postprocess in light of this "new constellation of concepts," he aims to "reground postprocess in a posthuman model of networks to ultimately argue that the subject of writing is the network that inscribes the subject as the subject scribes the network" (75).

Quite crucially, Hawk frames his effort as a "rearticulation of [Kent's] humanist position within the kinds of posthuman worlds rhetors inhabit today" and not as an argument with Kent. Or, as he affirms later, "This approach isn't a refutation of Kent's model of postprocess but an extension of his position beyond the limits of his passing hermeneutical theory." For Hawk, Kent's work "sets the conditions for these possible futures within our field." Other scholars might—and, I would venture, should— "continually reassemble it and see what future lines of thought and expression it makes possible in every new assemblage" (92). That postprocess had not (yet) been posthuman is not to say that it could not be(come) posthuman. Indeed, when one encounters an old text, one never encounters it in its original milieu but instead invariably opens up new textual possibilities. That is, "Rhetors can't go back to Heidegger and have him be the Heidegger of the 1920s or 1930s. It will always be Heidegger in this moment, in this gathered assemblage." And what is true of Heidegger is equally true of Kent and of postprocess: when, in 2011, "someone [say, Byron Hawk] writes about Kent circa 1999, it is no longer a Kent of the twentieth century, but, in this case, a Kent-Deleuze-Heidegger-Latour of this moment, in this edited collection, assembled with these other articles authors around postprocess and its matters of concern" (92). Of course, as I hope the reader will recognize, the transactive, reader-oriented and historically situated conception of textual meaning advocated by Hawk is characteristically postprocess.

While I think that Hawk's argument, on its own, offers a solid basis for considering posthuman visions of writing to be postprocess, I would like to turn to one other text connecting the conceptual constellations: Jennifer Rae Talbot's 2012 dissertation at Purdue University, *Re-Articulating Postprocess: Affect, Neuroscience, and Institutional Discourse.* (As an interesting historical footnote: Rickert was one of the co-chairs of Talbot's dissertation committee, alongside Jennifer Bay.) In that text, as I have here, Talbot sidesteps difficulties posed by the "diversity of definitions, applications, and implications that have emerged under the term [*postprocess*]" (2). For her, the ambiguity of the term's meaning(s) need not be a problem. Rather, she argues, "Growing ambiguity suggests that a theoretical term is actually doing important work to accommodate shifts in situation, and working through concepts and definitions in a complex and nuanced way" (154–55). And, furthermore, in a fascinating argument, she credits "the very contentiousness of the term" *postprocess* with "grant[ing] it the disciplinary traction" that it would need in order to endure (156). If the term had been more easily dismissed—or less obviously offensive (in both senses: violent and outrageous)—it might not have endured long enough to achieve its ultimate function.

For Talbot, "postprocess theory is most productively considered as a placeholder term within which a shift from humanist to posthumanist theories about writing continues to develop" (vi). Following Kent, she sees postprocess as an effort to "incorporat[e] a post-Cartesian subjectivity into rhetoric and composition." But, because postprocess "is part of a broader cultural shift that is still taking place"—an incomplete and ongoing project—its meanings and associations cannot help but evolve, as well (2). Two key points emerge here. First, by Talbot's account, the status of *postprocess* as a placeholder "does not at all mean that the term is empty—rather, it is [a] term that marks the space for something to become" (128). Second, Talbot follows the editors of *Beyond Postprocess*, who had also seen *postprocess* as a placeholder, rather than a signifier attached to an "easily defined moment or codifiable method." However, whereas they had simply indicated that postprocess would open onto "something beyond," Talbot identifies a conceptual destination: posthumanism (Dobrin, Rice, and Vastola 2).

Talbot explains the evolution of postprocess, as well as its relationship to Process in provocative and engaging ways. Just as I have distinguished between (social turn) post-process and (paralogic, externalist) postprocess, Talbot also identifies stages in the development of postprocess. In particular, she suggests that "notions of subjectivity are growing more complex through the progression from the social turn into postprocess" (123). In other words, she sees "social constructivism as a kind of proto-postprocess" inasmuch as it "broadens the conception of the writing subject to include social factors (21–22). Even while separating postprocess out from other "social" approaches, however, Talbot still frames postprocess as a "'complex extension' of process theory that is *still in progress*" (13).

For Talbot, much like Brooke and Rickert, Kent "makes an explicit but still insufficient move away from the Cartesian subject." In her estimation, though, the problem is not so much that he disregards technology as that he disregards embodiment and affect (14). In particular, his version of triangulation (and, I would add, the *principle* of charity) is too reliant on "conceptual and linguistic models" that are "abstract and disembodied" (30). Even so, in a later text drawing from her dissertation research, Talbot concedes, "Each iteration of postprocess theory has more deeply integrated the role of affect and the body into the construction of the writing subject, and has more widely distributed the component elements of cognition" ("Pedagogy" 165). And so, Talbot ultimately lays postprocess theory "*alongside* developments in neuroscience, regarding each as an iteration of a broader cultural and philosophical shift" toward posthumanism, "or, more specifically, a shift from a situation model to an ecology of assemblage model" (155).

Throughout this book, I have labored to apply a consistent, clear, and simple definition of postprocess as an externalist, paralogic view of writing. Of course, externalism can take multiple forms, and I have focused on two: semantic externalism, which can account for the "what" of mental states, and vehicle externalism, which better accounts for the "how" of mental states. Without question, when Reed Way Dasenbrock, Russell Hunt, Thomas Kent, David R. Russell, and the scholars I will discuss in the next section began "externalizing" composition scholarship, they primarily worked from semantic externalist principles. Still, in my estimation, their views are compatible with models of the vehicle externalism, colloquially known as the "extended mind." To give but one example: Kent is more attentive to physical matter than he is often credited with being. Explaining the nature of externalism, he writes, "No split exists between our minds and the minds of others and objects in a shared world," and he criticizes Stanley Fish's view of interpretive communities because it "cannot account for objects in the world or the minds of others" (*Paralogic Rhetoric* 92, 79).

Furthermore, as Hawk and Talbot demonstrate, and as Rickert and Brooke reluctantly concede, early postprocess theories seem to call out for more and more fully externalist perspectives. Indeed, as Marilyn Cooper has admitted, scholars had to "struggle to see relationships as primary, rather than focusing on—especially on—the human actors relating to human and nonhuman others, and even harder to see writing as part of a whole, interrelated, ceaselessly changing environment" ("Foreword" xiv). Arriving at conclusions that may now seem obvious was far from easy; doing so required considerable, sustained, collective effort. Ultimately, I agree with Talbot's argument: semantic externalist (postprocess) arguments helped prepare a space in which subsequent vehicle externalist (but still postprocess) ones could be accepted. And, I would also affirm Hawk's central claim: the core tenets of postprocess can be reconfigured to be(come) posthuman. Therefore, I believe assimilating ecological and posthuman theories of composition into the rubric of postprocess does justice to all three distinct discourses.

How Invention Became Postprocess: The Gradual Acceptance of Externalism

In this section, I examine early externalist works to construct a genealogy of contemporary inventional theories. In the process, I hope the reader may note the degree to which disciplinary "common sense" has shifted during the last thirty years. While the externalism advocated in early works once had to be justified strenuously, many current texts simply presuppose it.

The first major wave of scholarship on externalist composition began in October 1985 with Reither's "Writing and Knowing," which carries the subtitle "Toward Redefining the Writing Process." In that text, Reither demonstrates the inter-animating and co-constitutive roles of writing and its context, noting, "Writing is not merely a process that occurs within contexts. That is, writing and what writers do during writing cannot be artificially separated from the social-rhetorical situations in which writing gets done, from the conditions that enable writers to do what they do, and from the motives writers have for doing what they do." And, furthermore, he contends, "Writing is, in fact, one of those processes which, in its use, *creates* and *constitutes* its own contexts" (621).

Reither concedes that Process research "has taught us so much." But, given this strength, it has also "bewitched and beguiled" scholars into accepting a "truncated view" of writing as "a self-contained process," one which "begins naturally and properly with probing the contents of the memory and the mind" (622). In contrast, Reither notably identifies writing as "a more multi-dimensioned process" than had been commonly imagined. He also asserts that the process in question "begins long before it is appropriate to commence working with strategies of invention"—thereby identifying a conceptual lack in prior inventional schemes. He therefore encourages other scholars to develop a different theory of process, one operating at a different scale. He states, "The 'micro-theory' of process now current in composition studies needs to be expanded into a 'macro-theory' encompassing activities, processes, and kinds of knowing that come into play long before the impulse to write is even possible" (623).

In "Writing and Knowing," Reither focuses primarily on the classroom utility of his preferred pedagogical method, collaborative investigation, and only briefly gestures toward an externalist vision of invention. In contrast, his presentation at CCCC 1986, "Academic Discourse Communities, Invention, and Learning to Write" directly critiques the dominant inventional theories of the time. According to Reither, "If the current textbook advice of our discipline reflects up-to-date belief, compositionists appear to view invention as a strictly private, individual, cognitive act rather than a socio-cognitive, intersubjective act" (9). Throughout the course of that presentation, though, Reither examines the "reciprocal" relationship between two primary "levels" of academic discourse communities, the workshop and the discipline. By his estimation, the discipline "*authorises* the activities of the workshop, and in so doing both *drives* and *constrains* it"; in contrast, the workshop "*feeds* and *shapes* the discipline" (4–5). That is, the established knowledge base and acceptable research methods of a discipline dictate what can be studied and what can be said about those objects of inquiry. But, what individual researchers identify in their research and argue in their scholarship can, of course, re-shape what is known and accepted by the collective body of scholars in the discipline. Thus, the *workshop* and *discipline* are not places but rather "rhetorical situations or states of mind," defined primarily by "what disciplinary activity [the scholar] is engaged in at the moment"—whether they are evaluating the ongoing conversation or attempting to enter into it (7).

In recognizing the reciprocal relation between discipline and workshop, Reither is forced toward a conclusion regarding invention: workshop writers "get [their] information, ideas, [and] arguments . . . interactively, out of [their] transactions with knowledgeable peers and superiors in our workshops and in the discipline's literature. We do not—we cannot—get them in circumstance of conversational dissociation from others" (9). He offers an externalist vision of cognition by quoting from Clifford Geertz, who suggests that human thought amounts to "a traffic in what have been called . . . significant symbols—words for the most part but also gestures, drawings, musical sounds, mechanical devices . . . or natural objects" and, furthermore, "from the point of view of any particular individual, such symbols are largely given." One's cognitive apparatus draws from an array of external objects and symbols that one neither creates nor controls, and so "thinking is always thinking *in terms of* and *in relation to* others' thinking" (11). And, working from these premises, Reither affirms, "Invention cannot be a strictly private act"; it "cannot occur in a social vacuum" (10–11).

James E. Porter would also publish an externalist-leaning inventional theory in his 1986 "Intertextuality and the Discourse Community." Porter argues directly against those who would "teach writing only as the act of 'bringing out what is within,'" contending that to do so is to "risk undermining our own efforts" (42). Notably, he borrows the phrase "bringing out what is within" from David Bartholomae, and thus the obvious reading of that phrase in its "original source" would seem to be as a critique of expressivism. However, I think that Porter aims at something more ambitious: a critique of the internalism on which expressivism (typically) relies. Throughout his article, he demonstrates the interdependency of all texts, insofar as none can exist without precursors, nor can readers understand texts without background knowledge. He also privileges the role of situation and audience in expression, arguing, "In essence, readers, not writers, create discourse" ("Intertextuality" 34, 38). Even so, Porter is careful to avoid an (and perhaps *the*) "extreme" interpretation of post-structuralist thought: that the author is so thoroughly constrained by external factors that she or he has no remaining agency. He acknowledges that writers "are constrained insofar as we must inevitably borrow the traces, codes, and signs which we inherit and which our discourse community imposes." But, in the next breath, he also foregrounds the role of the author: "We are free insofar as we do what we can to encounter and learn new codes, to intertwine codes in new ways, and to expand our semiotic potential" (41).

In 1987 Karen Burke LeFevre would offer the most detailed and explicit analysis of socially conceived invention to date—both then and now. In the first "body" chapter of *Invention as a Social Act*, LeFevre enumerates the features of the conventional, Platonic (i.e., introspective) vision of invention. Then, in the following one, she explains what it means to conceive of writing in three other ways: as social; as dialectical, in the sense that the individual and the social collective are "coexisting and mutually defining"; and as an act. She identifies the first canon as both a finding and a making of subject matter and further asserts: "Invention . . . is, I think, best understood as occurring when individuals interact dialectically with socioculture in a distinctive way to generate something (2, 33). LeFevre places a concerted emphasis on the multiplicity of human actors within the inventional schema and exhibits comfortability with open-ended indeterminacy. In her model, one aims to generate "something," though its nature remains unclear and possibly unknowable.

Given the increased complexity LeFevre attributes to it, invention no longer appears as an appropriate task for a single writer. It necessarily becomes an act in which individuals commune—either mediated by texts or more directly, through dialogue. Subsequent scholars would identify even LeFevre's model of invention as too narrow—particularly for its anthrocentrism and its privileging of conscious intention over contingency and accident. However, her work nonetheless marks an important transformation in the discipline: the last gasps of one paradigm and the birth of another.

LeFevre's vision of the social appears to have derived from (internalist) collaborative learning scholars (121), but she herself points toward the next major development in inventional research—an (externalist) ecological understanding. In her conclusion, she writes, "We should study the ecology of invention— the ways ideas arise and are nurtured or hindered by interaction with social context and culture" (126). Subsequent scholars likely would not have arrived at (or, at the very least, accepted) these more complex conceptions of invention without first extending the definition one crucial removal—from the individual to the group.

LeFevre's turn toward an ecological approach occurs both hastily and very late in her text; in contrast, in her 1986 "The Ecology of Writing," Marilyn Cooper would investigate the ecological components of composing in a much more extensive and rigorous fashion. And, insofar as her ecological model explains where ideas come from, it is a theory of invention at its core. She begins her foundational article, "The Ecology of Writing," by asserting that "the time has come for some assessment of the benefits and limitations of thinking of writing as essentially—and simply—a cognitive process" (364). While she acknowledges the "undoubtedly beneficial changes" brought forth by cognitive models, she immediately criticizes them for "blind[ing] us to some aspects of the phenomena we are studying." The problem, she argues, "has nothing to do with [the model's] specifics." Instead, the problem with cognitivism is "the belief on which it is based—that writing is thinking, and, thus, essentially a cognitive process." This viewpoint "obscures many aspects of writing we have come to see as not peripheral" (365). Her work would, then, attempt to illuminate (or, un-obscure) the nature and functions of those non-peripheral but conventionally ignored elements. More precisely, she opposes depictions of the author as isolated and/ or solitary, working "within the privacy of his own mind" (365). Cooper asserts, instead, that the primary tools of thought—languages and texts—are themselves socially constituted (or what Bakhtin would call dialogic): words carry with them the traces of their prior application. No one can have an idea without relying upon, extending, or contending with the thoughts and ideas of others (369). Cognition is, in short, inherently and inexorably distributed. Therefore, she reasons, "Language and texts are not simply the means by which individuals discover and communicate information, but are essentially social activities, dependent on social structures and processes not only in their interpretive *but also in their constructive phases*" (366, emphasis added). Invention, too, has social elements. Writing does not *become* social in being shared; it is (to bring back a term from the 1980s) always already social: "Ideas result from contact. . . . Ideas are also always continuations. . . . In fact, an individual impulse or need"—to write, for instance, "only becomes a purpose when it is recognized as such by others" (369).

The term *social* does appear frequently within Cooper's text, and, as I've discussed in this book's Introduction, her work was somewhat unsurprisingly filtered into the scholarly conversations on social constructionism and discourse communities. It's worth pausing, then, to explain briefly what Cooper seems to have seen as the major implications of her work. While she admits an apparent similarity between an ecological conception of writing and what was then called a contextual approach, she carefully delineates their distinctions. Contextual models, she suggests, "abstract writing from the social context in much the way that the cognitive process model does," treating a given context as though it were "unique, unconnected with other situations" (367). While contextual models, like the Burkean pentad, may be useful for categorizing situational elements, they are less useful for demonstrating the causal relations between situations. "In contrast," she argues, "an ecology of writing encompasses much more than the individual writer and her immediate context" (368).

An ecologist explores how writers interact to form systems: all the characteristics of any individual writer or piece of writing both determine and are determined by the characteristics of all other writers and writings in the system." And, furthermore, an ecological model sees all of these elements as being "inherently dynamic." While these "dynamic interlocking systems" may pre-exist a particular act of writing, they "are not given, not limitations on writers; instead they are made and remade by writers in the act of writing" (368). And, Cooper writes in a forceful, concise sentence, "Furthermore, the systems are concrete." That is, stated differently, "they are not postulated mental entities, not generalizations" (369). They have physical presence. One can point to (at least some) of their elements or aspects. Ultimately, Cooper wishes to reconceive both the writer and writing itself. In place of the cognitivist "solitary author," the ecological model would project "an infinitely extended group of people who interact through writing, who are connected by the various systems that constitute the activity of writing." And, in place of the cognitivist view of writing "simply [as] a way of thinking," it would posit writing as "more fundamentally a way of acting" (374).

Ecological theories figure invention less as a bringing forth of resources out of oneself (the individualistic, internalist definition) or even out of a group of people (the social or collaborative view) but imagine the canon's functions more rhizomatically. That is, ecological theorists ask which resources can be connected to the self, either ephemerally or indefinitely, in order to produce some sort of novel item, to assemble a set of pre-existing items for alternate usage, or even to rearticulate a given object in wholesale fashion for an alternate purpose. The resources that one might employ are practically limitless, they assert, and the writing process functions best when one acknowledges and responds to the indefinitely many affordances and constraints that existence accords her. As a result, a common trope of recent scholarship is that one's historical predecessors did not externalize their theories *enough*. Expressivists were purportedly too concerned with the self; collaborative learning enthusiasts and even early ecological thinkers were purportedly too concerned with human actors (c.f., Syverson, *Wealth* 24, criticizing Cooper); though relying on complexity theory some other ecological theorists didn't make their works complex enough (c.f., Hawk, "Toward a Rhetoric" 846, criticizing Syverson); and some depictions of ecology fail to trouble the subject-object distinction adequately and to recognize the role of attention in determining the salience of ecological factors (Rickert, *Ambient Rhetoric* xi–xii).

While attending to situated, contingent variables, ecological composition also posits uncertainty and precarity as both inputs and outputs of the writing process. In Mark C. Taylor's words, "The moment of writing is a moment of complexity"; it is comprised of an indeterminate number of connected parts, some of which act sequentially while others act in parallel fashion. Most importantly, the self-organization and interaction of parts within complex networks produce effects which "are not necessarily reducible to the interactivity of the components or elements in the system" (198, 172). That is, because it is complex, one cannot predict the outcome of writing by assessing or measuring ingredients as one would when baking a cake; the process is substantially more chaotic. No process can guarantee the production of a given, desired result. In this light, the postprocess mantra that writing cannot be taught but can be learned—each time, anew—is more readily understandable (c.f., Olson, "Why Distrust" 426; Kent, "Principled Pedagogy" 432).

Ecological composition and posthumanism are similarly indebted to methods of systems-thinking, especially cybernetics, and the distinction between their approaches is largely a difference in emphasis, with the latter studying the body itself more closely and privileging the role of technology more heavily. Many of the best ecological thinkers hardly discuss IT; for instance, the word *technology* does not appear in Cooper's text at all. In contrast, one's relation to technology is the primary philosophical question posed by certain posthumanists. As N. Katherine Hayles notes, "The posthuman implies not only a coupling with intelligent machines but a coupling so intense and multifaceted that it is no longer possible to distinguish meaningfully between the biological organism and the informational circuits in which the organism is embedded" (35). But, of course, any spectrum has an indefinite number of middle points. Thus, one should not be surprised when Collin Gifford Brooke frames his efforts in *Lingua Fracta* as an effort to "reimagine the [rhetorical] canons ecologically and technologically" (28). Likewise, at the end of *The Wealth of Reality* (subtitled *An Ecology of Composition*), Syverson notes, "The understanding we gain from studying composing situations as complex ecological systems should help us as we consider the changes wrought by new technologies" (*Wealth* 205). For her, after all, a complex writing ecology would include, at minimum, five inexorably interconnected dimensions: the temporal, the spatial, the psychological, the social, and the physical-material—which includes technology (18–22).

Both models, ecology and posthumanism, base their arguments concerning writing on a conception of mind: cognition as a necessarily plural act (or response, or interaction), accomplished by an indefinite number of human and non-human actors that have become localized and functional in collaborative effort. As even the name of the field, posthumanism, suggests, to imagine thought in this way is, to a very large degree, to reconceptualize the nature of personhood, such that many of the most common phrases no longer seem apt. One is not simply a subject but also an object, both actor and acted upon; nor is the subject/object simply or solely human, given its what-externalism and sometimes literal incorporation of technological artifacts (e.g., pacemakers, anti-depressants, or even headache medications). Posthumanism, like ecology, is a disavowal of boundaries, and John Muckelbauer and Debra Hawhee therefore define it as "an attempt to engage humans as distributed processes rather than as discrete entities" (768). Via the topoi or "places," inventional theories hold a long-standing relationship to spatiality, but when humans link up with connected informational devices, and especially when they enter into and/or co-construct cyberspace, they encounter immaterial environments with "the potential for a complete reimagining of invention," ones that are, as Jeff Rice notes, "layered, confusing, and constantly changing" ("Networked Boxes" 305). Through a form of wired (or, increasingly, wireless) how-externalism, the mind traverses an indefinite number of informational circuits more or less simultaneously and conducts complicated operations with previously unthinkable rapidity. One cannot generalize about how ideas emerge in such contexts, except to say that their origins extend outside the writer's own skull.

EXTERNALIST INVENTION IN PRACTICE: RIP-MIX-BURN AND ASSEMBLAGE

Ecological and posthuman theories of composing are not theories of the first canon so much as theories involving or affecting it. One would be more accurate in calling them theories of the (necessarily plural) inventing actors or actants. Much like other branches of postprocess theory, neither offers much in the way of positive approaches to creation or discovery; they are post-pedagogical in that their tenets seem to deny the possibility of universal or even generalizable directives. Because they value connectedness and relationality so seriously and thereby deny the autonomy of the mind, neither asserts that one inventional success can serve as precedent for any other. Put simply, the conditions enabling a given invention will never emerge again in precisely the same form. By Brooke's estimate, though, the value of ecology lies precisely in "its ability to focus our attention on a temporarily finite set of practices, ideas, and interactions" without concerning itself with their stability or recurrence (*Lingua Fracta* 42). A given method or pedagogy is not transferable or portable to other contexts; kairos reigns. Yet, kairos, now understood as a spatio-temporal situation in which a rhetor is enmeshed and from which her or his actions cannot be isolated, does not negate the art of invention but instead serves as its ground (Rickert, *Ambient Rhetoric* 77–78, 82; Hawk, "Post-Technê" 381). Stated more directly: kairos enables invention; invention does not find or encounter or stumble into kairos. Of course, from an externalist perspective, every inventional act is caught up in its own surroundings by default, inasmuch as no mind can think in isolation. Figuring invention as a combination of "consciously taught elements" (e.g., topoi, pre-writing) and responsiveness, Hawk therefore contends that one must engage in "continual, situated invention—that is, remaking techniques for every new situation." If one could articulate a postprocess model for invention, it would be this: new each time, constantly evolving in response to situational constraints ("Post Technê" 388–89).

Postprocess theory has earned a reputation for being abstract, vague, inapplicable—even nihilistic in disavowing the writer as subject of the writing act.

And, of course, such views are not necessarily unfair. Even its defenders have been forced to concede, as Breuch does, that postprocess theory suggests few "concrete assignments or classroom environments" (127). To many compositionists, especially those favoring certainty and mastery, a command of conventions and rules, the theoretical advances offered by ecological and posthuman accounts may seem to present theoretical surrender or decline. But, I want to argue the opposite: the greatest contribution of these models may be their "revaluing of partiality" (Brooke, "Forgetting" 791). Inventions (both rhetorical and otherwise) reconfigure the nature of existence, and in so doing change what one might imagine or expect. Francis Bacon, the English statesman, scoundrel, and scholar (not to be confused with the twentieth century painter of the same name) states this matter well: "*Ars inveniendi adolescit cum inventis*," that is, the art of invention grows with inventions (741). Taking for granted its situated status and provisional nature, an acknowledgement that one cannot control the inventional process, then, seems to me a more intellectually honest approach. In foregrounding contingency, profound uncertainty, randomness, and openness, and in learning how to enable, channel, or direct forces beyond one's direct control, the writer allows herself to be re-written, re-wired, re-paired.

The preceding pages seem to suggest that the art of invention is dead while the practice—and, even more importantly, the experience—of invention is alive and well. The latter parts are certainly true, but the former is not necessarily. Postprocess approaches do not deny the utility of pre-writing, or heuristics, or the Burkean pentad but provide a more complex appraisal of their operations and a more robust framework for their application in particular instances. And, furthermore, models for posthuman and/or ecological invention already exist. Believing that digitally networked writing ecologies are here to stay, I would like to focus on two promising, contemporary approaches to invention that might serve as examples for future inventional innovations: Alex Reid's rip-mix-burn approach, which draws heavily from Gregory L. Ulmer's prior theorizing, especially his 2003 textbook, *Internet Invention*; and Johnson-Eilola and Stuart Selber's notion of the assemblage. Since each approach presupposes externalism and relies upon ecological and/or technological affordances, neither can present universal prescriptions for pedagogy. Even so, each illustrates the applications of an inventional theory attuned to its environs.

While introducing the un-hyphenated term *postprocess* in her 1994 book *Literacy, Ideology, and Dialogue*, Irene Ward notes, "Recently, several compositionists have challenged the process paradigm, attempting to institute a postprocess, postmodern pedagogy" (129). More specifically, Ward refers to Gregory L. Ulmer, William A. Covino, and Kent. In a subsequent sentence, though, Ward designates Ulmer and Covino as being *postmodern* scholars and singles out Kent as the *postprocess* one. I believe that Ulmer's work also deserves the latter appellation, though. Because his theorizing attends so carefully and commonly to invention, now seems an appropriate time to turn to it.

Ulmer primarily derives his principles from French post-structuralist philosophy, especially the works of Roland Barthes and Jacques Derrida, and so the particular lexicon he employs differs considerably from Kent's Anglo-American analytic one. Even so, his work clearly presumes an externalist conception of mind and denies that writing arises primarily from directed, intentional, conscious action (and thus that it can be taught, at least as *teaching* is typically conceived). Thus, it can and should be considered postprocess, according to the stipulative definition I am applying. His thinking on invention also directly aligns with my analysis in this chapter. In his 2003 textbook, *Internet Invention*, Ulmer explicitly states, "Invention is an ecological process" (27).

Postprocess and/or postprocess-compatible tenets form the groundwork of Ulmer's two primary inventional schemes, *heuretics* and *choragraphy*, which have been variously applied by a host of subsequent scholars, including Caddie Alford ("Creating"), Sarah J. Arroyo (*Participatory Composition*), Hawk ("Hyperrhetoric"), Michael Jarrett (*Drifting on a Read*), Jeff Rice (*The Rhetoric of Cool*), Rickert ("Toward the Chōra), and Madison Percy Jones ("Writing Conditions"). Ulmer's persistent efforts to rethink traditional (or classical) rhetorical theories for the age of electronic media (or what he has called the *electrate*, as opposed to the literate, apparatus) have also informed Brooke's work in *Lingua Fracta: Toward a Rhetoric of New Media*, most notably his theorizing of a *proairetic* approach to invention (which I examined in Lotier, "Around 1986" 375–76).

In simple terms, heuretics is a specific approach to reading, which differs considerably from the more common hermeneutic approach. As Ulmer points out, hermeneutic interpretation is oriented toward answering the question, "What might be the meaning of an existing work?" In contrast, heuretic invention asks, "Based on a given theory, how might *another* text be composed?" (Ulmer, *Heuretics* 5). Thus, in the words of Michael Jarrett, it "push[es] reading (consumption) so far and so hard that it [becomes] writing (production)" ("Elvis" 144). In many respects, heuretics resembles what Muckelbauer has elsewhere called "productive reading," a "style of engagement . . . [that] reads in order to produce different ideas, to develop possible solutions to contemporary problems, or, as importantly, to move through contemporary problems in an attempt to develop new questions ("On Reading" 73–74). As Muckelbauer points out, scholars demonstrate a (largely unexamined) tendency to refer to interpretive or critical texts as "readings" of prior works. Thus, he concludes, "Although reading and writing are different activities, common usage demonstrates that this difference is not reducible to the logic of consumption (reading) versus production (writing)." Rather, quite importantly, "the former practice [reading] is inventive while the latter [i.e., writing] is not an invention ex nihilo" (93).

Ulmer acknowledges the medieval origins of heuretics; it is a mode of reading as well suited toward scribal or print-based texts as electronic ones. However, he frames chorography "specifically [as] an *electronic* rhetoric" (*Heuretics* 34). It follows the "associational," linking logic of digital texts by playing upon the materiality of language. For instance, one of its characteristic tactics involves employing all the various meanings of a word, rather than selecting just one of them. In other words, it uses puns as though they were hyperlinks (34, 48). A chorographic author thus "has a different relationship to language and discourse," as compared to conventional conceptions; "it is that neither of writer nor reader but of 'active receiver'" (38).

While Ulmer occasionally pauses to consider the conceptual underpinnings of his models, his texts are often more literary and/or performative than they are explanatory; he aims to invent an electronic rhetoric by applying its principles, instead of merely contemplating what they might entail. Theorists working from his tenets have demonstrated their externalism in direct terms, though. Jarrett, for example, demonstrates that terms and concepts (what Ulmer calls "premises," while noting the pun of terrain and argumentative logic also present in the Greek *topoi*) offer the materials that we "reason with, and through." And, from Jarrett's perspective, Ulmer's chief insight is that "only by making [our premises] explicit, by putting our premises into the writing apparatus and thus external to our minds"—or, I would suggest, within the extended purview of our externalized minds—"can we perceive how they function" ("Elvis" 244). In Rickert's words, chorographic models "attribute inventional agency to non-human actors such as language, networks, environments, and databases" and thus "transform our sense of what is available . . . as a means for rhetorical generation" ("Towards the Chōra" 253). As I've previously noted, Rickert himself might not characterize choric inventional schemes as *postprocess*. But, they are quite clearly externalist—and thus postprocess according to my own classificatory scheme. They deny the existence of a "clear demarcation of 'in here' and 'out there'"—that is, a separation between mind and world—and demonstrate that invention does not result from "following a method, in some linear sense, but [from] being immersed in, negotiating, and harnessing complex ecologies of systems and information" ("253).

Before proceeding onward, I would like to focus on one last application of Ulmer's inventional thinking, the rip-mix-burn approach that Alexander Reid theorizes in *The Two Virtuals* (2007). For what it's worth, Reid credits Ulmer with having (pre-emptively) applied his rip-mix-burn approach in *Internet Invention*. But, because it is more a perspective on cognition and invention than an inventional approach or method *per se*, I would separate it out from both heuretics and chorography.

In my estimation, Reid's work represents the earliest fully articulated approach to vehicle-externalist composition pedagogy, one that "account[s] for the radical exteriorization of the subject" and "the rhizomatic distribution of the compositional process" (*Two Virtuals* 24). He does not, however, categorize it as *postprocess*, and he actively rejects calling it *post-process*, for entirely reasonable reasons. In a 2007 blog entry, Reid acknowledges "many varieties of post-process composition," which represent "the various ways that rhet/comp scholars have moved beyond, built upon, and/or rejected the dominant writing process school of thought." However, he specifies that, for him, "post-process is a recognition of the social and cultural dimensions of writing." It draws from "Berlin's social-epistemic rhetoric," which is "strongly Marxist," and also "represents the impact of Foucault and cultural studies on our understanding of the role of ideology/power in discourse and representation." This definition, I would note, accords very closely with my own usage of the term to denote the "leftwing trajectory of the social turn." While Reid acknowledges that his own scholarship is "post-process in the sense that I continue to teach writing by asking students to study writing, both the object and the practice," he also places himself outside of that category. Indeed, even more strongly, he states, "I'm thinking about writing in a way that's really not even in a category of composition theory as far as I know" ("[post-] post-process composition"). That assessment may strike some readers as hyperbolic. I myself find it fair and tenable. Hawk's efforts to re-articulate a vehicle-externalist definition of postprocess, which has informed my own thinking about what is and is not postprocess, was published four years later. In 2007, so far as I know, there really *wasn't* a term for what Reid was doing. I am applying my own label to it retro-actively.

As I've previously mentioned, Reid doesn't present rip-mix-burn as an approach to invention; like posthumanism and ecological composition, it's really more of a broad theoretical disposition with ramifications for (what used to be called) *invention*. As Reid is forced to concede, it represents an "approach to composition in which one can articulate a process, replete with mechanisms, but do so without reducing writing to a discrete set of practices. That is, unlike invention, arrangement, and revision, ripping, mixing, and burning are not steps, not even recursive steps" (*Two Virtuals* 143). Some readers will no doubt recognize, *ripping, mixing,* and *burning* as the terms used to describe a specific, nebulously legal but commonplace early 2000s process: taking music from one physical manifestation, such as a legitimately purchased compact disk (ripping); arranging various ripped songs into a specified order (mixing); and then moving the new collection of tracks to another, specially purchased, "burnable" CD (burning). Taking these terms from their original, narrow meanings and applying them to "composition in a broader sense," Reid writes,

> *Ripping* describes the practice of pulling on informational resources whether they are sensed, remembered, or from some pre-existing media; *mixing* then describes the process by which this ripped data connects in a rhizomatic network where each new connection holds the potential for unexpected mutation; finally, by *burning* the composition, the mixture of data becomes compressed into a material form that can be communicated across a network. In this way, the process can begin anew. (18)

From his perspective, all writing derives from these practices. But, equally importantly, he reasons, "There is no cognition except this kind" (130). All thought is embodied and distributed across a technological apparatus—including though hardly limited to symbol systems like writing.

Reid's perspective has serious ramifications for what was formerly called invention—and for writing more generally. By his account, nothing that might be construed as a "creative" action comes from nowhere; any new text arises, whether in part or in whole, from a selection of pre-existing elements: ripping should be construed as "integral to the composition process and thus unavoidable" (133). Rather than imagine ripping as the original act(ion) of writing, though, Reid frames it as something that "creates conditions" for novelty to emerge, especially as pre-existing elements are mixed, "creat[ing] the possibility for information to flow from one into the other causing mutation" (130–31). Something new and interesting might emerge in this process, of course, but in crediting its creation to an individual human, Reid suggests that one should not "mistake the legal fiction of authorship, necessary for copyright and the media marketplace, with the material processes of composition, which indicate that thought and creativity are processes distributed across culture and technologies" (8). He thus suggests that any pedagogy accepting a rip-mix-burn logic would need to rethink its definitions of plagiarism (133). And, in this way, his thinking aligns with that of Johnson-Eilola and Selber.

In "Plagiarism, Originality, Assemblage," Johnson-Eilola and Selber trumpet the virtues of the assemblage, a distinctly postmodern medium, which makes no distinction whatsoever between "invented" and "borrowed" content (375). The name of this concept seems to impend doom for the first rhetorical canon (as traditionally imagined), insofar as it implies a privileging of assembly over and against invention. Of central importance, if one considers the assemblage to be a valid form of writing, then one acknowledges that students may write productively without producing anything new at all. Even so, this allowance does not necessarily lead to the death of invention altogether—as though such a thing were possible; instead, as with all forms of writing, this mode carries with it its own theory of creation. In producing an assemblage, the primary role of the writer is to distribute; invention is secondary and, in some instances, either incidental or non-existent. But, as information economist Fritz Machlup demonstrated so long ago, information distribution is its own kind of production (*Production* 7). Because ideas lack material form, they are endlessly reproducible at effectively zero cost. Thus, in a very real way, each new idea that a given person learns adds to the sum total of existing ideas in the universe. But, from a less economic and more rhetorical perspective, one might also note that, through each situational re-deployment, an idea is born anew. Fitting a concept to its kairos is an artistic act, and that idea really is different—even new—each time it rediscovers and reasserts its force.

Extending a robust discourse on plagiarism and ownership in student writing that has thoroughly unsettled inherited notions of textual originality and borrowing/theft, Johnson-Eilola and Selber contend that the distinction between these two poles is "not only problematic but also counterproductive" (376). They therefore attempt to imagine a pedagogy—and, more broadly, a form of writing—that would elide the difference. In so doing, they reconceive the value of information production and distribution, privileging "effect in context," what a work does, over "performance," or how it was created. Johnson-Eilola and Selber state, "Creativity, in this rearticulation, involves extensive research, filtering, recombining, remixing, the making of assemblages that solve problems" (400). The success or failure of a work, becomes something that, at best, an instructor cannot judge alone and, at worst, cannot judge at all. The value of the work must be found in its operations with(in) the world, not in the sophisticated and elegant (though largely hypothetical) brilliance of its machinery.

Given the massive repository of information that new technologies make available, students often have perfectly good reasons for re-purposing other people's ideas, rather than generating their own. Selber and Johnson-Eilola therefore urge instructors to profit from this development, rather than blindly opposing it out of habit. Instead of always pushing students to develop "fresh insights" (or whichever term is fashionable at the moment) one might offer lessons on how to find good, reusable content—which is not so very different from teaching one to cite sources, ultimately, except that it does away with the false premise that those one credits themselves worked alone. Or, as Jim Ridolfo and Dànielle Nicole Devoss demonstrate, one might instruct students on how to contribute to or otherwise enhance the networks in which and of which they partake by producing re-workable content for others to engage ("Composing for Recomposition").

In sum, to practice the art of invention, one need not imagine the writer as the source of all ideas, original though some may seem. Externalization hardly represents the demise of the first canon. Instead one might see a student writer as a node in a more complex network, one through whom ideas pass, and one that alters or enhances many of them, one who both draws from and contributes to the overall ecology.

Eric Charles White articulates the thesis of his *Kaironomia: On the Will-to-Invent* in simple terms: "Invention must constantly be renewed" (8). Emphasizing the centrality of kairos, the opportune moment, he suggests that each rhetorical situation is unprecedented, wholly unique, and therefore those hoping to persuade cannot rely on precedent (13–14). A "systematic treatise on the management of the opportune" could never exist, he argues (20). But, even for those less inclined to believe in the radical singularity of the now, his thesis would seem to bear weight. Old methods lose their force; the world changes; new ways of being and living and thinking emerge; and all of these must have some impact on communicative practices. Invention must be renewed. It remains in a state of becoming, tethered somehow to and yet remaining indistinguishable from the nature of its constituent electracy, which is itself birthing and being born. Whatever invention will be, it is presently being and becoming; if you want to see it, look within you, or around you, or in the in-between.

CODA: BUT, WHAT IF WE DON'T (NEED TO) CALL IT *INVENTION?*

In this chapter, I have traced a rupture in inventional thinking that very few scholars—except those contributing to it—and perhaps even some of them—recognized while it was occurring: a shift from internalist assumptions to externalist ones. When I began writing the first version of what would become this chapter, sometime in the winter of 2014, I did not (so far as I can recall) yet know that postprocess was a thing that existed. I had, presumably, read the term here and there; I know, for example, that I had already read Dobrin's *Postcomposition* and my grad-school cubicle-mate's copy of Hawk's *Counter-History*, both of which use the term. But, I had never seriously considered postprocess as a disciplinary movement or the ramifications that it might provoke.

At that time, I had set myself a relatively clear task: to write a history of inventional thought from the 1970s to what was then the present day. To do so, I scoured disciplinary databases for articles with *invention* as a keyword, and I read them all. I had not yet read Lauer's "Rhetorical Invention: The Diaspora," and so I did not yet know that 1986 marked the year in which inventional research became increasingly hard to find. But, as I compiled an archive, I reached a similar conclusion on my own. I had an advantage (a technological affordance) that Lauer did not when she wrote her 2002 chapter, though. I had the ability to track citations, moving forward in time. I could start with a canonical text on invention, say, Richard E. Young's "Arts, Crafts, Gifts, and Knacks," then determine quickly every text that had ever cited it. What I found was something quite like what Lauer herself found: that scholarship on rhetorical invention moved into a diaspora. But, what I found differed from her account in one crucial way: I discovered a number of authors who were citing inventional scholarship but who didn't, at first glance, appear to be talking about *invention* at all. At minimum, many of them weren't using the word. Instead, they talked about *posthumanism* and *materiality* and *ecologies*.

They had shifted their vocabularies.

I didn't yet have a framework for making sense of how important that shift might be. I didn't yet know that postprocess might be defined most aptly *as a vocabulary*. I didn't understand why theorists might *relexicalize*, swapping one set of terms for another. But, I registered the change in terminology all the same.

At the end of this chapter's previous section, I elected to repeat the sentence that concludes an earlier version of this account (i.e., Lotier, "Around 1986"). That sentence reads, "Whatever invention will be, it is presently being and becoming; if you want to see it, look within you, or around you, or in the in-between." I still mostly agree with that sentiment. But, with a bit of historical distance, I would like to affirm another point, as well. Yes, whatever (what we once called) invention will be, it is presently being and becoming. It is being renewed, reconfigured, recomposed. What has conventionally been called the First Canon is evolving, as we reconsider our notions of what the mind is and how the mind works and as new technologies emerge that reconfigure the possible and the imaginable.

But, this time around, I want to say something a bit stronger: *invention* may no longer be the best word to characterize that particular aspect of writing, of what we used to (and still do) call *the writing process*. Indeed, if the postprocess thinking that I have examined in this chapter proves anything, it's that we don't *need* that word. It's not (always) necessary. We have other words now that operate within alternate conceptual constellations. Those new words accord better with how the mind works (via embodied and distributed cognitive apparatuses) and how we now understand writing to proliferate, to circulate, to participate in our thinking. And those new terms give us other insights, allowing us to think other thoughts. If the Age of *Invention* is over after more than two millennia—and I have no authority to proclaim it, so I merely pose the *if*—then so be it.

CHAPTER 7.
LEAVING MATTERS OPEN AT THE CLOSE

A common critique of postprocess scholarship is that its insights are not so very different—certainly not radically so—from those espoused by Process scholars, especially those writing and teaching and theorizing in the early days of Process. This is, I think, a fair point. What became postprocess is one of the many hypothetical or potential extensions of Process that existed at the origins of the earlier approach. Gary A. Olson has admitted as much: "What changes when you are operating from the assumptions of post-process theory is that you are likely to conform even *closer* to the original goals of the process approach because you will have come to terms with the thoroughly rhetorical—that is, radically contextual—nature of writing and the teaching of writing" ("Why Distrust?" 427). By Olson's account, postprocess differs considerably from what (actually existing) Process all too often became, though it resembles what (an Edenic) Process may have once been and what it could have remained. Rather than frame postprocess as a *break* from Process or an *extension* of it, two metaphors that assume the stability of Process, one might frame postprocess instead as an *intensification* of certain internal tendencies, thereby attributing to Process a dynamism that might result (via some indeterminate, complex series of events) in its own transformation.

Indeed, it's possible that the existence of postprocess may have led some scholars to return to Process texts with renewed vigor and renewed focus. Sidney Dobrin argues something very similar:

> Posts are really discursive demarcations more than anything else; posts mark a period in which conversations initiate about not only what we have been doing but what we are still very much currently doing. This conversation occurs in a reflexive, critical way that was not possible during the period prior to the post. This is what is hopeful about the post: the possibility of seeing and knowing the effects of that which is posted becomes greater. (*Postcomposition* 196)

In other words, asserting a *post* is a performative gesture, one intended to change a state of affairs at least as much as it is intended to describe that state of affairs. This is no small point. One of the (very few) merits of the term *postprocess*, then, is that it opened up a space for further reflection and analysis and engagement on *Process*. It led scholars to understand the merits, as well as the drawbacks, of Process more fully. I value Dobrin's perspective on *posts*, and I'll apply it to postprocess itself shortly.

However, in fairness to postprocess, I think one ought to consider it on its own terms, as well. I have attempted to do that throughout this book. As Reed Way Dasenbrock suggested before *postprocess* became the name for the phenomenon in question: it is "far from being purely a negative critique" ("Forum" 103). It really does offer a specific and robust vision of how written communication occurs, and, though it does not directly suggest a narrow set of pedagogical applications, certain logical entailments do seem to follow. Rather than affirm postprocess in terms of how it benefits Process, then, one might re-frame it as a lateral gesture, a side-stepping, a separation that is neither an outright dismissal nor a rejection: postprocess as a new (enough) vocabulary, another way of talking and writing that enables new ways of thinking. Postprocess was that which could de-center "the fundamental observation that an individual produces text by means of a writing process," shifting its place in the field's collective perceptual field "from figure," the point of focus, "to ground," that which remains but recedes from attention (Petraglia, "Is There Life?" 53).

In writing this book, I strove to analyze postprocess without addressing its relation to Process more than absolutely necessary. Paul Lynch argues, "The prefix *post* never really escapes the gravity of the word to which it is attached. To be postprocess is to operate out of the terms of process" (*After Pedagogy* 7). I certainly agree with the first part, but I would quibble with the second. It is true that those opposing postprocess have forced it to validate itself within the vocabulary supplied by Process—an impossible task, something it cannot possibly do. Rather, as I have previously quoted from Richard Rorty, "The trouble with arguments against the use of a familiar and time-honored vocabulary is that they are expected to be phrased in that vocabulary," and thus they are unable to demonstrate the limitations of prior concepts, "for such use is, after all, the paradigm of [what is presently understood to be] coherent, meaningful, literal speech" (*Contingency* 8–9). I have framed postprocess as an alternate vocabulary, though, one capable of implicitly demonstrating the limitations of Process by enabling new and compelling insights about writing. To the extent that postprocess has succeeded, it has not done so by criticizing Process in the language of Process but by doing something else entirely and demonstrating the utility of that something else. So, I would affirm something very similar-sounding to Lynch's second claim—and yet importantly different from it in meaning. By his account, "To be postprocess is to operate out of the terms of process." By my estimation, in contrast, to be postprocess is to operate *outside* of the terms of Process, to whatever extent possible, given the constraints and normalizing tendencies of disciplinary discourse.

And yet, although I wished to avoid talking about Process, I could not help but do so. In those minimal gestures, I hope I have demonstrated that Process (theories, pedagogies, and the movement itself, to whatever extent any of those can be said to have existed) suffered from two competing tendencies: dispersal and sedimentation. On the one hand, the word *Process* came to mean everything and thus nothing. In effect, because it was also a temporal indicator denoting a period set apart from its current-traditional predecessor, *Process* meant *something that compositionists are doing now.*

On the other hand, although the insight that writing is a process, rather than a product, had once spurred radical change, it could not maintain such inertia indefinitely. In Marilyn Cooper's words, "Revolution dwindle[d] to dogma," or, in Joseph Petraglia's words, "the mantra 'writing is a process'" came to be seen as "the right answer to a really boring question" (Cooper, "Ecology" 364; Petraglia, "Is There Life?" 53). Eventually, in Olson's words, "the vocabulary of process" proved itself to be "no longer useful," which is not to say that it was *never* useful. Of course, it was. But, its diminished utility need not have represented "a reason to despair." Instead, it offered "an invitation to rethink many of our most cherished assumption about the activity we call 'writing'" ("Toward" 9). It offered the opportunity for *relexicalization,* to borrow a term from Karen Kopelson ("Back" 602). Or, in Louise Wetherbee Phelps' words, scholars were given the opportunity to *proliferate their interpretants*: to see that writing is a process, and a product, and an ecology, and a network, and an event, and an activity, and an interaction, and a negotiation, and a visual artifact, and on, and on (*Composition* 46).

One of the merits of the term *postprocess*, I might suggest, is that it makes very little sense as a metaphor for writing; unlike *Process*, it fits very poorly in a *writing is X* construction. Nor does it come pre-packaged (or, perhaps, retro-actively packaged) with a concomitant metaphor—that *writing is a product*—as current-traditionalism did. Thus, inasmuch as postprocess (the signified, the vocabulary, the theory with a very small *t*) denies the existence of writing-in-general, affirming instead its radical situation-specificity, it is very well suited to proliferate interpretants. It resists sedimentation. If one endorses the supposition that no X can sufficiently fill the *writing is X* slot, one can start to ask the sort of interesting questions Petraglia seemed to invite: an un-ending series of *what is it?*

In her chapter "Why Composition Studies Disappeared and What Happened Then" and again in a 2002 interview with Mary Jo Reiff and Anis Bawarshi, Susan Miller offers a realpolitik critique of postprocess, objecting not to its principles so much as to its potential economic ramifications. Curiously, Miller had established herself as a strident critic of "sanctified composition studies," which, by her estimation has tended to rely on ethical arguments about the intrinsic value of the so-called "writing life," and thus to justify itself as creating better, more ethical subjects via writing ("Why" 50, 53). In its place, she advocated "a different writing studies" that might focus its attention on "situated literacies" and "very well-developed and smartly managed, indigenous writing practices, even those in academic disciplines that vehemently ignore insight and consciousness," in other words, one that "directs attention to practices rather than an interiorized writing life" (53–55). This sounds quite a lot like the form of Writing Studies I explored in Chapter 5, which traces its genealogy through postprocess. And yet, in both of the aforementioned places, Miller condemns postprocess because, she alleges, it offers insufficient grounds for universities to employ writing instructors.

In the book-chapter version of this proposition, she states, "Without a stake in a general theory of how composing and texts work, there is no justification—as some already suspect—for hiring *composition* specialists. . . . There will certainly be no reason to support graduate degrees in *composition studies*" ("Why" 55; emphasis added). In the latter interview, she reasons, "To assert that [postprocess scholars] are not experts about the writing process and that no one can be is to announce that there will be no reason to hire faculty members in *composition* at any institution. I am very cautious about the implications of saying that we don't study writers in the process of writing. If you don't, then what is your career-long, Ph.D. trained expertise?" (Bawarshi and Reiff, "Composition"; emphasis added). I cannot help but note that Miller continues to speak of the purportedly eclipsed composition studies even within a new writing studies regime, thereby indicating an inability or unwillingness to move her thinking beyond it. As Dobrin might point out, she also presumes that scholars of writing must study *writers*, rather than writing itself (i.e., texts, however broadly defined). If they were to depart from studying "writers in the process of writing," she suggests, they would no longer have an object of examination nor any trained expertise. To be direct: I think there are compelling reasons for rejecting Miller's rationale. In particular, I would like to question her realpolitik critique.

Inasmuch as postprocess proliferates interpretants and offers a conceptual space for questioning the utility of generic first-year writing courses, it opens up in(de)finitely many possible lines of analysis: it invites more research, more theorizing, and more teaching. It shows that writing is more difficult, more contingent, more situation-specific and activity-system dependent than Process theories had imagined. The same is true of writing instruction: it is more difficult, more contingent, more situation-specific and/or activity-system dependent than Process theories had imagined. Postprocess suggests that you need to study and teach writing in the myriad places where it arises. No single site deserves special (and thus invariably undue) privilege, not even the hallowed first-year writing classroom. Certainly, the researching and theorizing and teaching that it calls out for may occur beyond the narrow, conventional bounds of composition studies. It may occur in departments of writing studies, or further afield, in the disciplines. But, I suspect that such a development would prove to be a net-gain for writing instructors, even if they are, to some extent, scattered to the winds, carrying the seeds of postprocess with them where they go.

Throughout this book, I have argued that postprocess ideas have ascended during the last thirty years, even if the word *postprocess* seldom appears within our collective scholarship anymore. These days, relatively few scholars would disagree that "writing constitutes a specific communicative interaction occurring among individuals at specific historical moments and in specific relations with others and with the world." Most of those assenting to that claim would accept a corollary: "because these moments and relations change," no generalized theory "can capture what writers do during these changing moments and within these changing relations" (Kent, "Introduction" 1–2). Fewer still would deny that readers and writers co-construct the meanings of texts, or that "when we write, we interpret our readers, our situations, our and other people's motivations, the appropriate genres to employ in specific circumstances, and so forth" (2). And, hardly any would deny that the material conditions in which one writes, the words one employs, and the physical or imagined presence of one's readers all affect that which is written. In 1999, Thomas Kent could tenably suggest, "This [final] claim is a commonplace idea nowadays" (3). It is even more broadly agreed-upon now.

In other words, though the collective body of scholars would (and should) find reasons to criticize and reframe some of the foregoing statements, there's a general agreement that writing is public, interpretive, and situated. Externalist suppositions now inform many, many more theories of writing—and particularly theories of what was once called *invention*—than they did in the 1980s, even if their externalism isn't identified *as such*. And, on top of all that, the argument that there's no such thing as Writing-in-General, and thus one cannot teach it for "nothing exists to teach," has also gained widespread assent, as evidenced by numerous entries in *Naming What We Know* and *Bad Ideas about Writing* (Kent, *Paralogic Rhetoric* 161).

Relatively few scholars address postprocess anymore. Those that have done so in the last decade have tended to consign postprocess to the discipline's "deep familiar" (Rule 36), to align their thinking with postprocess principles while distancing themselves from the category itself (Duffy, 418; Rule 104), to place their theorizing very conspicuously *Beyond Postprocess*, or to question whether postprocess may be dead (Heard, 285). I understand, and accept, and even support the logic of each of those choices. But, if we are now post-postprocess (and I suspect we are), then we now encounter the opportunity explained by Dobrin: to explore "what we have been doing but what we are still very much currently doing . . . in a reflexive, critical way that was not possible during the period prior to the post." As I've tried to show in the book, postprocess is indeed "what we are still very much currently doing," even if it's seldom acknowledged as such. I want to suggest some ways, then, of exploring it in a reflexive and critical way. But, I also want to offer some methods for responding to whatever will come next and, eventually, writing its history. As one might expect, many of these will be methods I have employed or attempted to employ in writing this very book.

First, for the sake of accounting for large-scale or broad transformations in disciplinary thought and/or for documenting the formation, re-formation, and/or evolution of publics, I strongly recommend citational tracking. This action, I believe, will be as useful in re-assessing postprocess as in analyzing whatever movements/theories/attitudes arise next. Rhetoricians and compositionists have long been enthralled by the metaphor of the Burkean Parlor—a space for ongoing conversation in which participants enter and exit according to their availability, needs, and whims. But, while that metaphor accounts for some aspects of how scholarly conversations occur, its spatial emphasis (a parlor is physically situated and its existence is presumed to be stable) may blind us to many non-trivial features of actually existing scholarly discourses in our wired world. There isn't just one parlor; they are multiple. The many parlors that presently exist are distributed across and time space. Few conversants actually remain in one place for very long; they pass from parlor to parlor. But, it's not equally easy to pass from each to each. Some parlors will stay open longer than others. Some will be more crowded than others. Some will be dominated by the loudest voices; some will be less hierarchical. A conversation begun in one parlor may migrate to another, then to another, then to another. As that migration occurs, some conversants may travel together, but some may not. The conversations occurring simultaneously in different parlors may be making similar points but with different terms, or they may be making different points with the same terms, but one cannot know if either of those is true at first glance. What counts as an obvious or boring remark in one parlor may prove to be wildly interesting in another. All of that is to say: if one wants to trace out a given conversation, one faces a complex challenge in determining where and when and for how long to look. Even recognizing who is and is not participating in a given conversation is a more difficult task than we have often presumed.

If one wants to make a general claim about a highly dispersed, decentralized, and discontinuous scholarly conversation, one needs to have some basis for accounting for that phenomenon's particulars. Citational tracking—backward and forward in time, from author to author and back again recursively—offers those willing to attempt it a basis for making (more) accurate claims about generalized but dispersed phenomena. I hope that this book, taken as a whole, offers a basis for understanding the utility of this citational tracking approach, oriented toward accounting for the conduct of publics. But, to give but one more example of why this approach matters, I'll turn to my favorite book ever written on writing instruction, Lynch's *After Pedagogy*.

Lynch begins his book by accepting the fundamental correctness of postprocess and postpedagogical arguments that directly undermine what has commonly been called *writing instruction* and/or *pedagogy* (xv). Even so, he asks a reasonable question: "What next?" (31). How does one teach, if teaching is impossible? I find his answer, that pedagogy should be reimagined as a form of response, extremely compelling (54). Even so, I believe that Lynch clears the ground for his own intervention a bit too thoroughly. I also find aspects of his argument lacking on historical grounds, even if I very much agree with his separate theoretical claims.

Lynch's basic complaint with postprocess—which he mostly associates with Kent's work—is that it over-emphasizes the radical singularity of each act of communication and thus "de-emphasizes" the role of experience and learning (89). From his perspective, Kent does not adequately address the relationship between prior theories and passing theories, particularly the way that passing theories become the fodder for subsequent prior theories (or, in non-Davidsonian terms: how what you learn *this time* helps you *next time*). Even in statements where Kent seems to do so, Lynch believes that his "emphasis . . . is misplaced" (90). In other words, Lynch never accuses Kent of not having done something; he accuses him of not having done it *enough*. Lynch thus turns to the work of John Dewey, which he believes offers a corrective: a robust philosophy of experience.

In some instances, I think that Lynch misreads Kent, wanting to see over-emphasis and under-emphasis where they're actually more evenly weighted. From my perspective, then, he doesn't need Dewey to correct an error in Kent's work, *per se*, because that error doesn't exist. (Although, to be sure, Dewey may offer a more thorough account of the issue in question, as does Lynch himself.) In a passage from *Paralogic Rhetoric* that Lynch quotes, Kent writes, "Once communication takes place . . . the passing theory, in a sense, disappears *to become a part of a prior theory* that may or may not be used in future communicative situations" (Kent, *Paralogic* 87; emphasis added). In his next sentence, Lynch writes, "For Dewey, such experiences do not disappear so much as become available means for the shaping of future practice" (Lynch, *After Pedagogy* 90). But,

Kent never says that the passing theory disappears altogether. It only disappears to the extent that, once communication takes place and communicants go their separate ways, it no longer counts *as a passing theory* because the passing moment is past. It is now "a part of a prior theory that may or may not be used" in the future—something quite similar to it becoming "available means for the shaping of future practice."

As I have explained previously, Kent assumes that—regardless of how much background knowledge one acquires—communicative interaction will invariably involve hermeneutic guessing. By Lynch's account, though, he "fails to distinguish between shots in the dark and informed hypotheses" (92). But, that criticism strikes me as not-quite-right, either. At several places in the book Lynch cites, Kent argues that one learns to become a "better guesser" in engaging with one's "neighbors"—i.e., those that one engages with regularly (*Paralogic Rhetoric* 31, 37, 39, 72, 118). And, though I hesitate to stress the point, Kent had already addressed Lynch's primary criticisms (before they were ever raised) elsewhere. In his Introduction to *Post-Process Theory*, for instance, he acknowledges our ability to learn from experiences and reformulate subsequent plans accordingly, and he suggests that our guesses can become increasingly informed hypotheses as time moves along. He writes,

> Interpretation constitutes the uncodifiable moves we make
> when we attempt to align our utterances with the utterances
> of others, and these moves—I have called them "hermeneutic
> guesswork" do not constitute a process in any useful sense of
> the concept, except perhaps in retrospect. By "in retrospect,"
> I only mean that when we look back on a communicative
> situation, we can always map out what we did. We can always
> distinguish some sort of process that we employed. However,
> if we try to employ this process again, we can never be sure
> that it will work the way we want it to work. Of course, we
> will be better guessers the next time we write something in a
> similar situation; we will know what went wrong or right, and
> we will know the process we employed to produce a successful
> written artifact. (3)

Now, one could find other passages from other texts in which Kent says very similar things—even going so far as to note that our hypotheses can gradually become so informed that we stop recognizing them *as hypotheses*, at all ("Preface" xiii). But, to multiply such citations would hardly be in service of my primary point. To be clear, I am not trying to undermine Lynch's work as a whole—which, again, I think is stunningly good. Instead, I want to suggest that now is a good time to return to works that we think we know well. We may find that we have not known them as we thought we did.

In narrating the history of any movement/theory/attitude, one will struggle to balance an emphasis on "representative" or "leading" individual scholars and the more general grouping—what has often been called the movement, but which I prefer to call the *public*. To demonstrate this point, I will use Lynch's work as a foil once more. However, I only do so out of respect. If he has fallen into this pitfall, then it must be a very hard one to avoid. Indeed, I worry that I have not always avoided it myself. Let me acknowledge, then, the board in my own eye before reaching for the speck in his.

In any case, Lynch identifies a fault in Kent's work and subsequently frames it as a fault with postprocess as a whole. That fault does not necessarily exist in Kent's work—at least not to the extent that Lynch claims. But, rigorously applied citational tracking can demonstrate an even more crucial point: the very thing that Lynch finds lacking in postprocess scholarship as a whole—a theory that can account for learning and experience—has been one of its persistent concerns. In offering this statement, I claim no special insight. I am about to refer to three obscure texts, two of which do not use the word *postprocess* at all. But, if I have seen farther than others, it is because I stood on the shoulder of giants while holding a telescope (i.e., the citation tracker) that someone else built.

Before postprocess was called *postprocess*, Reed Way Dasenbrock suggested that an externalist orientation toward writing could improve upon a social constructionist one because the former "model of interpretation," unlike the latter, "allows for the possibility of learning from experience" ("Do We Write?" 14). Of course, as a good proto-postprocess thinker, Dasenbrock would admit that no general explanation could account for how such learning occurs or how new knowledge affects future practice: "It remains open, and interestingly open, how much of the passing theory is reintegrated into the prior theory, how much one's beliefs are changed by the encounter with another's beliefs" (16). But, that concession is just another way of saying that situations vary and we cannot do anything other than guess, as best we can, at how to respond to them. In any case, for Dasenbrock, the merit of what came to be called *postprocess* was found in the very thing that, according to Lynch, it lacked.

Of course, to be fair to Lynch, Dasenbrock's works have mostly fallen out of circulation within the primary postprocess public(s). Even so, there's good reason to see him as a founding member of it/them. Before *postprocess* was the name for a certain disposition or attitude or viewpoint toward writing, Charlotte Thralls and Nancy Roundy Blyler referred to it as *the paralogic hermeneutic* approach in a 1993 text ("Social" 22). At that time, they identified two scholars working from that position: Kent and Dasenbrock. Thralls and Blyler also

195

distinguished Kent and Dasenbrock's views from those of social constructionists and of post-process scholars, whom they categorized as employing an "ideologic" social approach. And, notably, in a text published that same year, Dasenbrock acknowledged a public of two members—himself and Kent—studying Donald Davidson's philosophy within composition studies ("Myths" 31).

If one were to chart out the circulatory history of Dasenbrock's and Kent's (proto)postprocess texts, one might arrive at Anis Bawarshi's "Beyond Dichotomy: Toward a Theory of Divergence in Composition Studies" (1997). In that article, Bawarshi cites one of the Dasenbrock's texts and seven of Kent's, as well other early externalist articles—most notably (per the accounts I have narrated in this book) David R. Russell's "Vygotsky, Dewey, and Externalism" and Johndan Johnson-Eilola's "Control and the Cyborg." Bawarshi, in my estimation, anticipates many of Lynch's later argumentative gestures. He praises prior externalist scholars for demonstrating that "every communicative act is an interpretive act and thus is mediated by and unique to a particular moment, a particular object, and a particular set of people, each dynamically (re)constituting the other." And yet, precisely because it focuses so closely on what is new to each encounter, he believes that externalist composition scholarship "fails to adequately consider the interpretive baggage that we bring with us to every communicative interaction—those prior strategies or conceptual frameworks (gendered, racial, class-based)—that we carry with us from one communicative moment to the next" (71). In other words, while previous postprocess accounts "help us get beyond the social/self dichotomy created by the Cartesian split, they nonetheless do not account for how passing and prior theories interact, and so we are left with yet another dichotomy" (74). Bawarshi, for what it is worth, turns to genre theories as a means of accounting for how conventional (i.e., prior) and passing strategies of interpretation can interact profitably (74–80).

I do not intend to belabor the point, but, if one were to trace subsequent citations of Bawarshi's article, one might encounter Dobrin's "Going Public: Locating Public/Private Discourse," a chapter that "turn[s] to the work of postprocess writing theorists" so as to "propose an ecological model for understanding discourse" (216). There, Dobrin also addresses that the very thing that Lynch believes to be lacking in postprocess, an explanation of why "rhetorical sensitivity does not require the repeated reinvention of the wheel" and how "continuity stretches between experiences" (Lynch, *After Pedagogy* 89, 88). In stating his thesis, Dobrin writes, "In turn, I will consider that individual communicators rely on a host of prior discursive moments to develop passing theories for engaging particular communicative moments and at no time separate those prior theories into realms of public or private but instead rely on all prior theories to enter into any communicative scenario" ("Going Public" 216). Later, elaborating on the ramifications of this view, Dobrin addresses something "it might seem reasonable to assume," namely "that each communicative scenario requires the individual to develop an internalized or private theory for engaging each new communicative scenario"—in other words, that one must invariably form one's prior and passing theories on one's own or alone (221). However, as Dobrin rightly points out, an externalist perspective suggests that what appears to be "the private"—that is, a function of the self alone—is always invariably a function of "the public"; one's private thoughts are only private to the extent that they have been "privatized" (221–22). If all of this is true, Dobrin concludes, there is no prior theory (nor any passing theory that adjusts it) that is not in some indeterminate way a function of experiences in prior communicative interactions (222). Furthermore, if one's ability to communicate is a function of one's ecology, it is important to affirm that "from moment to moment, the web of discourse maintains operational integrity through its relationships with users of discourse, the place in which those users of discourse use discourse, and its own shifting (lack of) form" (225). Ecologies are inherently dynamic, but they still demonstrate persistence. Things change at micro scales so that they can remain the same at macro scales.

Certainly—and let me be very clear on this point—there is almost no way that one would ever *find* all of the texts that I've just analyzed, were it not for citational tracking, nor would one automatically presume their inter-relations, at first glance. To reconstruct the public after the fact, one must reconstruct its archive of texts, which were published at odd intervals and not always in the likeliest of places. If one were only working in the manner of conventional genealogists, starting with the new and moving toward the old, I'm not sure that one would see what I have now made visible. But, starting with a few early texts (those of Kent and Dasenbrock) and seeing who cited them, and who subsequently cited *them*, and so on, one arrives at novel conclusions.

So, that's part one of my research ethic: if you'd like to make a claim about a generalized phenomenon, attend as carefully as possible to its particulars. Consider treating scholarly movements or commonplace theories as though they were publics and track citations. And of course, along the way, try to read source texts as charitably as possible.

Second, especially as new movements and/or theories and/or attitudes emerge, I hope that we may be patient with them. They are unlikely to emerge fully formed; they may experience growing pains. Scholars expressing broad-scale agreement will almost certainly disagree on particulars—and they should. Demands for consensus are stultifying, costly, and unnecessary. It is good that we disagree with one another charitably; such disagreement can be an engine of progress.

197

Furthermore, if new ideas do not seem immediately clear or transparently obvious, we would do well to remember that ideas we take to be *clear* are usually just commonplace assumptions that have been expressed with conventional terms applied in conventional ways. But, words are not neutral vehicles, and none is inherently more clear or transparent than any other. At first, scholars attempting to move away from (whatever they take to be) dominant conceptions will likely employ dominant terms under erasure, acknowledging their inadequacy but not yet dispensing with them, either because they do not feel empowered to do so or because they do not yet know how to do so. Or, they may indeed employ alternate vocabularies to indicate concepts not wholly comprehensible within the dominant lexicon. It must be possible—and I hope it will prove to have been—to demand rigor and exactitude of such thinkers without pulling their ideas back toward the status quo.

And, of course, I hope that we may find ways to value alternate ways of thinking, even if they do not present obvious or direct pedagogical applications at first glance.

Third, I hope we may attend to how phenomena appear at differing levels of scale and from different perspectives. Sometimes it's more productive to flatten distinctions and demonstrate similarity; sometimes the opposite is true. Postprocess scholarship was commonly faulted for claiming to diverge from Process scholarship while still resembling it in certain respects. The same, I suspect, will be true of whatever comes next. In some ways it will seem to resemble some strands of Process (if not the whole thing) and some strands of postprocess (if not the whole thing) and perhaps even some strands of current-traditionalism (though probably not the whole thing, one hopes). One will be able to frame the new as, in some sense, an extension of the old; in some sense, a break from the old; in some sense, an intensification of the old; and so forth down the line. Indeed, it's likely that all will be true—in some sense, of course.

Each of the various histories of whatever comes next will be what George Pullman has called a "rhetorical narrative": "a motivated selection and sequencing of events that sacrifices one truth in order to more clearly represent another" ("Stepping" 16). As Pullman carefully demonstrates, though, "Rhetorical narrative is not bad historiography; it is the inevitable result of the search for coherence and unity among disparate texts and practices—the inevitable oversimplification that language always performs on experience" (21–22). Historians, then, might offer different critiques of those with whom they disagree. To say that an argument is over-simplified is to say nothing much at all. One would be better served to explain why the over-simplification that one wishes to present is better than the over-simplification presented by another—on what basis, for what reasons. Even among rhetorical narratives, some claims are better than others, and we can help subsequent scholars along by explaining the criteria for judgment that we have applied.

As a corollary, any account of a multiplicity or multitude will likely require criteria for assessing the commonality of certain premises and/or principles and/or practices. In terms of accounting for historical change, in particular, one needs some basis for saying: things generally used to be (done) one way; now they're generally (done) some other way; therefore, it's safe to say that we have moved from one period/vocabulary/viewpoint to another. One of the best ways of doing so, I think, is to focus less on what a given period/vocabulary/viewpoint values or validates and more on what it excludes or treats as anomalous. To be sure, though, these conventions are just as likely to be *unformulated* or tacit as they are to be *formulated* or explicit. I have previously noted, for example, that Process-era, internalist visions of *invention* often blinded scholars to the relevant, related properties of externalist approaches. Those conventions were largely unformulated, but they still produced real effects. Indeed, because the connection between internalism and invention was so fundamental, some externalist approaches were even treated as "challenge[s] [to] invention" (Atwill, "Introduction" xvi).

I have also suggested that postprocess theories, on the whole, show much greater concern for situatedness, materiality, and the role of writing ecologies in textual production than did their Process predecessors. Though she has established herself as a sensible and well-versed critic of postprocess elsewhere ("Writing"), Laura R. Micciche provides some useful examples for proving my point about historical transformation. In *Acknowledging Writing Partners*, Micciche notes (rightly though sadly) that "male theorists appear with regularity" in the discourses of "object-oriented ontology, actor-network and post-process theories as well as theories of materialism more generally in composition studies," whereas female scholars remain under-cited in these domains, despite their considerable contributions (30–31). She then turns to the scholarship of some authors closely associated with the Process movement, including Mina Shaughnessy and Janet Emig, as well as a few that I would personally categorize as postprocess or proto-postprocess, most notably Ann Berthoff, Marilyn Cooper, Linda Brodkey, and Margaret Syverson. Those scholars, she shows, were notably "sensitive to small moments, idiosyncrasies, and the flotsam of writing." However, as she also concedes, they tended to treat these things as the "marginalia of composing," oddities and quirks, rather than considering how they might be foregrounded or centered in conceptions of text production (25).

To admit as much is not to fault them. It is instead to suggest that their work strained against the pressure of "dominant ideologies of authorship" that discounted their insights about material, affective, and embodied states as anomalous or "small and inconsequential" (37, 30). According to the logic I have applied in writing this book, then, it's reasonable to assume that those earlier scholars worked during a period (whatever one wants to call it) in which writing was presumed primarily to arise via conscious, individualized, internalist cognition. In contrast, Micciche, who can affirm that writing is "curatorial, distributed, and immersive" without feeling any compulsion to justify her position, presently works in another (41).

Finally, as I conclude my own contribution to this conversation, I want to affirm my desire for more analysis, more engagement on the topics I have explored here. At the start of this book, I acknowledged the complementary roles that generalized and localized histories can play. I have attempted to write a general account here that might still attend to localized specifics, as much as possible, given my constraints. I acknowledge that alternate accounts of the period I have surveyed may add nuance and complexity and depth to the stories I have told. I hope they will.

At its close, then, I want to leave this text open.

I hope that mine won't be the last voice on the subjects I've considered.

I hope that someone will take up the strands I've left frayed here and tie some of them together.

Someone else may find holes in the fabric I've woven and attempt to patch them.

Another may tear the whole thing apart.

Another may pick up the scraps and quilt them together with some seemingly mis-matched pieces.

Still others may arise—of whom this tattered metaphor offers no account.

Who's to say?

We can't know.

In any case, I leave this text open, and I welcome others to engage it and refine it and expand it and even, where it's wrong, to rebuke it.

We don't yet know enough about how our discipline's thinking has evolved over the last thirty or so years. We don't agree about enough, and we haven't yet publicly disagreed about enough.

There is more to be written.

I leave it for others to write.

WORKS CITED

Adler-Kassner, Linda, and Elizabeth Wardle, editors. *Naming What We Know: Threshold Concepts in Writing Studies.* Utah State UP, 2015.

Alexander, Kara Poe, and Danielle M. Williams. "DMAC after Dark: Toward a Theory of Distributed Invention." *Computers and Composition*, vol. 36, 2015, pp. 32–43, https://doi.org/10.1016/j.compcom.2015.04.001.

Alford, Caddie. "Creating with the 'Universe of the Undiscussed': Hashtags, Doxa, and Choric Invention." *Enculturation: A Journal of Rhetoric, Writing, and Culture*, 2016, http://enculturation.net/creating-with-the-universe-of-the-undiscussed.

Allison, Libby, et al., editors. *Grading in the Post-Process Classroom.* Boynton/Cook, 1997.

Anson, Chris M. "Process Pedagogy and Its Legacy." *A Guide to Composition Pedagogies*, 2nd ed. Eited by Amy Rupiper Taggart, et al. Oxford UP, 2013, pp. 212–30.

Arrington, Phillip K. "A Most Copious Digression: An Erasmian Analysis of the Rhetoric of Virginia Woolf's Comments on Letters in *Jacob's Room*." *College Literature*, vol. 45, no. 3, 2018, pp. 543–66.

———. "The Traditions of the Writing Process." *Freshman English News*, vol. 14, no. 3, 1986, pp. 2–10.

———. "Tropes of the Composing Process." *College English*, vol. 48, no. 4, Apr. 1986, pp. 325–38, https://doi.org/10.2307/377252.

Arroyo, Sarah J. *Participatory Composition: Video Culture, Writing, and Electracy.* Southern Illinois UP, 2013.

Atkinson, Dwight. "L2 Writing in the Post-Process Era: Introduction." *Journal of Second Language Writing*, vol. 12, no. 1, Feb. 2003, pp. 3–15, https://doi.org/10.1016/S1060-743(02)00123-6.

Atwill, Janet M. "Introduction." Atwill and Lauer, pp. xi–xxii.

Atwill, Janet M., and Janice M. Lauer. *Perspectives on Rhetorical Invention.* Tennessee Studies in Literature, vol. 39. U of Tennessee P, 2002.

Bacon, Francis. *The Advancement of Learning. The Rhetorical Tradition: Readings from Classical Times to the Present,* 2nd ed. Eited by Patricia Bizzell and Bruce Herzberg. Bedford/St. Martins, 2001, pp. 740–44.

Ball, Cheryl E., and Drew M. Loewe, editors. *Bad Ideas about Writing.* West Virginia U Libraries Digital Publishing Institute, 2017, https://textbooks.lib.wvu.edu/badideas/badideasaboutwriting-book.pdf.

Ballif, Michelle, editor. *Theorizing Histories of Rhetoric.* Southern Illinois UP, 2013.

Bawarshi, Anis. "Beyond Dichotomy: Toward a Theory of Divergence in Composition Studies." *JAC: A Journal of Composition Theory*, vol. 17, no. 1, 1997, pp. 69–82.

———. *Genre and the Invention of the Writer: Reconsidering the Place of Invention in Composition.* Utah State UP, 2003.

———. "Writing Post-Process: Agency and the Teaching of Writing." *Kansas English*, vol. 83, no. 1, Winter 1997–1998, pp. 68–76.

Bawarshi, Anis, and Mary Jo Reiff. "Composition and the Cultural Imaginary: A Conversation with Susan Miller." *Composition Forum*, vol. 13, no. 1–2, 2002, pp. 1–22.

Berlin, James A. "Contemporary Composition: The Major Pedagogical Theories." *College English*, vol. 44, no. 8, 1982, pp. 765–77, https://doi.org/10.2307/377329.

The Bible. New International Version, International Bible Society, 1984.

Bird, Barbara. "Interchanges: Writing about Writing as the Heart of a Writing Studies Approach to FYC." *College Composition and Communication*, vol. 60, no. 1, Sept. 2008, pp. 165–71, *JSTOR*, http://www.jstor.org/stable/20457051.

Bizzell, Patricia. "Cognition, Convention, and Certainty: What We Need to Know about Writing." *Pre/Text*, vol. 3, no. 3, 1982, pp. 213–43.

———. "Composing Processes: An Overview." *The Teaching of Writing*, edited by Anthony Petrosky and David Bartholomae. U of Chicago P, 1986, pp. 49–70.

Blyler, Nancy Roundy. "Process-Based Pedagogy in Professional Writing." *The Journal of Business Communication*, vol. 24, no. 1, Winter 1987, pp. 51–60, https://doi.org/10.1177/002194368702400113.

———. "Reading Theory and Persuasive Business Communications: Guidelines for Writers." *Journal of Technical Writing and Communication*, vol. 21, no. 4, 1991, pp. 383–96, https://doi.org/10.2190/JUBY-56UX-7RNW-NB2M.

———. "Research in Professional Communication: A Post-Process Perspective." *Post-Process Theory: Beyond the Writing-Process Paradigm*, edited by Thomas Kent. Southern Illinois UP, 1999, pp. 65–79.

———. "Shared Meaning and Public Relations Writing." *Journal of Technical Writing and Communication*, vol. 22, no. 3, 1992, pp. 301–18, https://doi.org/10.2190/XT47-79UB-UK8A-02KJ.

———. "Teaching Persuasion as Consensus in Business Communication." *The Bulletin*, Mar. 1993, pp. 26–31.

———. "Theory and Curriculum: Reexamining the Curricular Separation of Business and Technical Communication." *Journal of Business and Technical Communication*, vol. 7, no. 2. Apr. 1993, pp. 218–45, https://doi.org/10.1177/1050651993007002003.

Blyler, Nancy, and Charlotte Thralls. Preface. Blyler and Thralls, pp. xi–xv.

Blyler, Nancy Roundy, and Charlotte Thralls, editors. *Professional Communication: The Social Perspective*. Sage, 1993.

Breuch, Lee-Ann M. Kastman. "Post-Process 'Pedagogy': A Philosophical Exercise." *JAC*, vol. 22, no. 1, 2002, pp. 119–50.

Broadhead, Glenn J., and Richard C. Freed. *The Variables of Composition: Process and Product in a Business Setting*. Southern Illinois UP, 1986.

Brooke, Collin, and Thomas Rickert. "Being Delicious: Materialities of Research in a Web 2.0 Application." Dobrin, Rice, and Vastola, pp. 163–79.

Brooke, Collin Gifford. "Forgetting to be (Post)Human: Media and Memory in a Kairotic Age." *JAC*, vol. 20, no. 4, 2000, pp. 775–95.

———. *Lingua Fracta: Toward a Rhetoric of New Media*. Hampton, 2009.

Burnett, Rebecca E., and Lee-Ann Marie Kastman. "Teaching Composition: Current Theories and Practices." *Handbook of Academic Learning: Construction of Knowledge*, edited by Gary D. Phye. Academic Press, 1997, pp. 265–305.

Butts, Jimmy. "The More Writing Process, the Better." Ball and Loewe, pp. 109–16.

Carillo, Ellen C. "Reading and Writing Are not Connected." Ball and Loewe, pp. 38–43.

Carter, Michael. "Ways of Knowing, Doing, and Writing in the Disciplines." *College Composition and Communication*, vol. 58, no. 3, Feb. 2007, pp. 385–418. JSTOR, http://www.jstor.org/stable/20456952.

Caudery, Tim. "What the 'Process Approach' Means to Practising [sic] Teachers of Second Language Writing Skills." *TESL-EJ: The Electronic Journal for English as a Second Language*, vol. 1, no. 4, June 1995, http://www.tesl-ej.org/wordpress/issues/volume1/ej04/ej04a3/.

Ching, Kory Lawson. "Theory and Its Practice in Composition Studies." *JAC*, vol. 27, no. 3/4, 2007, pp. 445–469.

Clark, Andy. *Natural Born Cyborgs: Minds, Technologies, and the Future of Human Intelligence*. Oxford UP, 2003.

Clark, Andy, and David J. Chalmers. "The Extended Mind." *The Extended Mind*, edited by Richard Menary. MIT Press, 2010, pp. 27–42.

Coe, Richard M. "Eco-Logic for the Composition Classroom." *College Composition and Communication*, vol. 26, no. 3, 1975, pp. 232–37, https://doi.org/10.2307/356121.

———. "Write a Letter to Deanne." *Inkshed: Newsletter of the Canadian Association for the Study of Writing and Reading*, vol. 8, no. 2, Mar. 1989, pp. 20–21.

Connors, Robert J. "The Abolition Debate in Composition: A Short History." *Composition in the Twenty-first Century: Crisis and Change*, edited by Lynn Z. Bloom et al. Southern Illinois UP, 1996, pp. 47–63.

———. "Composition Studies and Science." *College English*, vol. 45, no. 1, 1983, pp 1–20, https://doi.org/10.2307/376913.

———. "Current-Traditional Rhetoric: Thirty Years of Writing with a Purpose." *Rhetoric Society Quarterly*, vol. 11, no. 4, 1981, pp. 208–21. JSTOR, https://www.jstor.org/stable/3885599.

———. "The New Abolitionism: Toward a Historical Background." Petraglia, pp. 3–26.

Cooper, Marilyn M. "Context as Vehicle: Implicatures in Writing." *What Writers Know: The Language, Process, and Structure of Written Discourse*," edited by Martin Nystrand. Academic Press, 1982, pp. 105–28.

———. "The Ecology of Writing." *College English*, vol. 48, no. 4, 1986, pp. 364–75. JSTOR, http://www.jstor.org/stable/377264.

———. Foreword. Weisser and Dobrin, pp. xi–xviii.

Cooper, Marilyn M., and Michael Holzman. *Writing as Social Action*. Heinemann, 1989.

Crowley, Sharon. "Around 1971: The Emergence of Process Pedagogy." *Composition in the University: Historical and Polemical Essays*. U of Pittsburgh P, 1998, pp. 187–214.

Dasenbrock, Reed Way. "Do We Write the Text We Read?" *College English*, vol. 53, no. 1, 1991, pp. 7–18, https://doi.org/10.2307/377963.

———. "Forum: *Paralogic Rhetoric: A Theory of Communicative Interaction* by Thomas Kent." *Rhetoric Society Quarterly*, vol. 23, no. 3/4, Summer-Autumn 1994, pp. 103-05. JSTOR, http://www.jstor.org/stable/3886146.

———. "The Myths of the Subjective and of the Subject in Composition Studies." *Journal of Advanced Composition*, vol. 13, no. 1, 1993, pp. 21–32.

Davila, Bethany. "Review: *The End of Composition Studies*, by David W. Smit." *Composition Studies*, vol. 34, no. 2, 2006.

Davis, D. Diane. "Finitude's Clamor; Or, Notes toward a Communitarian Literacy." *College Composition and Communication*, vo. 53, no. 1, Sept. 2001, pp. 119–45, https://doi.org/10.2307/359065.

Dejoy, Nancy. "I Was a Process-Model Baby." Kent, *Post-Process Theory*, pp. 163–78.

Descartes, René. "Discourse on the Method of Rightly Conducting the Reason and Seeking for Truth in the Sciences." *Discourse on the Method and Meditations on First Philosophy*. Edited by David Weissman. Yale UP, 1996, pp. 3–48.

Dobrin, Sidney I. *Constructing Knowledges: The Politics of Theory-Building and Pedagogy in Composition*. State U of New York P, 1997.

———. "Going Public: Locating Public/Private Discourse." *The Private, the Public, and the Published: Reconciling Private Lives and Public Rhetoric*, edited by Barbara Couture and Thomas Kent. Utah State UP, 2004, pp. 216–229.

———. "Paralogic Hermeneutic Theories, Power, and the Possibility for Liberating Pedagogies." Kent, *Post-Process Theory*, pp. 132–48.

———. *PostComposition*. Southern Illinois UP, 2011.

———. "Review: English Departments and the Question of Disciplinarity." *College English*, vol. 59, no. 6, Oct. 1997, pp. 692–99, https://doi.org/10.2307/378289.

———. "Writing Takes Place." Weisser and Dobrin, pp. 11–26.

Dobrin, Sidney I., and Christian R. Weisser. *Natural Discourse: Toward Ecocomposition*. State U of New York P, 2002.

Dobrin, Sidney I., J. A. Rice, and Michael Vastola, editors. *Beyond Postprocess*. Utah State UP, 2011.

Dobrin, Sidney I., J. A. Rice, and Michael Vastola. "Introduction: A New Postprocess Manifesto: A Plea for Writing." Dobrin, Rice, and Vastola, pp. 1–20.

Downs, Douglas, and Elizabeth Wardle. "Teaching about Writing, Righting Misconceptions: (Re)envisioning 'First-Year Composition' as 'Introduction to Writing Studies.'" *College Composition and Communication*, vol. 58, no. 4, June 2007, pp. 552–84. JSTOR, http://www.jstor.org/stable/20456966.

Drew, Julie. "Book Reviews: *Literacy, Ideology, and Dialogue: Toward a Dialogic Pedagogy*." *Composition Studies*, vol. 23, no. 1, Spring 1995, pp. 160–62.

Duffy, William. "Collaboration (in) Theory: Reworking the Social Turn's Conversational Imperative." *College English*, vol. 76, no. 5, May 2014, pp. 416–35. JSTOR, http://www.jstor.org/stable/24238154.

Edbauer, Jennifer. "Unframing Models of Public Distribution: From Rhetorical Situation to Rhetorical Ecologies." Rhetoric Society Quarterly, vol. 35, no. 4, 2005, pp. 5–24. JSTOR, http://www.jstor.org/stable/40232607.

Ede, Lisa. *Situating Composition: Composition Studies and the Politics of Location.* Southern Illinois UP, 2004.

Ede, Lisa, and Andrea Lunsford. *Singular Texts/Plural Authors: Perspectives on Collaborative Writing.* Southern Illinois UP, 1990.

Eldred, Janet Carey, and Peter Mortensen. "Coming to Know a Century." *College English*, vol. 62, no. 6, July 2000, pp. 747–55, https://doi.org/10.2307/379011.

Ewald, Helen Rothschild. "Iowa State University: Course Syllabus and Critical Statement." *Composition Studies/Freshman English News*, vol. 23, no. 2, 1995, pp. 45–52.

———. "Waiting for Answerability: Bakhtin and Composition Studies." *College Composition and Communication,* 44.3, 1993, 331–48. JSTOR, http://www.jstor.org/stable/358987.

———. "What We Could Tell Advanced Student Writers about Audience." *Journal of Advanced Composition*, vol. 11, no. 1, 1991, pp. 147–58.

Faigley, Lester. "Competing Theories of Process: A Critique and a Proposal." *College English,* vol. 48, no. 6, 1986, pp. 527–42, https://doi.org/10.2307/376707.

Fish, Stanley. *Is There a Text in This Class?: The Authority of Interpretive Communities.* Harvard UP, 1980.

Fleming, David. *From Form to Meaning: Freshman Composition and the Long Sixties, 1957–1974.* U of Pittsburgh P, 2011.

Fogarty, Daniel. *Roots for a New Rhetoric.* Columbia UP, 1959.

Foster, David. "More Comments on 'Social Construction, Language, and the Authority of Knowledge: A Bibliographic Essay.'" *College English*, vol. 49, no. 6, Oct. 1987, pp. 709–711, https://doi.org/10.2307/377813.

———. "What Are We Talking about When We Talk about Composition?" *Journal of Advanced Composition*, vol. 8, no. 1/2, 1988, pp. 30–40.

Foster, Helen. *Networked Process: Dissolving Boundaries of Process and Post-Process.* Parlor Press, 2007.

Fraiberg, Allison. "Houses Divided: Processing Composition in a Post-Process Time." *College Literature*, vol. 29, no. 1, Winter 2002, pp. 171–80. JSTOR, https://www.jstor.org/stable/pdf/25112627.pdf.

Freadman, Anne. "Anyone for Tennis?" *The Place of Genre in Learning: Current Debates,* edited by Ian Reid. Deakin UP, 1987, pp. 91–124.

Freed, Richard C., and Glenn J. Broadhead. "Discourse Communities, Sacred Texts, and Institutional Norms." *College Composition and Communication*, vol. 38, no. 2, May 1987, pp. 154–65, https://doi.org/10.2307/357716.

Fulkerson, Richard. "Composition at the Turn of the Twenty-First Century." *College Composition and Communication*, vol. 56, no. 4, 2005, pp. 654–87. JSTOR, https://www.jstor.org/stable/pdf/30037890.pdf.

———. "Composition Theory in the Eighties: Axiological Consensus and Paradigmatic Diversity." *College Composition and Communication*, vol. 41, no. 4, Dec. 1990, pp. 409–29, https://doi.org/10.2307/357931.

———. "Four Philosophies of Composition." *College Composition and Communication*, vol. 30, no. 4, Dec. 1979, pp. 343–48, https://doi.org/10.2307/356707.

————. "Of Pre- and Post-Process: Reviews and Ruminations." *Composition Studies*, vol. 29, no. 2, Fall 2001, pp. 93–119. JSTOR, http://www.jstor.org/stable/4350 1490.

Gallagher, Chris. "Once More Unto the Historiographic Breach: A Response to Rebecca Brittenham." *JAC*, vol. 21, no. 4, 2001, pp. 841–50.

Gibson, William. "The Science in Science Fiction." *Talk of the Nation*. Natl. Public Radio. 30 Nov. 1999. Radio.

Goggin, Maureen Daly, and Susan Kay Miller. "What Is NEW about the 'New Abolitionists': Continuities and Discontinuities in the Great Debate." *Composition Studies*, vol. 28, no. 2, Fall 2000, pp. 85–112. JSTOR, http://www.jstor.org/stable /43501463.

Gold, David. "Remapping Revisionist Historiography." *College Composition and Communication*, vol. 64, no. 1, Sept. 2012, pp. 15–34. JSTOR, https://www.jstor.org /stable/23264915.

Hairston, Maxine. "The Winds of Change: Thomas Kuhn and the Revolution in the Teaching of Writing." *College Composition and Communication* vol. 33, no. 1, 1982, pp. 76–88. JSTOR, https://www.jstor.org/stable/357846.

Hall, Jonathan. "Toward a Unified Writing Curriculum: Integrating WAC/WID with Freshman Composition." *The WAC Journal*, vol. 17, Sept. 2006, pp. 5–22. https:// doi.org/10.37514/WAC-J.2006.17.1.01.

Hardin, Joe Marshall. "Puttng Process into Circulation: Textual Cosmopolitanism." Dobrin, Rice, and Vastola, pp. 61–74.

Harrington, Elbert W. "A Modern Approach to Invention." *Quarterly Journal of Speech*, vol. 48, no. 4, 1962, pp. 373–78, https://doi.org/10.1080/00335636209382563.

Hass, Robert. "Meditation at Lagunitas." *The Apple Trees at Olema: New and Selected Poems*. HarperCollins, 2010, p. 79.

Hawk, Byron. *A Counter-History of Composition: Toward Methodologies of Complexity*. U of Pittsburgh P, 2007.

————."Hyperrhetoric and the Inventive Spectator: Remotivating *The Fifth Element*." *The Terministic Screen: Rhetorical Perspectives on Film*, edited by David Blakesley. Southern Illinois UP, 2003, pp. 70–91.

————. "Reassembling Postprocess: Toward a Posthuman Theory of Public Rhetoric." Dobrin, Rice, and Vastola, pp. 75–93.

————. *Resounding the Rhetorical: Composition as a Quasi-Object*. U of Pittsburgh P, 2018.

————. "Stitching Together Events: Of Joints, Folds, and Assemblages." *Theorizing Histories of Rhetoric*, edited by Michelle Ballif. Southern Illinois UP, 2013, pp. 106–27.

————. "Toward a Post-*Technê*—Or, Inventing Pedagogies for Professional Writing." *Technical Communication Quarterly*, vol. 13, no. 4, 2004, pp. 371–92, https://doi .org/10.1207/s15427625tcq1304_2.

————. "Toward a Rhetoric of Network (Media) Culture: Notes on Polarities and Potentiality." *JAC*, vol. 24, no. 4, 2004, pp. 831–50.

Hayles, N. Katherine. *How We Became Posthuman: Virtual Bodies in Cybernetics, Literature, and Informatics*. U of Chicago P, 1999.

Haynes, Cynthia. "Postconflict Pedagogy: Writing in the Stream of Hearing." Dobrin, Rice, and Vastola, pp. 145–62.

Heard, Matthew. "What Should We Do with Postprocess Theory." *Pedagogy: Critical Approaches to Teaching Literature, Language, Composition, and Culture*, vol. 8, no. 2, 2008, pp. 283–304, https://doi.org/10.1215/15314200-2007-041.

Horne, Miriam E. "Inkshed: History as Context." *Inkshed: Newsletter of the Canadian Association for the Study of Language and Learning*, vol. 23, no. 1, Spring 2006, pp. 5–12.

———. *Writing in a Community of Practice: Composing Membership in Inkshed*. Inkshed, 2012.

Horner, Bruce. "Rewriting Composition: Moving beyond a Discourse of Need." *College English*, vol. 77, no. 5, May 2015, pp. 450–79. JSTOR, https://www.jstor.org/stable/44075076.

Hunt, Russell A. "Afterword: Writing Under the Curriculum." *Writing Centres, Writing Seminars, Writing Culture: Writing Instruction in Anglo-Canadian Universities*, edited by Roger Graves and Heather Graves. Inkshed Press, 2006, pp. 371–83.

———. "Language Development in Young Children and in the Composition Classroom: The Role of Pragmatics." CCCC Annual Convention, 29 March 1984, New York. Address.

———. "Literature Is Reading Is Writing." *Inkshed: A Canadian Newsletter Devoted to Writing and Reading Theory and Practice*, vol. 2, no. 6, Dec. 1983, pp. 5–8.

———. "Process vs. Genre." *Inkshed: A Canadian Newsletter Devoted to Writing and Reading Theory and Practice*, vol. 8, no. 2, Mar. 1989, pp. 14–18.

———. "Reading as Writing." *Sentence Combining: A Rhetorical Perspective*. Eited by Donald A. Daiker et al. Southern Illinois UP, 1985.

———. "Re: Questions Concerning Your Scholarship." Received by Kristopher M. Lotier, 2 November 2018.

———. "Speech Genres, Writing Genres, School Genres, Computer Genres." *Learning and Teaching Genre*, edited by Aviva Freedman and Peter Medway. Boynton/Cook/Heinemann, 1994, pp. 243–61.

———. "Texts, Textoids, and Utterances: Writing and Reading for Meaning, In and Out of Classrooms." *Constructive Reading: Teaching beyond Communication*, edited by Deanne Bogdan and Stanley B. Straw. Heinemann-Boynton/Cook, 1993, pp. 113–29.

———. "Traffic in Genres, In Classrooms and Out." *Genre and the New Rhetoric*, edited by Peter Medway and Aviva Freedman. Taylor and Francis, 1994, 212–30.

———. "What Is 'Inkshedding?'" 16th Annual Inkshed Working Conference, Mont Gabriel, Quebec, Canada, 6–9 May 1999. Paper presentation.

Hunt, Russell A., and Douglas Vipond. "Contextualizing the Text: The Contribution of Readers, Texts, and Situations to Aesthetic Reading." Annual Meeting of the American Educational Research Association, 22 April 1987, https://eric.ed.gov/?id=ED284298. Poster Session.

———. "Crash-Testing a Transactional Model of Literary Reading." *Reader*, vol. 14, 1985, pp. 23–39.

―――. "Evaluations in Literary Reading." *TEXT*, vol. 6, no. 1, 1986, pp. 53–71.

―――. "Point-Driven Understanding: Pragmatic and Cognitive Dimensions of Literary Reading." *Poetics*, vol. 13, June 1984, pp. 261–77.

Hunt, Russell A., et al. "Social Reading and Literary Engagement." *Reading Research and Instruction*, vol. 26, no. 3, Spring 1987, pp. 151–61.

Hurley, Susan. "The Varieties of Externalism." *The Extended Mind*, edited by Richard Menary. MIT Press, 2010, pp. 101–154.

Jameson, Fredric. *Postmodernism, or, The Cultural Logic of Late Capitalism*. Duke UP, 1991.

Jarrett, Michael. *Drifting on a Read: Jazz as a Model for Writing*. State U of New York P, 1999.

―――. "Elvis (The Florida School Remix)." *New Media/New Methods: The Academic Turn from Literacy to Electracy*, edited by Jeff Rice and Marcel O'Gorman. Parlor Press, 2008, pp. 141–165.

Jensen, Kyle P. *Reimagining Process: Online Writing Archives & the Future of Writing Studies*. Southern Illinois UP, 2015.

Johnson, Barbara. *The Critical Difference: Essays in the Contemporary Rhetoric of Reading*. Johns Hopkins UP, 1985.

Johnson-Eilola, Johndan. "Control and the Cyborg: Writing and Being Written in Hypertext." *Journal of Advanced Composition*, vol. 13, no. 2, 1993, pp. 381–99.

―――. "The Database and the Essay: Understanding Composition as Articulation." *Writing New Media: Theory and Applications for Expanding the Teaching of Composition*, edited by Anne Frances Wysocki, et al. Utah State UP, 2004, pp. 199–236.

―――. *Datacloud: Toward a New Theory of Online Work*. Hampton, 2005.

Johnson-Eilola, Johndan, and Stuart Selber. "Plagiarism, Originality, Assemblage." *Computers and Composition*, vol. 24, 2007, pp. 375–403, https://doi.org/10.1016/j.compcom.2007.08.003.

Jones, Madison Percy. "Writing Conditions: The Premises of Ecocomposition." *Enculturation: A Journal of Rhetoric, Writing, and Culture*, 2018, http://enculturation.net/writing-conditions.

Jones, Steven Jeffrey. "The Logic of Question and Answer and the Hermeneutics of Writing." *Journal of Advanced Composition*, vol. 8, no. 1/2, 1988, pp. 12–21.

Kent, Thomas. "Externalism and the Production of Discourse." *Journal of Advanced Composition*, vol. 12, no. 1, 1992, pp. 57–74.

―――. "Formalism, Social Construction, and Interpretive Authority." Blyler and Thralls, pp. 79–91.

―――. "Genre Theory in the Area of Business Writing." *The Technical Writing Teacher*, vol. 14, no. 2, Spring 1987, pp. 232–42.

―――. *Interpretation and Genre: The Role of Generic Perception in the Study of Narrative Texts*. Bucknell UP, 1986.

―――. Introduction. Kent, *Post-Process Theory*, pp. 1–6.

―――. "On the Very Idea of a Discourse Community." *College Composition and Communication*, vol. 42, no. 4, Dec. 1991, pp. 425–445. JSTOR, https://www.jstor.org/stable/357995.

———. "Paragraph Production and the Given-New Contract." *The Journal of Business Communication*, vol. 21, no. 4, 1984, pp. 45–66, https://doi.org/10.1177/0021943 68402100405.

———. "Paralogic Hermeneutics and the Possibilities of Rhetoric." *Rhetoric Review*, vol. 8, no. 1, Autumn 1989, pp. 24–42. JSTOR, https://www.jstor.org/stable /465679.

———. "Paralogic Rhetoric: An Overview." Olson, pp. 143–52.

———. *Paralogic Rhetoric: A Theory of Communicative Interaction*, Bucknell UP, 1993.

———, editor. *Post-Process Theory: Beyond the Writing-Process Paradigm.* Southern Illinois UP, 1999.

———. "Preface: Righting Writing." Dobrin, Rice, and Vastola, pp. xi–xxii.

———. "Principled Pedagogy: A Reply to Lee-Ann M. Kastman Breuch." *JAC*, vol. 22, no. 2, 2002, pp. 428–433.

———. "The 'Remapping' of Professional Writing." *Journal of Business and Technical Communication*, vol. 21, no. 1, Jan. 2007, pp. 12–14, https://doi.org/10.1177 /1050651906293506.

———. "Response to Reed Way Dasenbrock." *Rhetoric Society Quarterly*, vol. 23, no. 3/4, 1994, pp. 105-07, https://doi.org/10.1080/02773949409391000.

———. "Schema Theory and Technical Communication." *Journal of Technical Writing and Communication*, vol. 17, no. 3, 1987, pp. 243–52.

———. "Six Suggestions for Teaching Paragraph Cohesion." *Journal of Technical Writing and Communication*, vol. 13, no. 3, 1983, pp. 269–74.

———. "Talking Differently: A Response to Gayatri Chakraborty Spivak." *JAC*, vol. 11, no. 1, Winter 1991, pp. 185–91.

Killingsworth, M. Jimmie. "Discourse Communities: Local and Global." *Rhetoric Review*, vol. 11, no. 1, 1992, pp. 110–22.

Kirsch, Gesa E. "Ethics and the Future of Composition Research." *Composition Studies in the New Millennium: Rereading the Past, Rewriting the Future*, edited by Lynn Z. Bloom, et al., pp. 129–42.

Kopelson, Karen. "Back at the Bar of Utility: Theory and/as Practice in Composition Studies (Reprise)." *JAC*, vol. 28, no. 3/4, 2008, pp. 587–608.

Kostelnick, Charles. "Process Paradigms in Design and Composition: Affinities and Directions." *College Composition and Communication*, vol. 40, no. 3, Oct. 1989, pp. 267–81, https://doi.org/10.2307/357774.

Koupf, Danielle. "Proliferating Textual Possibilities: Toward Pedagogies of Critical-Creative Tinkering." *Composition Forum*, vol. 35, Spring 2017, http://composition forum.com/issue/35/proliferating.php.

———. "Scrap Writing in the Digital Age: The Inventive Potential of Texts on the Loose." *Enculturation: A Journal of Rhetoric, Writing, and Culture*, 2019, http:// enculturation.net/scrap-writing.

Kuhn, Thomas. *The Structure of Scientific Revolutions.* U of Chicago P, 1962.

Kyburz, Bonnie Lenore. "Meaning Finds a Way: Chaos (Theory) and Composition." *College English*, vol. 66, no. 5, 2004, pp. 503–523, https://doi.org/10.2307 /4140732.

Langer, Judith A. "Musings." *Research in the Teaching of English*, vol. 18, no. 2, May 1984, pp. 117–18.

Langer, Judith A., and Arthur N. Applebee. "Musings." *Research in the Teaching of English*, vol. 18, no. 1, Feb. 1984, pp. 5–7.

Lauer, Janice M. "Composition Studies: Dappled Discipline." *Rhetoric Review* vol. 3, no. 1, 1984, pp. 20–29.

———. "Heuristics and Composition." *College Composition and Communication*, vol. 21, no. 5, 1970, pp. 396–404, https://doi.org/10.2307/356091.

———. *Invention in Rhetoric and Composition*. Reference Guides to Rhetoric and Composition. Parlor Press; The WAC Clearinghouse, 2004. https://wac.colostate .edu/books/referenceguides/lauer-invention/.

———. "Rhetorical Invention: The Diaspora." Atwill and Lauer, pp. 1–16.

LeFevre, Karen Burke. *Invention as a Social Act*. Southern Illinois UP, 1987.

Liebman-Kleine, Joanne. "In Defense of Teaching Process in ESL Composition." *TESOL Quarterly*, vol. 20, no. 4, Dec. 1986, pp. 783–88.

Lotier, Kristopher M. "Around 1986: The Externalization of Cognition and the Emergence of Postprocess Invention." *College Composition and Communication*, vol. 67, no. 3, Feb. 2016, pp. 360–84. JSTOR, https://www.jstor.org/stable/24633885.

Lynch, Paul. *After Pedagogy: The Experience of Teaching*. NCTE, 2013.

Lynch, Paul, and Nathniel Rivers, editors. *Thinking with Bruno Latour in Rhetoric and Composition*. Southern Illinois UP, 2015.

Lynn, Steven. "Reading the Writing Process: Toward a Theory of Current Pedagogies." *College English*, vol. 49, no. 8, Dec. 1987, pp. 902–10, https://doi. org/10.2307/378122.

MacDonald, Brock. "Farewell to Inkshed." Email on CASLL-L Listserv, 10 April 2017.

Machlup, Fritz. *The Production and Distribution of Knowledge in the United States*. Princeton UP, 1962.

Maimon, Elaine P., et al. *Readings in the Arts and Sciences*. Little, 1984.

Massey, Lance. "Book Review: *Networked Process: Dissolving Boundaries of Process and Post-Process*." *Composition Studies*, vol. 36, no. 2, 2008, pp. 157–60.

———. "The (Dis)Order of Composition: Insights from the Rhetoric and Reception of *The Making of Knowledge in Composition*. *The Changing of Knowledge in Composition*." Edited by Lance Massey and Richard C. Gebhardt. Utah State UP, 2011, pp. 305–322.

Matsuda, Paul Kei. "Process and Post-Process: A Discursive History." *Journal of Second Language Writing*, vol. 12, no. 1, Feb. 2003, pp. 65–83.

Mays, Chris. "Writing Complexity, One Stability at a Time: Teaching Writing as a Complex System." *College Composition and Communication*, vol. 68, no. 3, 2017, pp. 559–585. JSTOR, https://www.jstor.org/stable/44783580.

McComiskey, Bruce. *Teaching Composition as a Social Process*. Utah State UP, 2000.

Meyer, Leonard. *Music, the Arts, and Ideas*. U of Chicago P, 1994.

Micciche, Laura R. *Acknowledging Writing Partners*. The WAC Clearinghouse; UP of Colorado, 2017, https://doi.org/10.37514/PER-B.2017.0872.

———. "Writing Material." *College English*, vol. 76, no. 6, 2014, pp. 488–505. JSTOR, https://www.jstor.org/stable/24238199.

Miller, Susan. *Textual Carnivals: The Politics of Composition*. Southern Illinois UP, 1991.

———. "Why Composition Studies Disappeared and What Happened Then." *Composition Studies in the New Millennium: Rereading the Past, Rewriting the Future*, edited by Lynn Z. Bloom et al. Southern Illinois UP, 2003, pp. 48–56.

Mills, Barriss. "Writing as Process." *College English* vol. 15, no. 1, 1953, pp. 19–26.

Miranda, Lin-Manuel. "Hurricane." *Hamilton: An American Musical: Original Broadway Cast Recording*. Atlantic, 2015.

Muckelbauer, John. *The Future of Invention: Rhetoric, Postmodernism, and the Problem of Change*. State U of New York P, 2008.

———. "On Reading Differently: Through Foucault's Resistance." *College English*, vol. 63, no. 1, 2000, pp. 71–94, https://doi.org/10.2307/379032.

Muckelbauer, John, and Debra Hawhee. "Posthuman Rhetorics: 'It's the Future, Pikul.'" *JAC* vol. 20, no. 4, 2000, pp. 767–74.

Mueller, Derek, et al., editors. *Cross-Border Networks in Writing Studies*. Inkshed, 2018.

Murray, Donald M. "Teach Writing as Process, Not Product." *Cross-Talk in Comp Theory: A Reader*. 3rd ed., edited by Victor Villanueva and Kristin L. Arola. NCTE, 2011, pp. 3–6.

Neel, Jasper. "Review: *Composition as a Human Science*, by Louise Wetherbee Phelps." *College Composition and Communication*, vol. 41, no. 1, Feb. 1990, pp. 94–96.

Ngai, Sianne. *Our Aesthetic Categories: Zany, Cute, Interesting*. Harvard UP, 2012.

Nietzsche, Friedrich. "On Truth and Lies in a Nonmoral Sense." *Philosophy and Truth: Selections from Nietzsche's Notebooks of the Early 1870s*, edited and translated by Daniel Breazeale. Humanities Press, 1977, pp. 79–97.

Nystrand, Martin. Personal Webpage. https://english.wisc.edu/staff/nystrand-p-martin-marty/.

———. "Rhetoric's 'Audience' and Lingustics' 'Speech Community': Implications for Understanding Writing, Reading, and Text." *What Writers Know: The Language, Process, and Structure of Written Discourse*, edited by Martin Nystrand. Academic Press, 1982, pp. 1–28.

———. "Sharing Words: The Effects of Readers on Developing Writers." *Written Communication*, vol. 7, no. 1, Jan. 1990, pp. 3–24, https://doi.org/10.1177/0741088390007001001.

———. "A Social-Interactive Model of Writing." *Written Communication*, vol. 6, no. 1, 1989, pp. 66–85, https://doi.org/10.1177/0741088389006001005.

———. "The Social and Historical Context for Writing Research." *Handbook of Writing Research*, edited by Charles A. MacArthur et al. Guilford Press, 2006, pp. 11–27.

———. *The Structure of Written Communication: Studies in Reciprocity between Writers and Readers*. Emerald, 1986.

Nystrand, Martin et al. "Where Did Composition Studies Come From?" *Written Communication*, vol. 10, no. 3, July 1993, pp. 267–333, https://doi.org/10.1177/0741088393010003001.

Nystrand, Martin, and Margaret Himley. "Written Text as Social Interaction." *Theory into Practice*, vol. 23, no. 3, 1984, pp. 198–207.

Olson, Gary A. "Extending Our Awareness of the Writing Process." *Journal of Teaching Writing*, vol. 5, no. 2, Fall 1986, pp. 227–36.

———. "Fish Tales: A Conversation with 'The Contemporary Sophist.'" *Journal of Advanced Composition*, Vol. 12, no. 2, 1992, pp. 253–77.

———, editor. *Rhetoric and Composition as Intellectual Work*. Southern Illinois UP, 2002.

———. "Toward a Post-Process Composition: Abandoning the Rhetoric of Assertion." Kent, *Post-Process Theory*, pp. 7–15.

———. "Why Distrust the Very Goals with Which You Began?" *JAC*, vol. 22, no. 2, Spring 2002, pp. 423–28.

Paré, Anthony. "Toward a Post-Process Pedagogy; or, What's a Theory Got to Do with It?" *English Quarterly*, vol. 26, no. 2, Winter 1994, pp. 4–9.

Pell, John. "Review: Dobrin, Sidney I. *Postcomposition*." *Composition Forum*, vol. 27, Spring 2013, https://compositionforum.com/issue/27/pell-postcomposition-review.php.

Pender, Kelly. "Philosophies of Invention Twenty Years after *The Making of Knowledge in Composition*." *The Changing of Knowledge in Composition: Contemporary Perspectives*, edited by Lance Massey and Richard C. Gebhardt. Utah State UP, 2011, pp. 63–83, https://doi.org/10.2307/j.ctt4cgjw0.8.

Pepper, Stephen C. *World Hypotheses: Prolegomena to Systematic Philosophy and a Complete Survey of Metaphysics*. U of California P, 1942.

Petraglia, Joseph. "Introduction: General Writing Skills Instruction and Its Discontents." Petraglia, pp. xi–xvii.

———. "Is There Life after Process? The Role of Social Scientism in a Changing Discipline." Kent, *Post-Process Theory*, pp. 49–64.

———, editor. *Reconceiving Writing, Rethinking Writing Instruction*. Erlbaum, 1995.

———. "Spinning Like a Kite: A Closer Look at the Pseudotransactional Function of Writing." *JAC*, vol. 15, no. 1, 1995, pp. 19–33.

———. "Writing as an Unnatural Act." Petraglia, pp. 79–100.

Phelps, Louise Wetherbee. "Audience and Authorship: The Disappearing Boundary." *A Sense of Audience in Written Communication*, edited by Gesa Kirsch and Duane H. Roen, SAGE, 1990, pp. 153–74.

———. *Composition as a Human Science: Contributions to the Self-Understanding of a Discipline*. Oxford UP, 1988.

———. "The Dance of Discourse." *Pre/Text: The First Decade*. Victor J. Vitanza, editor. U of Pittsburgh P, 1993, pp. 31–64.

———. *The Development of a Discourse Model for Composition: Recursion in the Teaching Process*. MA Thesis. The Cleveland State University, 1976.

———. "Dialectics of Coherence: Toward an Integrative Theory." *College English*, vol. 47, no. 1, Jan. 1985, pp. 12–29. JSTOR, https://www.jstor.org/stable/377350.

———. "The Domain of Composition." *Rhetoric Review*, vol. 4, no. 2, Jan. 1986, pp. 182–95.

———. "Four Scholars, Four Genres: Networked Trajectories." Mueller, et al., pp. 81–122.

———. "Review: *The End of Composition Studies* by David W. Smit." *Rhetoric Review*, vol. 25, no. 2, 2006, pp. 211–14.

Porter, James E. "Intertextuality and the Discourse Community." *Rhetoric Review* vol. 5, no. 1, 1986, pp. 34–47.

Porter, Kevin. "Literature Reviews Re-Viewed: Toward a Consequentialist Account of Surveys, Surveyors, and the Surveyed." *JAC*, vol. 23, no. 2, 2003, pp. 351–77.

———. "The 'Neglected' Question of Meaning: Toward a Consequentialist Philosophy of Discourse." *JAC*, vol. 23, no. 4, 2003, pp. 725–64.

Preston, Jacqueline. "Project(ing) Literacy: Writing to Assemble in a Postcomposition FYW Classroom." *College Composition and Communication*, vol. 67, no. 1, 2015, pp. 35–63.

Prior, Paul. *Writing/Disciplinarity: A Sociohistoric Account of Literate Activity in the Academy*. Erlbaum, 1998.

Pullman, George L. "Rhetoric and Hermeneutics: Composition, Invention, and Literature." *Journal of Advanced Composition*, vol. 14, no. 2, 1994, pp. 367–87.

———. "Stepping Yet Again into the Same Current." Kent, *Post-Process Theory*, pp. 16–29.

Reid, Alexander. "(Post-) Post-Process Composition." *Digital Digs*, 26 July 2007, https://profalexreid.com/2007/07/26/post-post-proc-2.

———. *The Two Virtuals: New Media and Composition*. Parlor Press, 2007.

Reiff, Mary Jo. "Rereading 'Invoked' and 'Addressed' Readers through a Social Lens: Toward a Recognition of Multiple Audiences." *JAC*, vol. 16., no. 3, 1996, pp. 407–24.

Reither, James A. "Academic Discourse Communities, Invention, and Learning to Write." Annual Meeting of the Conference on College Composition and Communication, March 13–15, 1986. Paper presentation.

———. "Editorial Inkshedding." *Inkshed: Newsletter of the Canadian Association for the Study of Writing and Reading*, vol. 5, no. 4, Sept. 1986, p. 1–2.

———. "Editorial Inkshedding." *Inkshed: Newsletter of the Canadian Association for the Study of Writing and Reading*, vol. 5, no. 6, Dec. 1986, p. 1.

———. "Epistemic Newslettering; or, *Inkshed* as a Mode of Learning." *Inkshed: A Canadian Newsletter Devoted to Writing and Reading Theory and Practice*, vol. 4, no. 1, Feb. 1985, pp. 1–3.

———. "Time for the Revolution." *Inkshed: Newsletter for the Canadian Association for the Study of Writing and Reading*, vol. 8, no. 2, Mar. 1989, pp. 11–13.

———. "Writing and Knowing: Toward Redefining the Writing Process." *College English*, vol. 47, no. 6, Oct. 1986, pp. 620–28, https://doi.org/10.2307/377164.

Reither, James A., and Douglas Vipond. "Writing as Collaboration." *College English*, vol. 51, no. 8, 1989, pp. 855–67, https://doi.org/10.2307/378091.

Rice, Jeff. "Networked Boxes: The Logic of Too Much." *College Composition and Communication*, vol. 59, no. 2, 2007, pp. 299–311. JSTOR, https://www.jstor.org/stable/20457001.

———. *The Rhetoric of Cool: Composition Studies and New Media*. Southern Illinois UP, 2007.

Rickert, Thomas A. *Ambient Rhetoric: The Attunements of Rhetorical Being*. U of Pittsburgh P, 2013.

———. "Toward the Chōra: Kristeva, Derrida, and Ulmer on Emplaced Invention." *Philosophy and Rhetoric*, vol. 40, no. 3, 2007, pp. 251–273.

Ridolfo, Jim, and Dánielle Nicole DeVoss. "Composing for Recomposition: Rhetorical Velocity and Delivery." *Kairos* vol. 13, no. 2, 2009, http://kairos.technorhetoric.net /13.2/topoi/ridolfo_devoss/.

Rivers, Thomas M. "A Catalogue of Invention Components and Applications." *College English*, vol. 44, no. 5, 1982, pp. 519–28, https://doi.org/10.2307/376658.

Roberts, David D. "Readers' Comprehension Responses in Informative Discourse: Toward Connecting Reading and Writing in Technical Communication." *Journal of Technical Writing and Communication*, vol. 19, no. 2, 1989, pp. 135–48.

Rodrigue, Tanya K. "A Portrait of a Scholar . . . in Progress: An Interview with Louise Wetherbee Phelps." *Composition Forum*, vol. 27, Spring, 2013, http://composition forum.com/issue/27/louise-wetherbee-phelps-interview.php.

Roozen, Kevin, et al. "Writing Is a Social and Rhetorical Activity." Adler-Kassner and Wardle, pp. 17–34.

Rorty, Richard. *Contingency, Irony, and Solidarity*. Cambridge UP, 1989.

Rose, Shirley, et al. "All Writers Have More to Learn." Adler-Kassner and Wardle, pp. 59–70.

Rosenblatt, Louise M. "The Poem as Event." *College English*, vol. 26, no. 2, Nov. 1964, pp. 123–28, https://doi.org/10.2307/373663.

———. *The Reader, The Text, The Poem: The Transactional Theory of the Literary Work*. Southern Illinois UP, 1978.

———. "Viewpoints: Transaction Versus Interaction—A Terminological Rescue Operation." *Research in the Teaching of English*, vol. 19, no. 1, Feb. 1985, pp. 96–107.

Rule, Hannah J. *Situating Writing Processes*. The WAC Clearinghouse; UP of Colorado, 2019, https://doi.org/10.37514/PER-B.2019.0193.

Russell, David R. "Activity Theory and Its Implications for Writing." Petraglia, pp. 51–78.

———. "Activity Theory and Process Approaches: Writing (Power) in School and Society." Kent, *Post-Process Theory*, pp. 80–95.

———. "Looking beyond the Interface: Activity Theory and Distributed Learning." *Distributed Learning: Social and Cultural Approaches to Practice*, edited by Mary R. Lea and Kathy Nicoll. Routledge, 2002, pp. 64–82.

———. "Vygotsky, Dewey, and Externalism: Beyond the Student/Discipline Dichotomy." *Journal of Advanced Composition*, vol. 13, no. 1, 1993, pp. 173–97.

———. *Writing in the Academic Disciplines, 1870–1990: A Curricular History*, 2nd ed. Southern Illinois UP, 2002.

Sánchez, Raúl. "First, A Word." Dobrin, Rice, and Vastola. 183–94.

Sargent, M. Elizabeth, and Cornelia C. Paraskevas, editors. *Conversations about Writing: Eavesdropping, Inkshedding, and Joining In*. Nelson College Indigenous Press, 2005.

Schilb, John. "What's at Stake in the Conflict between 'Theory' and 'Practice' in Composition?" *Rhetoric Review,* vol. 10, no. 1, 1991, pp. 91–97.

Schuster, Charles I. "Review: *The Structure of Written Communication: Studies in Reciprocity between Writers and Readers,* by Martin Nystrand." *College Composition and Communication,* vol. 39, no. 1, Feb. 1988, pp. 89–91, https://doi.org/10.2307 /357830.

Shipka, Jody. *Toward a Composition Made Whole.* U of Pittsburgh P, 2011.

Skinnell, Ryan. "Who Cares If Rhetoricians Landed on the Moon? Or, a Plea for Reviving the Politics of Historiography." *Rhetoric Review,* vol. 34, no. 2, 2015, pp. 111–28.

Smit, David W. *The End of Composition Studies.* Southern Illinois UP, 2004.

———. "Hall of Mirrors: Antifoundationalist Theory and the Teaching of Writing." *JAC,* vol. 15, no. 1, 1995, pp. 35–52.

———. "Reply to Daniel J. Royer, 'Appealing to Philosophy in Composition Studies.'" *JAC,* vol. 15, no. 2, 1995, pp. 379–81.

Smith, Daniel L. "Ethics and 'Bad Writing': Dialectics, Reading, and Affective Pedagogy." *JAC,* vol. 23, no. 3, 2003, pp. 525–52.

Sommers, Nancy. "Response to Sharon Crowley 'Components of the Composing Process.'" *College Composition and Communication,* vol. 29, no. 2, 1978, 209–211, https://doi.org/10.2307/357318.

Spinuzzi, Clay. "Pseudotransactionality, Activity Theory, and Professional Writing Instruction." *Technical Communication Quarterly,* vol. 5, no. 3, Summer 1996, pp. 295–308, https://doi.org/10.1207/s15427625tcq0503_3.

Spray, William, and Anthony Rhinelander. *A History of St. Thomas University: The Formative Years, 1860–1990.* St. Thomas UP, 2014.

Styron, William. *The Confessions of Nat Turner.* Vintage, 1966.

Syverson, Margaret A. *The Wealth of Reality: An Ecology of Composition.* Southern Illinois UP, 1999.

Talbot, Jen. "Pedagogy and the Hermeneutic Dance: Mirroring, Plasticity, and the Situated Writing Subject." *Contemporary Perspectives on Cognition and Writing,* edited by Patricia Portanova et al. The WAC Clearinghouse; UP of Colorado, 2017, pp. 153–67, https://doi.org/10.37514/PER-B.2017.0032.2.08.

Talbot, Jennifer Rae. *Re-Articulating Postprocess: Affect, Neuroscience, and Institutional Discourse.* Diss. Purdue U, 2012.

Taylor, Mark C. *The Moment of Complexity: Emerging Network Culture.* U of Chicago P, 2001.

Thralls, Charlotte, and Nancy Roundy Blyler. "The Social Perspective and Pedagogy in Technical Communication." *Technical Communication Quarterly,* vol. 2, no. 3, Summer 1993, pp. 249–70.

———. "The Social Perspective and Professional Communication: Diversity and Directions in Research." Blyler and Thralls, pp. 3–34.

Tobin, Lad. "Introduction: How the Writing Process Was Born—and Other Conversion Narratives." *Taking Stock: The Writing Process Movement in the '90s,* edited by Lad Tobin and Thomas Newkirk. Boynton/Cook Heinemann, pp. 1–14.

Trimbur, John. "Consensus and Difference in Collaborative Learning." *College English*, vol. 51, no. 6, 1989, pp. 602–16. JSTOR, https://www.jstor.org/stable/pdf/377 955.pdf.

———. "Taking the Social Turn: Teaching Writing Post-Process." *College Composition and Communication*, vol. 45, no. 1, Feb. 1994, pp. 108–18, https://doi.org/10 .2307/358592.

Ulmer, Gregory L. *Heuretics: The Logic of Invention.* Johns Hopkins UP, 1994.

———. *Internet Invention: From Literacy to Electracy.* Pearson, 2002.

University of Florida Department of English. "Sid Dobrin." 2020. https://english.ufl .edu/sid-dobrin/. Accessed August 12, 2020.

Vipond, Douglas A. "Re: Questions Concerning Your Scholarship." Received by Kristopher M. Lotier, 15 October 2018.

Vipond, Douglas, and Russell A. Hunt. "The NEW 'Politics of Composition' and the OLD Need to 'Take Care of Business.'" *Dialogue: A Journal for Writing Specialists*, vol. 2, no. 1, 1995, pp. 53–64.

———. "Shunting Information or Making Contact?: Assumptions for Research on Aesthetic Reading." *English Quarterly*, vol. 20, no. 2, Summer 1987, pp. 131–36.

Ward, Irene. *Literacy, Ideology, and Dialogue: Towards a Dialogic Pedagogy.* State U of New York P, 1994.

———. "Review: *Paralogic Rhetoric: A Theory of Communicative Interaction*, Thomas Kent." *JAC*, vol. 15, no. 1, 1995, pp. 182–86.

Wardle, Elizabeth. "Can Cross-Disciplinary Links Help Us to Teach 'Academic Discourse' in FYC?" *Across the Disciplines: A Journal of Language, Learning, and Academic Writing*, vol. 1, 2004, https://doi.org/10.37514/ATD-J.2004.1.1.06.

———. Comment on "(post-) post-process composition" by Alexander Reid. 26 July 2007 at 9:51 p.m., https://profalexreid.com/2007/07/26/post-post-proc-2/.

———. Comment on "(post-) post-process composition" by Alexander Reid. 27 July 2007 at 10:32 a.m., https://profalexreid.com/2007/07/26/post-post-proc-2/.

———. Comment on "What Should College Students Write" by Alexander Reid. 25 July 2007 at 4:30 p.m., https://profalexreid.com/2007/07/24/what-should-col-2/.

———. "Continuing the Dialogue: Follow-Up Comments on 'Teaching about Writing, Righting Misconceptions.'" *College Composition and Communication*, vol. 60, no. 1, Sept. 2008, pp. 175–81. JSTOR, https://www.jstor.org/stable/20457053.

———. "'Mutt Genres' and the Goal of FYC: Can We Help Students Write the Genres of the University?" *College Composition and Communication*, vol. 60, no. 4, June 2009, pp. 765–89. JSTOR, https://www.jstor.org/stable/40593429.

———. "Understanding 'Transfer' from FYC: Preliminary Results of a Longitudinal Study." *WPA: Writing Program Administration*, vol. 31, nos. 1–2, 2007, pp. 65–85.

———. "You Can Learn to Write in General." Ball and Loewe, pp. 30–34.

Wardle, Elizabeth, and Linda Adler-Kassner. "Metaconcept: Writing Is an Activity and a Subject of Study." Adler-Kassner and Wardle, pp. 15–16.

Wardle, Elizabeth, and Doug Downs. "Reflecting Back and Looking Forward: Revisiting 'Teaching about Writing, Righting Misconceptions' Five Years On." *Composition Forum*, vol. 27, Spring 2013, http://compositionforum.com/issue/27/reflecting-back.php.

Warner, Michael. "Publics and Counter-Publics." *Public Culture*, vol. 14, no. 1, 2002, pp. 49–90.

Weisser, Christian R. "Ecocomposition and the Greening of Identity." Weisser and Dobrin, pp. 81–96.

Weisser, Christian R., and Sidney I. Dobrin. "Breaking New Ground in Ecocomposition: An Introduction." Weisser and Dobrin, pp. 1–9.

Weisser, Christian R., and Sidney I. Dobrin, editors. *EcoComposition: Theoretical and Pedagogical Approaches*. State U of New York P, 2001.

Whicker, John. "Narratives, Metaphors, and Power-Moves: The History, Meanings, and Implications of 'Post-Process.'" *JAC*, vol. 31, nos. 3/4, 2011, pp. 497–531.

White, Eric Charles. *Kaironomia: On the Will-to-Invent*. Cornell UP, 1987.

Williams, Andrea. "Voicing Scholars' Networked Identities through Interviews." Mueller, et al., pp. 46–80.

Witte, Stephen P., and David Elias. "Review: *The Structure of Written Communication: Studies in Reciprocity between Writers and Readers*." *Style*, vol. 22, no. 4, 1988, pp. 670–76.

Worsham, Lynn. "The Question Concerning Invention: Hermeneutics and the Genesis of Writing." *PreText*, vol. 8, nos. 3–4, 1987, pp. 197–244.

Yarbrough, Stephen R. *After Rhetoric: The Study of Discourse beyond Language and Culture*. Southern Illinois UP, 1999.

Yarnoff, Charles. "Contemporary Theories of Invention in the Rhetorical Tradition." *College English*, vol. 41, no. 5, 1980, pp. 552–60, https://doi.org/10.2307/375726.

Yood, Jessica. "A History of Pedagogy in Complexity." *Enculturation: A Journal of Rhetoric, Writing, and Culture*, 2013, http://www.enculturation.net/history-of-pedagogy.

Young, Richard E. "Paradigms and Problems: Needed Research in Rhetorical Invention." *Research on Composing: Points of Departure*, edited by Charles R. Cooper and Lee Odell. NCTE, 1978, pp. 29–47.

Young, Richard E. and Alton L. Becker. "Toward a Modern Theory of Rhetoric: A Tagmemic Contribution." *Harvard Educational Review*, vol. 35, no. 4, 1965, pp. 450–68.

Young, Richard, and Maureen Daly Goggin. "Some Issues in Dating the Birth of the New Rhetoric in Departments of English: A Contribution to a Developing Historiography." *Defining the New Rhetorics*, edited by Theresa Enos and Stuart C. Brown. SAGE, 1993, pp. 22–43.

Yuan, Rue. "Yin/Yang Principle and the Relevance of Externalism and Paralogic Rhetoric to Intercultural Communication." *Journal of Business and Technical Communication*, vol. 11, no. 3, July 1997, pp. 297–320.

INDEX